THE MARINE BOOK

A PORTRAIT OF AMERICA'S MILITARY ELITE

THE MARINE BOOK

A PORTRAIT OF AMERICA'S MILITARY ELITE

Chuck Lawliss

PHOTOGRAPHS BY THE AUTHOR

THAMES AND HUDSON
New York and London

FOR MY BROTHER LYNN
A HARD-CHARGING MARINE.
WHO WENT TO ONE WAR
TOO MANY.

*ONLY THE DEAD
HAVE SEEN THE END
OF WAR.*

— PLATO

ACKNOWLEDGMENTS

*T*his book could not have been written without the full cooperation of the Marine Corps. I was welcomed warmly and given kind, thoughtful attention by countless Marines, from the commandant to privates in the field. No access I requested was denied; no question I asked went unanswered. This cooperation does credit to the Corps and to the democracy it serves so well.

I am particularly grateful to Chief Warrant Officer Bill Henderson of the New York public affairs office who helped me every step of the way along a complex, demanding schedule and fielded numerous questions and requests with unflagging good humor. Special thanks also go to the staff of the Marine Corps Historical Center in Washington; Major Geoffrey P. Lyon, also of the New York public affairs office; Captain K. P. Murphy and Chief Warrant Officer Doug Hauth of the Ground Combat Center, Twenty-nine Palms, California; and Colonel Bill White (Ret.) of the Marine Corps Association.

The excellent drawings that accompany the Portraits in Green are the work of my dear friend Richard H. Brown.

PHOTOCREDITS

126, Goodyear Kirkham Collection; 164, David Luttenberger; cover, back, 26, 28, 37–44, 46, 47, 49, 50, 52, 55, 56(top), 57, 58, 61, 63–67, 69, 75, 76, 122, 124, 125, 129, Offical U.S. Marine Corps Photographs; 36, Naval Historical Foundation—Capertan Collection; 56(bottom), U.S. Naval Historical Center; 153, Offical U.S. Navy Photograph; 48, Springer/Bettman Film Archive; 35, Unknown; 21, World Wide.

CONTENTS

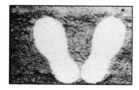

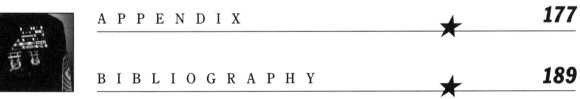

THE **MARINE** BOOK

A PORTRAIT OF AMERICA'S MILITARY ELITE

CHAPTER 1

PROUD TO CLAIM THE TITLE

The setting sun casts long shadows as the visitors gather on a grassy knoll in the small park that adjoins Arlington National Cemetery. Across the Potomac, the Washington Monument shimmers through the haze; farther away to the right is the dome of the capitol. The reviewing stand fills with officers in white dress uniforms and women in colorful summer silks and picture hats. There is an air of hushed expectancy. The visitors are here to see the Sunset Parade, a ceremony "in honor and in memory of the men of the United States Marine Corps who have given their lives for their country since November 10, 1775."

The park is dominated by a 100-ton bronze statue by Felix de Weldon, nine years in the making. It depicts the flag-raising on Iwo Jima, perhaps the most memorable image of World War II. The statue is of heroic dimensions. Counting its base, it stands 78 feet tall. The six figures in battle fatigues and helmets would be 32 feet tall if they weren't bending to lift the 60-foot flag pole. The flag on the pole is a real one, 10 by 19½ feet, and it flies twenty-four hours a day by presidential decree. On the black marble base, gold letters spell out the words used by Fleet Admiral Chester Nimitz to pay tribute to the Marines who fought on Iwo Jima: "Uncommon valor was a common virtue."

The parade begins. First to perform is the Marine Drum and Bugle Corps, the "Commandant's Own." These seventy-five Marines have been recruited from civilian drum corps and marching bands, and trained to excel in the famous "concert in motion." They play bugles that range from soprano to contrabass, and snare and bass drums, tympani, and the xylophone. They wear white pants and flame-red tunics decorated with gold braid.

The corps leads off its complex routine by playing and marching to "Barnum and Bailey's Favorite." Other selections, separated by intricate drum interludes, include "America the Beautiful," "Over the Rainbow," and the finale, "Stars and Stripes Forever" by John Philip Sousa, himself a Marine.

Officers' swords flash as the troops line up in front

OPPOSITE PAGE: The world famous Marine Band, "The President's Own," in formation in front of the Iwo Jima Monument.

Stepping out smartly, the Marine Corps Drum and Bugle Corps performs at the Sunset Parade at the Iwo Jima Monument, a popular weekly event in the summer.

of the reviewing stand for adjutant's call. Bayonets are fixed for the presentation of colors. Beside the American flag is the Battle Color of the Marine Corps: scarlet with bright gold fringe and trimmings, bearing a large Marine Corps emblem. From the pike, just below the top of the color staff, are suspended forty-seven streamers commemorating military campaigns in which Marines have fought with honor. The streamers are decorated with palms, oak leaf clusters, and stars, which represent more than four hundred awards and campaigns. Below the Battle Color, forty-seven engraved silver bands ring the staff, each naming a battle, campaign, or expedition for which a ribbon was awarded a place on the Battle Color.

The American flag and the Battle Color are carried by the Marine Corps Color Guard: the Color Sergeant of the Marine Corps, a bearer for the Battle Color, and two riflemen.

The troops stand at attention as the report is received by the commanding officer; then they march off to set the stage for the ten-minute precision routine of the Marine Corps Silent Drill Platoon. No verbal commands are given as the platoon executes one after another complex variation on the elements of the man-

ual of arms. Members carry the vintage M1 rifle, and much of the drill is performed with fixed bayonets. The high point of the drill is the inspection of arms, the rifles flipped high in the air to and from the inspecting officer.

The guests and spectators stand as honors are paid to the reviewing officer. The troops pass in review to the strains of "Semper Fidelis" and the "Marines' Hymn." All stand again for the memorial tribute to the Marine dead, and the retiring of the colors. Then the marchers parade around the field to the strains of "Colonel Bogey" and "Anchors Aweigh" before marching off to a reprise of "Semper Fidelis." A lone bugler blows taps; the notes seem to hang in the warm air. Darkness has fallen. The statue is now lit from below by powerful floodlights.

The Sunset Parade is a moving experience. The Marines have paid a woeful price over the years defending their country. Moreover, the parade is mili-

OPPOSITE PAGE: Across the back of the drum major of the Marine Corps Band is a sash listing all the major battles and campaigns of the Corps.

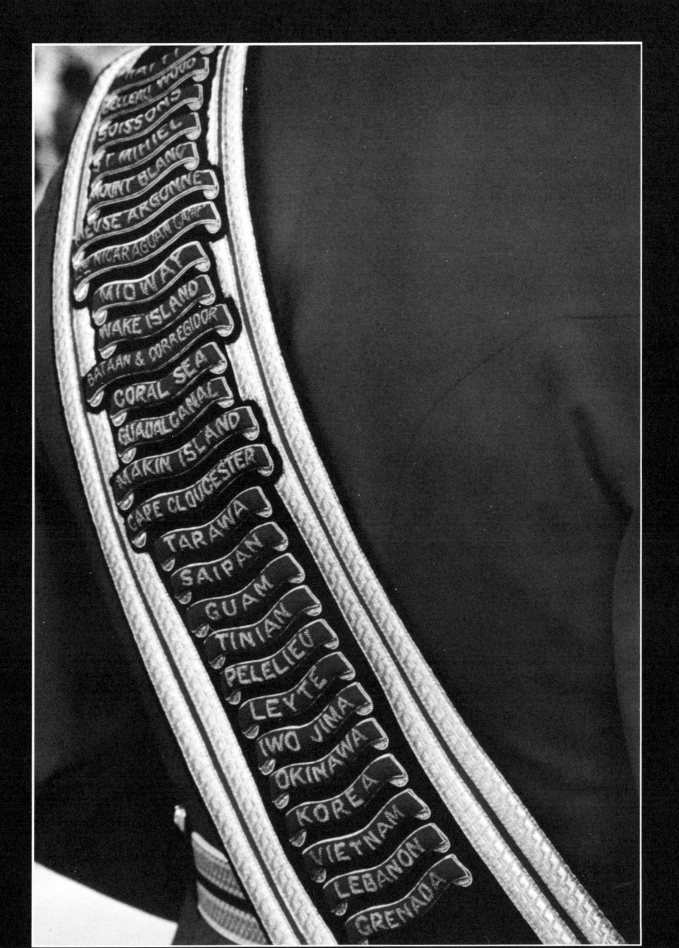

tary pageantry at its best. But the Sunset Parade is also thought-provoking, for it is a metaphor for the Marine Corps.

The juxtaposition of parade pomp and battlefield sacrifice is pure Marine Corps. From its inception, the Corps has been an elite fighting force with extensive ceremonial duties. Marines have been an integral part of formal rituals aboard Navy ships since the Revolution. Today they also stand guard at the White House and at U.S. embassies. Marines in their Dress Blues are a symbol of America throughout the world.

In this dual role, the Marines are unique. There is no counterpart here or abroad. British Commandos don't wear red coats and busbies and march in front of Buckingham Palace. The Garde Républicain did not fight in Indochina or Morocco.

Not only do Marines fight, they fight far more often and in far more places than any other branch of the service, having averaged nearly two engagements a year over their long history. The Marines have seen action in Africa, China, and Central America. They are remembered for Okinawa and Korea; the Marines remember that they fought in both places in the nineteenth century. As the United States grew as a world power, president after president would order: "Send in the Marines."

There are many unique aspects to the Marine Corps. Some are important, like its dual role. Some are minor; trivial to the layman, perhaps, but treasured by the Marines.

A keen observer at the Sunset Parade might have noted that the sergeants carried swords, the only noncommissioned officers in the armed forces ever authorized to carry what traditionally has been a commissioned officer's weapon. The privilege was granted to Marine sergeants in 1850, and they have carried them ever since as a symbol of leadership.

And what other branch of the service makes a big affair of its birthday? If an enemy wants to catch the Corps unaware, the night of November 10th is the best time to try.

There is a story behind the funding of the Iwo Jima statue. The Sunset Parade program notes, "The entire cost of the statue and the Memorial site was donated by the United States Marines, former Marines, Marine Reservists, friends of the Marine Corps and members of the Naval Service. No public funds were used."

What this comes down to is that the Marines built their own memorial. But this somewhat unusual act also is pure Marine Corps. The Marines have never been shy about calling attention to their record. In the words of a former commandant, General Clifton B. Cates:

"The Marine Corps has no ambition beyond the performance of its duty to its country. Its sole honor stems from that recognition which cannot be denied to a Corps of men who have sought for themselves little more than a life of hardship and the most hazardous assignments in battle."

Another reason for erecting the statue may be found in a comment made by James Forrestal, then Secretary of the Navy, at the time of the battle. "The raising of the flag on Mount Suribachi," he said, "means a Marine Corps for the next five hundred years."

Consider the figures in the statue. One represents Ira Hayes, a full-blooded Indian from Bapchule, Arizona. Another, Rene Gagnon, of French-Canadian ancestry, was from Manchester, New Hampshire. Two were Southerners: Franklin Sousley of Flemingsburg, Kentucky, and Harlan Block of Weslaco, Texas. One was a sergeant, Michael Strank, from Conemaugh in the coal-mining region of Pennsylvania. The sixth man was a Marine only in spirit. Pharmacist's Mate 2nd Class John Bradley of Appleton, Wisconsin, was one of the unsung Navy medical corpsmen who accompanied the Marines into battle. Three of the men—Sousley, Strank, and Block—would be killed before the fighting on Iwo Jima ended. Together the six were a cross section of the Marine Corps; indeed, of America itself.

The phrase "former Marines" in the list of who paid for the statue also is worthy of note. The Marines believe there is no such animal as an ex-Marine: "once a Marine, always a Marine." It makes no difference if a man served three years or thirty, he will consider himself a Marine for the rest of his days. Former Marines also tend to see themselves as the keepers of the faith, and any criticism of the Corps will bring down their righteous wrath. This, too, is a unique Marine quality. Other ex-servicemen often find former Marines as incomprehensible as foreigners.

The Corps also has the support of many men who never wore the green but think of themselves as Marines, or at least near-Marines. Like Notre Dame, the Corps is cheered on by its "subway alumni."

The flag of Mount Suribachi on Iwo Jima, a World War II image symbolizing the heroism of the Marine Corps.

But the Sunset Parade metaphor can be taken only so far. Combat and ceremony—"shoot and salute" in the parlance of the Corps—are the two extremes; and Marines spend much of their service life doing other things. And metaphors oversimplify. The psychology of the Marine Corps is too complex, too filled with paradoxes to fit easily into any metaphor.

Marines present a stern military visage, but behind it they are deeply suspicious. They feel surrounded by those who want to either usurp their duties and privileges or eliminate them altogether. This suspicion is not unfounded. The Corps has been under attack many times through the years from the other services, Congress, and a surprising number of presidents, including Andrew Jackson, Teddy Roosevelt, and Harry Truman.

In *A History of Militarism,* Alfred Vaghts may have caught the essence of the Marines' problem: ". . . the Marines [are] a curiously amphibian force, which owes its origin, if not its continued existence, more to political considerations than to military designs." The Corps does seem to be perpetually caught up in "political considerations" of one sort or another.

It has never been enough for the Marines to prove their worth in battle. The Army always has felt that fighting on land is its prerogative, and its alone. Army Green Berets, Special Forces, and Delta Forces now handle many of the special missions once entrusted to the Marines. The Air Force sees no reason why the Marines need their own planes. Even the Navy has been whittling away at some of the duties traditionally performed by Marines. One reason for the survival of the Corps, ironically, is that the other services don't trust one another, which prevents them from ganging up on the Marines.

In one of the periodic examinations of the role of the Marines, a senator told the Armed Forces Committee, "In the vast complex of the Department of Defense, the Marine Corps plays a lonely role." The Corps does see itself as alone, and, oddly enough, finds sustenance in its very loneliness.

Another Marine Corps paradox concerns its size. The Corps sees itself as small. The theme of its recruiting is "The Few. The Proud. The Marines." But the current active strength of the Corps is 198,000. True, the other services are more than twice as large, and Russia and China have standing armies larger than all the U.S. services put together. The Marines, however, are bigger than the British Army, and they dwarf the armed forces of any other country in the Western Hemisphere. Marine aviation would rank as the world's eighth-largest air force.

But elite forces are small, almost by definition, and the Corps treasures its elitism in all its ramifications beyond anything else.

The Corps also likes to posture itself as simple. The other services actively promote the multitude of skills they teach, while the Marines' recruitment advertisements suggest that "shoot and salute" pretty much describes the Corps's curriculum. In fact, Marines are trained in hundreds of skills, as many as any other service. The Corps simply doesn't want young people to enlist for the wrong reasons; they should enlist to be Marines, not to learn a trade.

Whatever their eventual specialty may be, all Marines are trained combat riflemen. All officers are trained platoon leaders. A Marine also may be trained as a computer operator, mechanic, photographer, or cook, but only after he has mastered the skills of combat. When John Lardner was a combat correspondent on Iwo Jima, he caught this essential difference: "In the Army, shock troops are a small minority supported by a vast group of artisans, laborers, clerks, and organizers. In the Marines, there are practically nothing but shock troops."

Public accolades to the Marines gall the Army, and for good reason. "Eliminate the Marine Corps and you no longer have a measuring rod to apply to the Army," said Senator Paul Douglas, himself a decorated Marine in World War II. "I sometimes suspect that is why some Army men want to eliminate the Marine Corps because they will not then be subject to the test of competition."

Marines are proud, and their pride sometimes gets them in trouble, especially in peacetime. Men in uniform in peacetime are an unpleasant reminder that war may come again. And it is only human to take a bit of enjoyment when the proud suffer a fall from grace. An example of the price of pride came in 1987 when four young Marines at the U.S. embassy in Moscow were accused of compromising security. The next week, the cover of *Time* magazine showed the face of a Marine sporting a black eye. The article was headlined, " 'And to Keep Our Honor Clean': The Marines struggle to live up to their hymn and their code of *Semper Fidelis.*"

Suddenly it wasn't four embassy guards that stood accused, but the whole Marine Corps. Apparently if one Marine trips, all Marines are stumblebums. This presumed collective guilt is an old stick, and the Marines have been beaten with it before. But they accept it with stoicism.

Do the Marines have a secret? If they do, it is one as old as war itself. Their secret is esprit de corps, the spirit of devotion of Marines for one another, their Corps, and its mission. Looked at another way, it is Marines honestly believing that they are the best fighting men in the world, and behaving accordingly.

Esprit powers the Marines in battle just as surely as it did the Spartans and the Praetorian Guard of ancient Rome. Esprit is the one quality that makes a good fighting force great. Without it, Marines would be just ordinary troops in green uniforms.

Esprit de corps, however, is not a phrase one hears often in the Marine Corps. It's too pretentious, too French. The Marines who wear the *fourragère* their predecessors earned capturing Belleau Wood refer to the decoration as "pogey rope." But then, "valor" and "courage" aren't everyday words in the Corps either. A Marine who demonstrates these qualities is a "hard-charger" or simply a "good Marine," even if he has the medals to vouch for his courage. "Hero" is another word the Marines rarely use.

This sense of brotherhood usually is expressed, "Marines look out for each other." This covers everything from barroom brawls, where to fight one Marine is to fight his fellow Marines, to never abandoning the dead and wounded on the battlefield. A poignant photograph from the Korean War shows bone-weary Ma-

John Lejeune's French ancestors migrated to Louisiana after the British won control of Canada. His father was a farmer who had been a Confederate officer. He wanted John to go to West Point; it seemed a good way for a young man to get an education at no cost. There was no vacancy at West Point, so he went to Annapolis instead. On a training cruise to the South Pacific, Lejeune was nearly killed in a hurricane at Samoa in 1889.

Lejeune was in command of the Marines who landed in Panama in 1903 to support the rebellion that would create Panama out of Colombia and permit the construction of the canal.

After Panama, Lejeune commanded the Marine Barracks in Washington. Then back to Panama again, to the Philippines, and in 1912 to Cuba to put down a revolution. In 1914 he commanded the Marines in the occupation of Veracruz, Mexico. He returned to Washington to serve as Assistant to the Commandant as America drew near to involvement in World War I.

Lejeune went to France in 1918, and was given command of the 4th Brigade, which had fought so gallantly ay Belleau Wood. Later he commanded the Second Division, composed of Marines and soldiers. The division under Lejeune broke the German line for the second time in the last eleven days of the war.

Lejeune, the first Marine general to command a division, or Army troops in battle, received the Distinguished Service Medal, the Badge of the Legion of Honor, and the Croix de Guerre for his service in France.

On July 1, 1920, John Lejeune became Commandant of the Marine Corps, a post he was to hold for eight years. He was a popular, forward-looking general who fought the Corps's battles in congressional cloakrooms and the White House.

Lejeune oversaw the development of the famous Orange Plan, a prescient assumption that the Marines would eventually fight the Japanese expansion in the Pacific. This, in turn, led the Corps to concentrate on amphibious warfare.

Lejeune's great contribution to the Corps was to give it a new vision of the future. In a 1922 memorandum Lejeune put forward a revolutionary concept declaring that it was vital to have "a mobile Marine Corps force adequate to conduct offensive land operations against hostile naval bases." It was accepted that the Marines would defend Navy bases, but Lejeune wanted something more. He wrote, "The primary war mission of the Marine Corps is to supply a mobile force to accompany the fleet for operations on shore in support of the fleet." The Fleet Marine Force was created, a permanent strike force to be kept in a state of readiness for operations with the fleet.

rines in retreat from the Chosin Reservoir. They are trudging through the snow beside a truck; from the truck protrude the feet of their dead comrades. The dead ride, the survivors walk. This image is as symbolic of the Corps as that of the flag-raising on Iwo Jima.

The motto of the Marine Corps is *Semper Fidelis,* Latin for "always faithful." (Until 1871 it was "First to Fight," a motto that still applies.) Through the years, Marines have shortened it to Semper Fi, and "Semper Fi, Mac" is the universal Marine greeting.

After the bombing of the Marine barracks in Beirut in 1982, the commandant visited the hospital to award the Purple Heart to the wounded. He stopped at the bed of a young Marine who had tubes in his throat and couldn't speak. After the medal was pinned to his

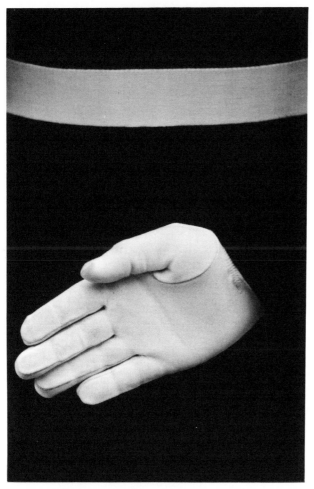

In Dress Blues, standing at parade rest presents this formal pose. Parades, reviews, and other ceremonial duties are part of the life of every Marine.

The Marine Corps emblem on the buckle of the Dress Blue belt is surrounded by oak leaves. The button device is the oldest in use in the armed forces.

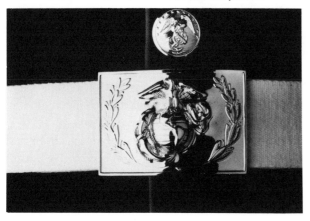

hospital gown, he motioned for a pencil and paper. He wrote something and handed the paper to the commandant. The message was two words: "Semper Fi."

Military experts agree that the larger the force, the harder it is to make it elite. William Manchester, a former Marine himself, wrote about the tricky business of instilling and maintaining esprit de corps in *Goodbye Darkness: A Memoir of the Pacific War:*

> General Eisenhower once said he doubted Marines were better fighters than his own Army Rangers. In a sense, he was probably right; if you tell picked men they are crack troops, they are likely to fight like an elite. The difference is that Ike's Rangers were a small band of commandos, while the Marine Corps, a *corps d'élite,* fielded six divisions in the Pacific—three corps, a whole army. Their élan helped shape the character of the war and determined the course of Nimitz's great drive across the central Pacific. It is, for example, a military maxim, repeated down through the ages, that casualties of 30 percent are usually the most a fighting unit can endure without losing combative spirit. Tarawa, where over 40 percent fell, proved that wasn't true of the Marine Corps. As we approached Japan, the casualty rates of our rifle regiments rose higher and higher. On Peleliu, the 1st Marines lost 56 percent of its men; on Iwo Jima, the 26th Marines lost 76 percent; on Okinawa, the 29th Marines lost 81 percent. Thus they seized islands whose defenders would have thrown other invaders back into the surf.

Of the many unique aspects of the Marines, by far the most significant is its ability to expand rapidly in time of war without losing or diluting its esprit de corps. In World War II the Corps increased in size tenfold, and more than fourfold in the Korean War. Some 447,000 Marines served in Vietnam. No other elite force in the world ever has attempted a comparable rapid expansion.

How are the Marines able to do this? Not by giving wartime recruits additional training. Boot camp now lasts eleven weeks. In the war, recruits were pushed through in eight, sometimes less. Advanced training also was cut to the bone. Standards for enlistments were lowered. Draftees were accepted. Despite everything, the Corps performed brilliantly.

The Marine Corps exudes an air of professionalism. A young man can be "in the Army" or "in the Navy," and that has a temporary ring to it. But he "is a Marine," and that suggests a lifetime commitment. The turnover in the Corps isn't significantly different from the other services, but the public regards Marines as professionals nonetheless.

This can be a problem. Americans have an ambivalent attitude toward professional military men. They consider them, at best, a necessary evil. It probably started with the "embattled farmer" fighting off the Hessian mercenary, then grew into the tradition of the citizen-soldier. The citizen-soldier goes off to war, does what he has to do, and comes home when it's over, never to fight again.

To study Marine history is to discern a recurring pattern: Marines distinguish themselves in war; their numbers are cut back sharply when the war is over; one of the other services moves to take them over; they pull in all their favors and survive a Congressional hearing. These brushes with extinction have caused the Marines to seek a role for themselves that would be immune from attack.

For a long time, the role of the Marines was to be the enforcer of American foreign policy wherever the need arose.

Later, between the World Wars, the Marines had the prescience to foresee the coming need for highly sophisticated amphibious landings, and were uniquely prepared for the war in the Pacific. But since the end of World War II, the dynamics of war have been changing.

The atomic bomb alone questions the validity of conventional warfare. But the changes are more complex than that. Korea wasn't a Marines kind of war. Nor was Vietnam. In both wars the Marines fought as divisions under the overall command of the Army. With the exception of Inchon, there was little need for their amphibious specialty. More often than not, the Marine air wings were under the command of the Army or Air Force. This kind of utilization only strengthens the argument for absorbing the Marines into the other services.

Once again, the Corps is asking itself some tough questions and coming up with intelligent answers. Its combat units have been restructured and renamed. They now can get into action anywhere in the world, fully equipped for sustained combat, with a speed that was undreamed of a few decades ago.

The Marine Corps today plays an important role in the nation's defense, and that of the free world. It describes itself as a "rapid deployment force" and is prepared to back up the claim. But even though the times are changing, Marines are still Marines, very much cast from the mold that was made before this country was a country. It takes an effort to get to know them and understand why they are unique, but the effort pays handsome dividends. The place to begin is, naturally, in the past.

The notes of Taps are sounded by a bugler. The cord on his shoulder is a fourragère, *originally awarded to the Marine units that fought at Belleau Wood.*

2★

THE OLD CORPS

From the Halls of Montezuma
To the shores of Tripoli...

The very first words of the "Marines' Hymn" speak of past glory—appropriately enough, for the past covers, and partly obscures, the Marine Corps like a mist from the sea. Reminders of the past are everywhere. The Dress Blue uniforms came from a 250-year association with the British Royal Marines. The officer's sword is patterned after one presented to Lieutenant Presley O'Bannon by the pasha of Tripoli. Over the bar in an enlisted men's club at a base in California are photographs of old-time Marine heroes: Smedley Butler, "Chesty" Puller, "Manila John" Basilone. Drill instructors proudly wear the antiquated

OPPOSITE PAGE: Somewhere in France, Marines present arms. Thinking them shock troops, the Germans called them teufelhunde—*devil dogs, an epithet proudly adopted by the Corps.*

field hat as a symbol of their authority. Marine slang is laced with words and phrases whose origins can be traced to duty in China and Haiti. This sense of history is unique to the Marines.

Marines love their past. They revel in it, sometimes to the point of obsession.

All Marines know Marine history. The Corps sees to that. Every recruit and officer candidate takes an extensive course in Marine history and traditions.

It is good to know something about the organization to which one belongs, but the Corps has more compelling reasons for spending valuable training time in history lessons. This historical indoctrination, the Corps believes, has three purposes: to make new Marines feel part of a continuing tradition; to give them a yardstick by which to measure themselves; and to inspire them in battle.

If a knowledge of Marine history is part of being a Marine, it also is part of understanding the Marines, for the Corps is very much a product of its past. Marine history as taught by the Corps is honor bright and a bit bowdlerized. In truth, there are villains as well as heroes, a wart here and there, and a few skeletons in the Corps's footlocker. But the story of an occasional fall from grace simply makes an incredible history more human.

The official birthdate of the Marine Corps is November 10, 1775, but its roots go back much further. The use of fighting men aboard ships was well established by the time of the Phoenicians, and their duties were remarkably similar to those of today's Corps—fighting in naval engagements, boarding enemy ships, and making raids into enemy territory. The Greeks and Romans picked up the idea of marines from the Phoenicians, and marines have been used by every maritime country since.

Official recognition of marines came first from Charles II of England. In 1664 he decreed the formation of the Admiral's Maritime Regiment, later renamed the Regiment of Marines, still later, the Royal Marines. In 1740 three regiments of marines were raised in the American colonies. An early commander was William Gooch of Virginia, and his troops became known as Gooch's Marines. A junior officer was George Washington's half-brother, Lawrence.

Gooch's Marines first saw action in England's war with Spain, attacking Cartagena, where Gooch was wounded. They also landed in the Spanish colony of Cuba and secured Guantanamo Bay for the British fleet. Later they were involved in several skirmishes with the French Navy.

In war and peace, one duty of Gooch's Marines was to be the security force aboard ship, making sure the sailors didn't get out of line. This led to bad feelings between the sailors and the marines, a mutual antipathy that lingers to this day.

The years in which American colonists served in the Royal Marines forged a link between American and British marines. Though enemies in the Revolution and the War of 1812, they fought side by side in Samoa, the Boxer Rebellion, World Wars I and II, and Korea. Today they work closely together in NATO. They share traditions: both services use the colors scarlet and gold; Royal Marines wear a device showing the Eastern Hemisphere; U.S. Marines wear one showing the Western Hemisphere. There is even an officer exchange program. A team of top runners from the Royal Marines comes to Washington, D.C., each fall to compete against a team from the Corps in the Marine Corps Marathon.

When the Revolution came, the Americans found they needed marines of their own. The Second Continental Congress on November 10, 1775, resolved that "two battalions of Marines be inlisted [sic] to serve for and during the present war between Great Britain and the colonies." Two weeks later Samuel Nicholas, a Quaker innkeeper, was commissioned the first Marine officer, and recruiting began at the Tun Tavern in Philadelphia.

The Marines first saw action on March 3, 1776. Captain Nicholas led 268 Marines ashore on New Providence Island in the Bahamas, capturing two forts, cannon, and a quantity of ammunition. On the way home, their ship, the *Alfred,* tangled with the British warship *Glasgow.* One Marine officer and six enlisted men were killed. John Hancock, President of the Continental Congress, sent his congratulations on the success of the foray. General George Washington stopped by the ship to pay his respects.

Nicholas and three hundred of his Marines fought with Washington's army at the second Battle of Trenton, the first of many times Marines would fight alongside soldiers. In the West, Captain James Willing led a company of Marines down the Mississippi on an old riverboat he renamed the *Rattletrap,* to harass British merchant ships around New Orleans. Later they marched north to join the forces of George Rogers Clark in fighting Indians near Lake Michigan.

Continental Marines fought in two Revolutionary War land actions. One was the abortive attempt to capture a British fort at Penobscot Bay in Maine; the other was an attempt to defend Charleston, South

In the 1880s Marines escort reveling sailors through the streets. Years of being the Navy's police force led to bad feelings between Marines and sailors.

Marines fire on the British at Penobscot Bay, Maine, in an unsuccessful attempt to seize a British fort in 1779. They were commended for a "forcible charge on the enemy."

Marines from John Paul Jones's ship Ranger *leave to raid the British port of Whitehaven on the Irish Sea, April 22, 1783. They spiked cannon and set fire to ships in the harbor.*

Carolina, against superior British forces. The Marines helped take the war to England. In April 1778, Marines from John Paul Jones's *Ranger* made two raids on English soil, and Marines from the frigate *South Carolina* made a landing on the Isle of Jersey in 1781.

The last engagement of any importance involving Continental Marines was the capture of the *Baille* in early 1783. The Treaty of Paris was signed April 11, 1783, ending the Revolution, and the new nation proceeded to disarm. The Army and Navy were disbanded, warships were auctioned off, and the Continental Marines ceased to exist. Major Nicholas returned to his tavern. At their height, the Marines had numbered 124 officers and some 3,000 men.

An old yarn has it that when the Revolution ended, the Army and the Navy took inventory and found some mules and a company of Marines left over. They flipped a coin. The Army won and took the mules.

The Barbary Coast pirates were responsible for the rebirth of the Marines. American ships in the Mediterranean had been attacked by the pirates off and on for five years before Congress in 1794 authorized the reactivation of the Navy and the construction of five frigates, each to carry a unit of Marines. On July 11, 1798, President John Adams signed into law *An Act for Establishing and Organizing a Marine Corps,* authorizing 33 officers and 848 men. The mission of the Corps included "any duty on shore as the President, at his discretion, shall direct." The act also stipulated that at sea the Marines would be under the command of the Navy; on shore, the Army. This

schizophrenia of command was to plague the Corps for years to come.

A new Marine uniform was created. Enlisted men wore short coats and trousers of blue edged in scarlet. Their hats had a yellow band and a cockade, and were worn with one side turned up. Officers wore long coats of blue with scarlet cuffs and gold epaulettes. Both uniforms had high, stiff leather collars, inspiring the Marine nickname, "leatherneck."

William Ward Burrows of Philadelphia was appointed Major Commandant. Within a few months, he recruited his quota of officers and men, a notable success considering that a private's pay was one dollar a week. A Marine band was formed, and the Marine headquarters was moved to Washington on a site "near the Navy Yard and within easy marching distance to the Capitol."

The first order of business for the Marines wasn't pirates. American ships were being raided by French privateers, and in 1798 President Adams acknowledged that the country was in an "undeclared naval war." Marines of the *Constitution* attacked French ships anchored at the Spanish island of Santo Domingo. They stormed the Spanish fort, spiked its guns, and made off with one of the French ships.

At sea, two French ships, the *Insurgente* and the *Vengeance,* were mauled by the *Constellation.* Eighty-five French ships had been captured when the hostilities ended in 1801. The Marine Corps was then trimmed to 26 officers and 453 men—an ill-considered move as it turned out.

1st Lieutenant, 1775

Sergeant, 1780

1st Lieutenant, 1810

Sergeant, 1834

Lance Corporal, 1851

Sergeant, 1859

Drum Major, 1875

Colonel, 1880

Sergeant, 1898

Captain, 1900

Corporal, 1918

Corporal, 1925

Technical Sergeant, 1938

Private, 1942

Corporal, 1943

Private, 1951

For years the threat of pirates had been used by Tunis, Morocco, Algiers, and Tripoli to coerce the United States and the European powers. To protect its ships in the Mediterranean, the U.S. was paying in tribute more than two million dollars a year—an amount more than one-fifth of the annual federal revenue. In 1801 Tripoli upped the ante; the U.S. refused to increase its tribute, and Tripoli declared war.

Four warships were dispatched to the Mediterranean to protect American interests. The frigate *Philadelphia* was captured by pirates after running aground. Marines were part of a force led by Stephen Decatur that slipped aboard the frigate and burned her to the waterline. A large ransom, however, was later paid for the captured crew.

America was up in arms. "Millions for defense but not one cent for tribute" was the belated rallying cry. But what ended the war with Tripoli was an amazing expedition led by Marine Lieutenant Presley O'Bannon and a U.S. diplomat and former Army general, William Eaton.

In Alexandria, Egypt, O'Bannon and Eaton recruited mercenaries to augment their Marines and marched them on a six-hundred-mile trek to Derna, Tripoli. They arrived on April 25, 1805, and attacked the city, supported by a bombardment from three warships. After several hours of fighting, O'Bannon was able to raise the American flag, the first time it had been raised in triumph on foreign soil. O'Bannon later was presented with a sword by the pasha of Tripoli.

War came again in 1812. Britain had been harassing U.S. merchant ships, treating America as if it were still a colony. Although the U.S. had only three first-line warships and the Marine Corps numbered fewer than 500 men, Congress declared war.

The Corps distinguished itself at sea and on land. A battalion fought at the Battle of Bladensburg in a futile attempt to keep the British forces out of Washington, and again in the defense of Fort McHenry, a battle that inspired Francis Scott Key to write "The Star-Spangled Banner."

In the Battle of New Orleans, 300 Marines, under the command of Major Daniel Carmick, fought beside Andrew Jackson. Carmick was mortally wounded, one of fewer than 100 American casualties. The British lost 2,036, and 500 were taken prisoner. A major triumph, but an unnecessary one, for a peace treaty had been signed in Europe before the battle began.

The war record of the Marines, however, was overshadowed by scandals. Commandant Franklin Wharton fled Washington just before the British attack. Court-martialed but acquitted, he resigned and died a year later. His successor, Major Anthony Gale, was cashiered for drunkenness after two years in office. Commodore Oliver Perry, the hero of Lake Erie, quarreled with the commander of his Marine detachment, Captain John Heath, who demanded a duel. Heath fired at Perry and missed; Perry refused to return fire. The newspapers had a field day with the affair.

Meanwhile, the role of the Marine Corps was being hotly debated in Washington. President Jackson wanted the Marines to be part of the Army. Congress prevailed, however, and on June 30, 1834, passed an act "for the better organization of the United States Marine Corps." It made the Corps responsible to the Navy, except on the order of the president. The Corps's strength was increased to 1,287, to be headed by a colonel commandant. Archibald Henderson, commander of the Marines aboard the *Constitution* during the War of 1812, was reappointed commandant.

It was a busy time for the Marines. They fought Cuban pirates in the early 1820s; evacuated 38 American sailors from the Falkland Islands in 1831; and fought pirates again in 1832, this time in Malay. In 1824, 30 Marines put down a riot of several hundred prisoners at the Massachusetts State Prison.

President Jackson in 1836 ordered the Marines to join with the Army to suppress an Indian uprising in the South. Commandant Henderson pinned a note to the door of his office: "Gone to fight the Indians. Will be back when the war is over."

The uprising had started when federal officials tried to force the Creeks of Georgia and Alabama and the Seminoles of Florida to reservations west of the Mississippi. The Army and Marines quickly rounded up the Creeks, and moved on to Florida. The Seminoles retreated to the Everglades, and six years of campaigning couldn't dislodge them. For his gallant leadership, Henderson was promoted to general, the first Marine so honored.

In 1843, some years after the importation of slaves had been declared illegal in America, Marines from the Navy's African Squadron were put ashore in Liberia to investigate slaver activity. Matthew Perry, the squadron commander, accompanied the Marines. They were questioning the Berribees, a tribe involved in the slave trade, when the chief, Ben Crack-O, attacked Perry. A Marine sergeant shot the chief dead. A battle broke out, but the Marines subdued the tribe without casualties. The Marines saw periodic action in Africa until 1860.

War with Mexico came in 1846, and the Marines were in the first battle, at Burrita, near the mouth of the Rio Grande. A brigade of Marines joined General Winfield Scott's army on its drive from Veracruz to Mexico City. They helped capture Chapultepec Castle —later misnamed "the Halls of Montezuma." Commandant Henderson's son was one of 26 Marine casualties at the castle. Pressing on to Mexico City, Marines helped break through a line of Mexican artillery and stop a charge of lancers.

The battle for Mexico City inspired an unknown Marine to write some lines of verse and set them to a march tune from the popular Offenbach opera *Genevieve de Brabant*. It caught on and later was adopted as the "Marines' Hymn."

Marines landed in Buenos Aires in 1852 to protect American lives and property from rioters. That same year Marines helped fight a fire that threatened to sweep through San Juan del Sur in Nicaragua. Between 1856 and 1860 they saw repeated action in the southern part of Nicaragua protecting workers of an American company building a railroad across the Isthmus of Panama.

A religious rebellion broke out in China in the 1850s, and some twenty million Chinese were killed before it ended. In 1856 American ships were fired on from forts on the Pearl River near Canton. Supported by a naval bombardment, Marines landed and captured one of four forts. The other three fell in the next two days, the Marines spiking the guns of the fort. Ten Marines and five hundred Chinese were killed.

As America approached civil war, the abolitionist John Brown and eighteen of his supporters seized the arsenal at Harper's Ferry in a scheme to arm runaway slaves. Brown was holding forty people hostage when a detachment of Marines arrived from Washington. Army Colonel Robert E. Lee led the Marines. When Brown refused to surrender, the Marines broke down the arsenal door. One Marine was killed in the brief battle.

At the beginning of the Civil War, the Marines numbered 93 officers and 3,074 men, and a number of officers resigned to fight for the South. At Bull Run,

near Manassas, Virginia, the first major battle of the war, a 353-man Marine unit was part of the 35,000 Union forces. After sustaining 44 casualties in three Confederate cavalry assaults, the Marines broke ranks and fled, the only such instance in Marine history.

Marines served on Navy ships, but the war at sea was a sideshow to the murderous land battles. One amphibious landing involving the Marines proved to be a fiasco. A Union force of 1,600, including 400 Marines, under the command of master politician and amateur general Ben Butler, landed at Wilmington, North Carolina, to capture Fort Fisher. The attackers reached the fort under a covering naval barrage, but Butler got cold feet and called the operation off. General A. H. Terry replaced Butler and the force was increased to 3,500 men. A second attack also misfired, and some 300 Marines and sailors were casualties. In the aftermath, Admiral Porter defended himself and the Navy by blaming the Marines.

The Corps did not distinguish itself in the war, in part because of its size. The maximum strength of the corps was 4,167 in a conflict that produced more than a million casualties.

The Marines were vulnerable, and trouble was not long in coming. On June 18, 1866, the House of Representatives agreed to consider a resolution on "the expediency of abolishing the Marine Corps, and transferring it to the Army."

Commandant Jacob Zeilin set about getting Marine support from high-ranking Navy officers, and was successful. Rear Admiral David Porter testified, "A ship without Marines is like a garment without buttons." The House Naval Affairs Committee voted down the resolution, recommending instead that the Marine "organization, as a separate Corps, be preserved and strengthened . . . and that its commanding officer hold the rank of brigadier general." Throughout its history, the Corps always has fought well in the corridors of the Capitol.

After the Civil War, the settlement of the West preoccupied America. The only wars most people were conscious of were with the Indians. But the Marines saw action, many times in many countries.

In the 1860s the Marines fought in Uruguay, Japan, and Formosa. In the 1870s, Hawaii, Korea, Colombia, and Mexico. In the 1880s, Hawaii again, Mexico, and Colombia. And in the 1890s, China, Nicaragua, Chile, Argentina, and Panama.

When the Marines landed in Panama, correspondent Richard Harding Davis cabled his newspaper, "The Marines have landed and the situation is well in hand." In a sentence, Davis captured an era of the Marines and gunboat diplomacy.

There were some unusual tasks to keep the Corps busy at home. Marines guarded the conspirators accused in the assassination of Abraham Lincoln. A few years later, Marines raided the Irishtown section of Brooklyn to search out and destroy illegal stills. They were called out again in 1877 when a nine-state railroad strike erupted into violence.

Charles Grymes McCawley succeeded General Zeilin as commandant in 1876 and was able to work some changes beneficial to the Corps. Naval Academy graduates were allowed to serve as Marine officers. Uniforms were standardized, and the lot of the enlisted man was improved. Plagued with complaints about the Marine Corps Band, General McCawley recruited a new director, John Philip Sousa.

Colonel Charles Heywood, commander of the Marines in Panama, succeeded McCawley in 1891. He started the practice of requiring examinations for the promotion of officers, and created several new Marine bases, including Parris Island, South Carolina. He insisted that every Marine work hard at physical fitness, marksmanship, and field tactics—a training regimen that continues today.

Commandant Heywood also had to fight off the Navy. A Navy-sponsored bill introduced in Congress called for combining the Marines with the Navy and giving Marine duties to the Army. After some vigorous lobbying by Heywood, the Military Affairs Committee killed the bill, noting that the plan would have the Navy create a new force "identical with the present Marines." The Navy made two more unsuccessful attempts before the turn of the century to eliminate, or sharply restrict, the Corps.

Interservice rivalry was forgotten temporarily when the battleship *Maine* blew up in Havana harbor, killing 238 sailors and 28 Marines. Cheered on by the Hearst press, Congress declared war on Spain on April 21, 1898.

President William McKinley was not enthusiastic about the war, but Teddy Roosevelt was. The young assistant secretary of the Navy urged Admiral Dewey to steam his Asiatic Squadron to the Philippines. The squadron arrived in Manila Bay on May 1, and after

eight hours of hard fighting the Spanish fleet surrendered. Marines were put ashore to seize control of the naval base at Cavite. Dewey then was ordered to wait until the Army arrived. The admiral later said, "If there were 5,000 Marines under my command at Manila Bay, the city would have surrendered to me on May 1."

In Cuba, a Marine battalion went ashore at Guantanamo Bay where the Navy wanted a coaling station. The landing was unopposed, but when the Marines marched on Cuzco, six miles away, they encountered stiff Spanish resistance. A naval bombardment fell short of the Spanish, landing dangerously close to the Marines. Sergeant John Quick improvised a signal flag, stood on a rock with Spanish bullets whizzing around him, and signaled the fleet to redirect its fire. Quick was awarded the Medal of Honor.

The Marines were in action in Cuba well before the Army arrived, and were in better physical condition: half of the Army troops were out of action with yellow fever and other tropical diseases; the Marine sickness level in Cuba was 2 percent.

The Filipinos thought the Americans were liberating them from the Spanish, and when they realized they were only changing masters, they rose up, attacking the Marines at Cavite. Admiral Dewey summoned another Marine battalion. By 1900 six Marine battalions were in combat.

The last island in the Philippines to be subdued was Samar, the home of the Moros, a legendary tribe of warriors. The Moros attacked an Army garrison, slaughtering many and torturing the rest to death. The Army commander, General "Hell-Roaring Jake" Smith, called in a Marine battalion led by Major Littleton Waller. "I want no prisoners," General Smith ordered. "I want you to burn and kill. The more you burn and kill, the better it will please me."

In a few weeks, Waller's troops drove the Moros deep into the jungle, where they scaled a two-hundred-foot cliff and captured the Moro stronghold.

The Marines then made an arduous march across the island to find the best route for a military telegraph, and it was a series of disasters. Waller blamed his eleven native guides and bearers. He held a quick field trial, then executed them all. On returning to Cavite, Waller and his officers were arrested by the Army and charged with murder. They were court martialed and acquitted, but the Army commanding

OPPOSITE PAGE: In Port-au-Prince, Haiti, circa 1916, three motorcyclists pose for a photographer. Here, as in many Latin countries, Marine units were sent in to protect American interests. THIS PAGE, ABOVE: Aboard the battleship California, the Marine detachment prepared to land at Corinto, Nicaragua, in August 1912. The old field hats now are worn only by drill instructors. THIS PAGE, BELOW: In search of Caco bandits, Marines patrol in Haiti in 1918. The Marines would stay in this troubled country until 1934. Mules were invaluable for toting supplies in the mountains.

was slowly but surely being drawn into war in Europe.

America tried to stay neutral, but the sinking of the *Lusitania* was the last straw. On April 6, 1917, Congress declared war on Germany and the Central Powers. The Marine slogan, "First to Fight," was bringing in a flood of enlistments, and Commandant George Barnett was determined that the first convoy to France would include a Marine expeditionary force.

Despite War Department protests that the Army had enough troops of its own, President Wilson approved, on May 29, the sending of the 5th Marine Regiment. It landed at St. Nazaire less than a month later. The 6th Marines followed, and joined with the 5th to form the 4th Marine Brigade.

The Marines in France were ordered to wear olive drab instead of Marine green to simplify the problem of supply. They also traded in their beloved field hats for overseas caps, and wore metal helmets in battle for the first time.

The Marines first saw action in the Amiens sector. On the edge of the Bois de Belleau, they filled a gap in the line left by a retreating French unit. A French officer told Colonel Wendell "Whispering Buck" Neville that it would be prudent to pull his Marines back from the edge of the woods. The colonel roared, "Retreat, hell! We just got here!"

On June 2 the Germans launched a major attack at the point where the Marines had dug in. They received a painful lesson in marksmanship; Germans were being shot before they came within eight hundred yards of the Marines. They attacked two more times, but the Marines held. The Germans dug in and set up machine-gun emplacements.

The Germans reported back to headquarters that they had encountered American "shock troops." The German soldiers called the Marines *teufelhunden*— "devil dogs"—and the Marines loved it. They later adopted the English bulldog as their official mascot, and young Marines still are having "Devil Dogs" tattooed on their arms.

Marines fighting in trenches in the Meuse-Argonne area in 1918. The offensive here involved the most American troops of any battle in history and ended World War I.

In the harsh winter of 1917–1918 a machine gun is moved up somewhere in France. The Corps struggled hard to keep Marine battalions from being used as Army replacements.

A smiling young Marine wearing a French-style overseas cap relaxes behind the lines. The inverted V on his sleeve means he has been overseas for at least six months.

The next day, the Marines were ordered to go in and clear the Germans out of the woods. Correspondent Floyd Gibbons reported hearing Sergeant Dan Daly, late of Peking, yell to his platoon, "Come on, you sons of bitches! Do you want to live forever?"

The Marines had Springfield 30-06 rifles and light machine guns, but few grenades and no mortars. They did know how to work in small-fire teams, though, and by nightfall had cleared part of the woods at the cost of 1,087 Marine casualties—a figure not to be surpassed until Tarawa.

They consolidated their position the next day, digging shallow rifle pits. One Marine referred to his pit as a foxhole. The name stuck. It took nearly three weeks of fierce fighting before the signal was flashed —"Woods now U.S. Marine Corps entirely."

After the battle, the French general in command decreed, "Henceforth, in all official papers, Belleau Wood shall bear the name 'Bois de la Brigade de Marine.'"

The battalions that fought at Belleau Wood were decorated by the French. Every Marine in the battalions was entitled to wear on his shoulder a *fourragère*, a braided cord symbolizing bravery in battle.

More importantly, Belleau Wood was to help shape the future of the Corps. In the past, Marines had been confined to fighting natives in obscure parts of the world. Now they had triumphed over a formidable enemy in a major action. The Corps would not be taken lightly again.

On July 15, 1918, the last German offensive of the war began, a massive strike toward the key city of Soissons. The 5th Marines were ordered up, the 6th placed in reserve, but both soon were in the thick of the battle. A Marine company commander, Captain Clifton Cates, sent a message from a trench under attack: ". . . I have only two men left out of my company and 20 out of other companies . . . I have no one on my left, and only a few on my right . . . I will hold." Two days of fighting cost 1,972 Marine casualties.

On the line again a few days later, the Marines were instrumental in winning the Battle of San Mihiel, the opening of the American Meuse-Argonne offensive. The offensive, lasting forty-seven days and involving 550,000 American troops, still is the largest land battle in U.S. military history.

There was friction in France between the Marines and General John Pershing, commander of the American Expeditionary Force. Pershing fought with the British and the French for the right to keep American units intact, yet he did not accord the Marines the same privilege.

The general reported to Washington that "while Marines are splendid troops, their use as a separate division is unadvisable." Pershing refused to let the 10th Marines, an artillery regiment, fight as a unit, parceling its officers out as replacements to Army units. Later, partly as a sop to the Marines, Pershing put Marine General John Lejeune in command of the Second Division.

Later an irate Pershing said, "Why in hell can't the Army do it if the Marines can? They are all the same kind of men. Why can't they be like Marines?"

As the war went into its final month, Marines led the attack on Mont Blanc, advancing nine kilometers in a single day and taking 1,700 prisoners. They crossed the Meuse at night, resuming their attack in the morning. But it was November 11, and at 11 o'clock the war was over.

The Marine Brigade became part of the Army of Occupation, not returning home until August 12, 1919. After reviewing the brigade on its return, President Wilson wrote Commandant Barnett, "The whole nation has reason to be proud of them."

In the war, the Corps had grown to 76,000, some 32,000 of whom had served in France. Of these, 11,366 were casualties; 2,459 Marines were killed or missing in action. Only 25 were taken prisoner.

A footnote to the war: Marines were sent in June 1918 to guard the American consulate at Vladivostok in the aftermath of the Russian Revolution. They were replaced in a few months by Army troops, but Marines guarded the Navy radio station in Vladivostok Bay until 1922.

From early 1917 until 1920, Marines were in Cuba, protecting American sugar interests. Spasmodic unrest kept the Marines in Nicaragua until 1933. If nothing else, these tours of duty were good training. The Marines learned jungle combat techniques, and experimented with their aircraft in close air support—lessons that would prove invaluable in the years to come.

Remembering those days, General H. M. Smith wrote, "If the Battle of Waterloo was won on the playing fields of Eton, the Japanese bases in the Pacific were captured on the beaches of the Caribbean."

The many prolonged Marine incursions in Latin America to protect American commercial interests, often in support of unpopular regimes, earned the Corps the sobriquet "Wall Street's police force." It

THIS PAGE: A vintage landing craft lands an artillery piece during maneuvers in 1924. Between the wars the Marines worked on perfecting their amphibious tactics. OPPOSITE PAGE: Marines jam the deck of a troopship bound for Nicaragua. Campaigns in Latin Americas in the 1920s and 1930s gave the Corps a trained cadre of leaders for World War II.

OPPOSITE PAGE, ABOVE: On maneuvers at Culebra, Puerto Rico, in 1924, Marines come ashore from an early landing craft, learning the lessons that paid off in the Pacific in World War II. OPPOSITE PAGE, BELOW: A historic photograph taken at Veracruz, Mexico. Left to right: Captain Fredrick Delano, Sergeant Major John Quick, Lieutenant Colonel Wendell Neville, Colonel John Lejeune, and Major Smedley Butler. Quick and Neville won the Medal of Honor; Butler earned two. Both Neville and Lejeune became Commandant of the Marine Corps.

also earned the Marines the dislike of many Latin Americans, a feeling that sometimes crops up today.

In the middle 1920s there was a civil war in China between Canton and the northern provinces. The Soviet-supported Cantonese threatened Shanghai in 1927. Marines, under the command of Smedley Butler, were sent in to protect the city's international settlement. Most of the Marines were sent home in 1929, leaving behind a force of "China Marines" to protect American interests.

The Corps, cut back from a wartime high of 76,000 to less than 20,000, once again was a small, exclusive military fraternity. There was good duty, at home and abroad. Even the Marine pay looked princely by Depression standards, and there was a waiting list to enlist.

As the decade wore on, war drew closer. Civil war broke out in Spain. Hitler and Mussolini sent troops to aid their fellow fascist, Generalissimo Francisco Franco. Japan invaded China. And Hitler was making his plans for the domination of Europe increasingly clear.

Only a few of the most prescient Marines sensed that this was the twilight of the Old Corps.

The Marine Armed Guard of the steamer Iping *patrolled the Yangtze River in the 1930s. The Japanese invasion of China made the lot of the legendary China Marines a lot tougher.*

3★

THEIR FINEST HOUR

General John A. Lejeune emerged from the World War a much-decorated and popular hero. His appointment as commandant on June 30, 1920, seemed a proper finale to a long and distinguished career, but his greatest service to the Corps lay before him.

The way wars were fought had been changed forever. For four years, great armies had been stalemated in the muddy trenches of Flanders, fighting a murderous war of attrition. Machine guns and barbed wire had practically neutralized the enemy's infantry. Artillery barrages had been ineffective against deeply entrenched troops. The tank was promising but hadn't proved itself. The airplane was becoming a factor; it could be a forward observer, drop bombs, and strafe enemy troops.

General Lejeune saw at first hand that the enormous price of the war stemmed from a lack of mobil-

---

OPPOSITE PAGE: A vintage poster shows a Marine on a battlefield, uniform tattered, bayonet fixed. The Old Corps's recruiting slogan: "First to Fight."

ity. The determining factor in France was sheer manpower and logistics, not brilliant commanders and brave troops, although there had been plenty of both.

Where did this leave the Marine Corps? Lejeune wondered. Mobility was the Marine hallmark. If warfare were to remain static, the best the Corps could hope for was to fight in separate units alongside the Army as it had done in France. But a great lesson of military history is that the dynamics of warfare constantly change; this lesson was not lost on Lejeune. He knew that it would be a fatal mistake to plan to fight the last war over again.

A catalyst to the general's thinking was a young officer, Earl Hancock "Pete" Ellis. While a student at the Naval Academy, Ellis became fascinated with Japan, its militarism and its growing sphere of influence. He was convinced that someday the United States would be drawn into a war with Japan, and that the war would involve the Japanese-controlled islands of the Pacific. He believed that the key to a U.S. victory in a war with Japan was the development of the techniques of amphibious warfare. He first articulated these theories in a lecture at the Naval War College in 1913.

Ellis's theories gained support among senior Marine officers. With the backing of Commandant Lejeune, Ellis developed and refined his ideas in a document called *Advance Base Operations in Micronesia,* better known as the Orange Plan. Despite the disinterest of the other services, Lejeune approved the Orange Plan in 1921, and set about getting the Corps ready to meet the challenge of the Japanese. A major step was changing the old Expeditionary Force into the Fleet Marine Force, and gearing it up for amphibious warfare.

Ellis should have been happy to have the Corps act on his vision. Instead, he became even more obsessed with the Japanese threat. In 1923 he took a one-year leave of absence to make, with the blessing of the Corps, an unofficial tour of the Japanese islands in the Pacific. He became ill and died at Koror, one of the Palau Islands, before completing his mission. The full story of the visionary Major Ellis and what he found in the islands is lost to history.

Colonel Robert Dunlap made an exhaustive study of the largest amphibious landing of the World War, the Allied invasion at Gallipoli. Dunlap was able to convince the Corps that Gallipoli had been right in concept, and failed only because the operation had been bungled.

The Marines held a series of landing exercises in Cuba and other locales in the early 1920s. They learned that their equipment wasn't up to the task, although much progress was made in improving landing techniques. In 1934, after years of intensive study, the Marines published the *Tentative Manual for Landing Operations,* an imaginative pioneer work. It spelled out every important aspect of landing operations: joint command, communications, ship-to-shore troop movements, naval gunfire and air support, and the organization of troops on shore. One military historian praised the manual as "the Pentateuch and Four Gospels" of modern amphibious warfare.

Andrew Higgins developed early prototypes that led to the famous LCIs of World War II: short, chunky boats with flat bottoms that could reach the beach, with hinged bows that dropped down to discharge Marines. In Florida a gifted amateur designer, Donald Roebling, developed a truly amphibious vehicle, with tanklike treads, for rescue work in the Everglades. The Marines heard about it and asked Roebling to develop a similar craft to their specifications. The re-

Lieutenant Colonel Earl "Pete" Ellis was convinced that the Marines would have to fight the Japanese. He died on the island of Kator in 1922 under mysterious circumstances.

sult was the Amtrack. It was capable of crossing over obstacles in the water and taking Marines right up on the beach.

War began in Europe on September 1, 1939. German troops invaded Poland, and two days later Britain and France declared war on Germany. The Marine Corps then numbered some 18,000, roughly the size of the New York City police force. President Franklin D. Roosevelt declared a limited national emergency, which included increasing the size of the Corps to 25,000. A year later the Marine Reserve was called up, some 250 officers and 5,000 men. Marine defense battalions were sent to the Pacific islands of Samoa, Midway, Johnston, and Palmyra. The 1st Marine Division was created and was sent to Tent City One, at what would become Camp Lejeune, North Carolina. The 2nd Division was formed on the West Coast.

In this rapid buildup, somehow the Corps managed to retain its essential character. Colonel Samuel B. Griffith, II, later wrote about this phenomenon in his book, *The Battle for Guadalcanal.*

They were a motley bunch. Hundreds were young recruits only recently out of boot training at Parris Island.

Others were older: first sergeants yanked off "planks" in Navy yards, sergeants from recruiting duty, gunnery sergeants who had fought in France, perennial privates with disciplinary records a yard long. These were the professionals, the "Old Breed" of United States Marines. Many had fought "Cocos" in Haiti, "bandidos" in Nicaragua, and French, English, Italian and American soldiers and sailors in every bar in Shanghai, Manila, Tsingtao, Tientsin and Peking.

They were inveterate gamblers and accomplished scroungers, who drank hair tonic in preference to post exchange beer ("horse piss"), cursed with wonderful fluency, and never went to chapel ("the God-box") unless forced to. Many dipped snuff, smoked rank cigars or chewed tobacco (cigarettes were for women and children).

They knew their weapons and they knew their tactics. They knew they were tough and they knew they were good. There were enough of them to fill out the Division and to impart to the thousands of young men a share both of the unique spirit which they animated and the skills they possessed.

Early in 1941 there were 25,000 British troops stationed in Iceland. Winston Churchill desperately needed them, and Roosevelt replaced them with the Marine 1st Provisional Brigade. The Marines turned Iceland over to the Army in March 1942, when their presence, too, was needed elsewhere.

The Japanese struck the Pacific Fleet at Pearl Harbor on the morning of December 7, 1941. In ninety minutes, three hundred Japanese carrier-based planes crippled the fleet.

Further west, the Japanese bombed Midway, Johnston, and Palmyra. On December 8 some 6,000 Japanese troops landed at Guam and overwhelmed the 130-man Marine garrison. At Wake, most of the Marine planes were destroyed on the ground; the few remaining held off the Japanese until December 22. (An apocryphal story has it that the last radio message received from the Marines at Wake was "Send us more Japs!")

In the Philippines, the 4th Marine Regiment arrived on December 1 and helped General Douglas MacArthur's forces in the defense of Bataan and Corregidor in 1942. Many Marines died on the Death March after their defeat.

The Joint Chiefs of Staff decided to commit the Marine Corps to the Pacific, anticipating that the "next year or so promises to comprise a series of landing operations from shipboard to small islands." The 1st Marine Division, commanded by General Alexander Vandegrift, was sent to New Zealand.

By late spring 1942 the Japanese offensive in the South Pacific had taken most of New Guinea and several of the Solomon Islands, including Guadalcanal, where an airfield was being built. Australia and New Zealand, their armies fighting in North Africa, were threatened by invasion.

Two decisive U.S. naval victories set the stage for a Marine offensive in the South Pacific. A task force commanded by Admiral Frank Fletcher intercepted a Japanese fleet headed for Port Moresby in southeastern New Guinea. In a four-day battle in the Coral Sea, May 4 to May 8, 1942, the U.S. fleet blocked Japan's southeastern push. It was an historic naval battle, the first ever fought entirely by aircraft.

Japan was preparing to invade Midway, one thousand miles northwest of Hawaii, unaware that the U.S. had broken its naval code. Admiral Chester Nimitz knew the plans of the Japanese fleet and was waiting

Commandant Alexander Vandegrift, right, with his generals. From the left: Henry Larsen, Roy Geiger, and Holland Smith, commander of Fleet Marine Force, Pacific.

★ MARINES IN THE MOVIES

The Marines always have been a popular subject for motion pictures. In fact, Thomas Alva Edison was the first to make a Marine movie. The Edison Studio filmed *Star Spangled Banner* in 1916, starring Paul Kelly as a swashbuckling Marine. Edison made three more Marine movies, including *The Marinettes,* as the World War I women's auxiliary was called. Through the years, more than 75 Marine movies have been made. Many were forgettable, a few downright silly, but a few became screen classics.

One classic was the 1922 *What Price Glory?* adapted from the hit Broadway play by Maxwell Anderson and Lawrence Stallings. In the film, Edmund Lowe was Captain Flagg and Victor McLaglen was Sergeant Quirt. It was remade in 1952 with James Cagney and Dan Dailey but it didn't have the bite or the popularity of the original. In another 1926 movie, Gene Tunney, the World War I Marine who defeated Jack Dempsey for the heavyweight boxing title, played himself in *The Fighting Marine.*

In the 1920s and 1930s, practically every Hollywood leading man turned up on the screen in Marine green: Jack Holt, William Boyd (later to become famous as Hopalong Cassidy), Richard Dix, Lon Chaney, Pat O'Brien, Richard Arlen, and Dick Powell were among the better known.

World War II brought a flood of Marine movies. A good one was the 1942 *Wake Island* starring Brian Donlevy, Robert Preston, Macdonald Carey, and William Bendix. One of the best wartime Marine movies was *Guadalcanal Diary,* with Preston Foster, Lloyd Nolan, Anthony Quinn, Richard Conte, and Richard Jaeckel.

Two wartime movies were about the Marine Raiders. In *Gung-Ho,* Randolph Scott played Evans Carlson, supported by Robert Mitchum, J. Carroll Naish, and Sam Levene. *Marine Raiders* starred Pat O'Brien and Robert Ryan.

John Garfield gave an excellent performance in the 1945 *Pride of the Marines* playing Al Schmid, a hero blinded on Guadalcanal. *Till the End of Time* focused on the problems of returning Marine veterans. Robert Mitchum and Guy Madison starred.

It comes as a surprise that John Wayne played a Marine in only two movies, but one was excellent and the other was outstanding, practically everyone's favorite Marine movie. *Flying Leathernecks* was inspired by Guadalcanal's Cactus Air Force. Wayne was ably supported by Robert Ryan and Don Taylor. The quintessential Marine movie was *Sands of Iwo Jima,* in which Wayne's portrayal of Sergeant Stryker forever captured the spirit of the Marine sergeant.

Leon Uris's best-selling novel *Battle Cry* became a fine movie starring Tab Hunter, Aldo Ray, and Van Heflin as "High Pockets," the battalion commander. In *Fighter Attack,* Sterling Hayden, a former Marine, played a role based on an OSS mission he personally had participated in. Jack Webb was a merciless D.I. in *The DI.* Tony Curtis played Ira Hayes, the full-blooded Indian Marine who helped raise the flag on Iwo Jima, in *The Outsider.*

One of the best films about Marines in World War II was *Hell in the Pacific* starring Lee Marvin, a former Marine who had been severely wounded on Saipan. Another fine film was *Halls of Montezuma.* In it Richard Widmark, Robert Wagner, and Jack Webb were good; Jack Palance was exceptional.

Other leading men playing Marines in that period included William Holden in *The Proud and the Profane;* Paul Newman in *Until They Sail;* Burt Lancaster in *South Seas Paradise;* John Payne in *Tripoli;* Clifton Webb as John Philip Sousa in *Stars and Stripes Forever;* Charlton Heston in *85 Days at Peking;* Alan Ladd and Sidney Poitier in *All the Young Men;* Cliff Robertson in *Inchon;* and Robert Conrad as Pappy Boyington in *The Black Sheep.*

Military movies fell out of favor during Vietnam and its aftermath. The 1980s, though, brought some excellent Marine films. In Stanley Kubrick's *Full Metal Jacket,* Lee Ermey, a former D.I. himself, does a tour de force as an old-school D.I., punching and bullying his recruits into shape for Vietnam.

It probably was inevitable for Clint Eastwood to play a Marine. As the veteran gunnery sergeant in *Heartbreak Ridge,* he found himself out of step with the modern Corps and out of touch with his ex-wife. All worked out satisfactorily, though, after Clint carried the day in the invasion of Grenada.

There seems to be an unquenchable thirst for Marine movies, and Hollywood apparently hasn't lost the knack of turning them out.

when planes from Japanese carriers struck Midway on June 4. Planes from the *Enterprise, Hornet,* and *Yorktown* hit the Japanese carriers while their planes were away. Four Japanese carriers were sunk, and most of their planes were shot down in the two-day battle, which ended the threat to Hawaii.

The Marines swung into action. Colonel Merritt "Red Mike" Edson led his 1st Raider Battalion ashore on Tulagi, near Guadalcanal, killing the 500 Japanese defenders. The nearby islands of Gavatu and Tanambogo also fell to the Marines. Then the main Marine force was put ashore at Guadalcanal.

The first great Marine amphibious campaign began on August 7, 1942, with deceptive ease. There were only some 2,200 Japanese on the island, many of them construction workers. By nightfall the 1st and 5th

Marines had established a strong beachhead. They captured the airfield the next day. Then the Japanese struck from the air. Forty bombers went for the transports. The Japanese shot down twenty-one of the ninety-three Navy carrier fighters. The Navy carriers, pleading a shortage of fuel, steamed south. That night a Japanese task force sunk more transports; the few remaining U.S. ships sailed away in the morning.

There were 11,125 Marines on Guadalcanal, 6,805 on the other islands. They were stranded, short of food and ammunition. The long ordeal began.

The Japanese Imperial General Staff committed 80,000 troops to the task of retaking Guadalcanal. They started to land in mid-August, a week after Vandegrift had radioed, "Airfield Guadalcanal ready for fighters and dive bombers." Two Marine squadrons

A machine gunner and riflemen ford a muddy stream in South Pacific campaign. Malaria and heat exhaustion often were as much a hazard as the Japanese.

flew in, nicknamed themselves "The Cactus Air Force" after the code word for Guadalcanal, and started blasting Japanese planes out of the sky.

Months of hard fighting lay ahead on Guadalcanal. More and more Japanese troops came ashore. Henderson field was bombed nightly, and Japanese warships came down the Slot between Tulagi and Guadalcanal to fire on Marine emplacements. On short rations, in jungle heat and tropical rains that destroyed clothing and equipment, a third of the Marines contracted malaria. (A Marine wasn't allowed off the line until his temperature reached 103 degrees.) But somehow the Marines managed to hang on, turning back attack after attack. By December, three more divisions had landed. What was left of the 1st Marine Division was relieved.

They had resented the Navy steaming off and leaving them stranded on Guadalcanal. Some Marines on the island created an unofficial medal that reflected their view of the Navy. Called the George Medal, it was inscribed *Faciat Georgius*—Latin for "Let George do it"—and depicted an admiral dropping a hot potato into the hands of a kneeling Marine; the ribbon was fashioned from Marine utility uniform material.

Historian Samuel Eliot Morison wrote of the battle: "Guadalcanal is not a name but an emotion, recalling desperate fights in the air, furious night naval battles, frantic work at supply and construction, savage fighting in the sodden jungle, nights broken by screaming bombs and deafening explosions of naval shells."

The six-month battle for Guadalcanal cost the Marines more than 3,000 casualties, not to mention 8,580 cases of malaria. The Japanese lost 25,000 troops, 600 planes, and 24 warships. The U.S. also lost 24 warships. But the Japanese had been stopped cold, never again to regain the initiative.

The Joint Chiefs developed two possible plans to defeat Japan. MacArthur insisted that the U.S. should drive north to New Guinea, then retake the Philippines as a base from which to invade Japan. The alternate plan, proposed by Admirals Halsey and Nimitz, would use the islands of the central Pacific as stepping stones to Japan. The Joint Chiefs compromised: they approved both plans.

Before the Americans could go their separate ways, though, they had to neutralize the large Japanese base at Rabaul, on New Guinea, 565 air miles from Guadal-

In the Gilberts, a Marine Corsair fighter is on the runway for takeoff. Part of the Devildog Squadron, the plane has flown 100 missions with more to come.

canal. The Marines moved up the Solomons, then seized the Russell Islands. In June 1943 they made a series of seven landings on New Georgia. The next step was a big one, Bougainville.

Bougainville was larger than Guadalcanal and was defended by an estimated 35,000 Japanese. The 3rd Marine Division landed November 1, with an Army division in reserve. A month and 1,841 Marine casualties later, Bougainville was secured. Airfields were quickly carved out of the jungle; three months later, Rabaul was bombed out of business.

By now the 1st Marine Division had been remanned and resupplied in Australia. New semi-automatic Garand M1's replaced the World War I Springfields the division had used on Guadalcanal. The day after Christmas, the division stormed ashore at Cape Gloucester on the island of New Britain. The landing was relatively unopposed, but stiff resistance developed from the 75,000 defenders. Three months passed before the Marines could turn the island over to the Army.

The planned two-pronged attack in the Pacific was confirmed at the Quebec Conference in August 1943. The Marine offensive would begin with the Gilberts, proceed to the Marshalls, then the Carolines. First stop: Tarawa.

Everything went wrong at Tarawa. A naval bombardment was to have knocked out the beach defenses; it didn't. The tide was thought to have been high enough for the landing craft to clear the coral reef

in the harbor; it wasn't. There was no air support. H-Hour was postponed twice because the Japanese shore batteries were still firing.

On the first wave, Higgins boats were stranded on the reef and blown apart. The survivors waded ashore in shoulder-high water, holding their rifles over their heads. The second wave also faltered and only a few hundred troops made it ashore, only to be pinned down by enemy fire under a wooden pier. They held on through the night.

The 1st Battalion, 8th Marines, spent the night in landing craft. They started in at daylight, taking heavy losses. Then the last Marine reserves were sent ashore.

A naval officer who witnessed the landing wrote in his log, "The water seemed never clear of tiny men . . . slowly wading beachward. . . . They kept falling, falling, falling . . . singly, in groups, and in rows." Correspondent Robert Sherrod told how the Marines trudged on, keeping their formation, "even disdainful of death . . . black dots of men, holding their weapons above their heads, moving at a snail's pace, never faltering."

It was touch-and-go on the beach all that day. The next morning, the Marines were able to fan out and secure the island. Three days of fighting had killed 984 Marines and wounded 2,072. Tarawa had taught the Corps some costly lessons.

Next stop: Kwajalein in the Marshalls. The attacking force was the 4th Marine and the 7th Army Divisions. A two-day bombardment preceded D-Day, January 31, 1944. Kwajalein was an atoll, a main island and a curved string of smaller islands. The 25th Marines took five small islands the first day. The other two, Roi and Namur, fell the second day, despite Japanese banzai attacks. The cost: 313 dead and 502 wounded. The Army suffered slightly fewer casualties taking the main island of Kwajalein.

Eniwetok in the Marshalls was tough to crack, and it took more than a thousand Marine and Army casualties to do it.

Other Japanese bases in the Marshalls, cut off from supplies and reinforcements, were bombed into ineffectiveness.

What was needed now were airfields in the Marianas to enable the new B-29s to bomb Japan and the Philippines. Part of the plan was to draw out the main Japanese battle fleet, inactive since Guadalcanal.

Three islands were selected for invasion: Saipan, Tinian, and Guam.

A task force of some 800 ships and 162,000 troops was assembled in the Marshalls, to be protected by Admiral Raymond Spruance's Fifth Fleet. This Joint Expeditionary Force was commanded by Admiral Kelly Turner, with General Holland Smith leading the Marines. An Army division was in reserve, another stood by in Hawaii.

Saipan, the headquarters of the Japanese Central Pacific Fleet, was defended by 30,000 troops. The Marines hit the beach at Charon Kanoa, suffering some 2,000 casualties the first day. Five battalion commanders were among the wounded. Reinforced by the Army's 27th Division, the Marines were making slow progress when the Navy got its wish—the Japanese fleet came out to fight. On June 19, fighters from carriers shot down 346 Japanese planes in the Battle of the Philippine Sea. Spruance pressed the attack and, at the cost of 100 planes, sank three Japanese carriers.

The battle was not going well on Saipan. Disgusted with the performance of the Army's 27th Division, General "Howlin' Mad" Smith, after conferring with Spruance and Turner, relieved its commanding general, Ralph Smith, with whom the Marine general had quarreled before. The shock of a Marine general relieving an Army general touched off a furor that almost got "Howlin' Mad" Smith relieved himself, and inflamed Army-Marine relations for years. But the decision stuck, and the 27th started to pull its weight, at least for a while. But on the night of June 27, General Smith warned the new Army general to expect a banzai attack. It came, swept over light Army defenses, and was stopped only by the 10th Marines firing 105mm howitzers at point-blank range.

At the northern tip of Saipan, hundreds of Japanese soldiers and civilians committed suicide by jumping off a 220-foot cliff into the sea. American casualties in the campaign were 16,525; 12,934 of them Marines.

The loss of Saipan and the disastrous defeat at sea were too much for Premier Hideki Tojo. His resignation was accepted by Emperor Hirohito.

At Guam, the Marines, commanded by General Roy Geiger, had a difficult landing. A point of land separated the two regimental landing beaches, and from there two 75mm cannons destroyed twenty-four landing craft before being silenced. The Marines on the beaches fought off a night counterattack, moving in-

Under heavy fire, Marines move off the beach at Tarawa and head inland. Miscalculations made Tarawa a near disaster as hundreds of men were killed wading ashore.

land the next morning. A few nights later, ten battalions of Japanese made a banzai charge. Some broke through to a field hospital, where wounded Marines, dressed only in their skivvies, fought them off. Long after the battle for Guam was over, Japanese soldiers were captured or killed in the hills; the last gave himself up in 1972. The price of Guam: 9,111 American casualties, most of them Marines.

Just south of Saipan lies Tinian, its flat cane fields perfectly suited for B-29 runways. Two Marine divisions, the 2nd and the 4th, landed from Saipan on July 20. They rolled Tinian up quickly, despite brisk resistance and a banzai charge. By August 12, 6,050 Japanese were dead and 225 were prisoners. Marine casualties: 290 dead, 1,515 wounded, and 24 missing.

In most wars there are meaningless battles. Peleliu was one. Originally the plan was to begin MacArthur's campaign to retake the Philippines by a landing on Mindanao; Peleliu was needed to protect the right flank. But Admiral Halsey, operating near the Philippines, concluded that Leyte, to the north, wasn't as well defended as Mindanao. Leyte was chosen as the invasion site, and Peleliu became of no importance. But the Marines were told to take Peleliu anyway. No one realized how well it was defended.

General MacArthur was only one of the people who decided to have the Marines take Peleliu, but many Marines blamed him anyway. There was bad blood between the general and the Marines dating back to France, where he let it be known that he felt the Marines had been overdecorated for Belleau Wood. In the Pacific, he was thought to have made up for it by decorating Marine units sparingly. Marines fighting on Bataan resented MacArthur's comparative safety on Corregidor, referring to him as "Dugout Doug."

After the horror of Tarawa, a ditty sprang up among the Marines. It was sung to the tune of "Bless 'Em All" and one of the verses was aimed at the general:

Oh, we sent for MacArthur to come to Tarawa
But General MacArthur said no.
He gave as his reason, it wasn't his season,
Besides there was no USO.

53

PORTRAIT IN GREEN:
JOHN BASILONE

John Basilone quit high school in Raritan, New Jersey, at fifteen, a big Italian kid with jug ears and a ready smile. He worked in a laundry and sold vegetables off a truck before joining the Army. Stationed in Manila, he was a Golden Gloves light-heavyweight champion. Here he met the great love of his life, the .30-caliber machine gun. He spent hours breaking down and reassembling his gun blindfolded; when he fired he would laugh with joy. His accuracy was amazing.

After his hitch was up, Basilone went home. His mother wanted him to get married and settle down, but he missed military life. He enlisted in the Marines in 1940. His buddies called him "Manila John."

On Guadalcanal, Basilone was a machine gunner in "Chesty" Puller's battalion defending Lunga Ridge near Henderson Field. A Japanese regiment was attacking, determined to take the field and drive the Marines off the island. On the second night of the battle there was a torrential rain, and the Japanese were storming the barbed wire forty yards in front of

Basilone. He repeatedly repaired guns, ducking back through the jungle to the company command post for more ammo belts and spare parts, fighting his way through infiltrating Japanese with his .45.

After one such trip, he learned the Japanese had overrun the section of machine guns on his right, killing two Marines and wounding three. The Japanese had tried to turn the guns on the Marines in the other pits, but the guns had jammed. Basilone and a private raced to the pit, found eight Japanese and killed them all. He got the guns working again, rolling from gun to gun, shooting up each belt as soon as his crews fed it into the breech. His two guns formed a cross fire at a gap in the barbed wire. After the battle, more than 800 dead Japanese were found in front of Basilone's position.

Manila John was awarded the Medal of Honor, the first enlisted Marine so honored in World War II, and sent home a hero. In September 1944 he joined the 27th Marines as they were preparing to invade Iwo Jima.

Basilone and his machine-gun platoon hit Red Beach on Iwo on February 19, 1945. They were up to their knees in volcanic ash; gunfire poured in from Japanese pillboxes and tanks. The platoon made it over a sand dune and saw a blockhouse. On top of it was a heavy machine gun. He ordered his men to dig in and he circled behind the blockhouse. Basilone's grenades put the blockhouse out of commission.

Minutes later, a mortar shell killed Manila John and four of his platoon. He was posthumously awarded the Navy Cross. A life-sized bronze statue stands in Raritan. Manila John is clad in battle dress, and cradled in his arms is a machine gun.

The Marines hit the beach on Peleliu on September 15, 1944, the landing preceded by a two-day naval bombardment which proved to be the least effective of the Pacific war. The first wave was met by light fire, then the beach became an inferno. Cannon knocked out 26 landing craft, and Japanese tanks and infantry attacked. The Japanese were stopped, but the Marines were way off schedule.

Peleliu marked a change in Japanese defensive tactics. No longer would they make an all-out defense on the beaches and, when that failed, die in a banzai charge. They now were dug into the coral hills in a network of interconnecting positions. They would let the Marines get ashore, then make them pay dearly. In taking a ridge called Bloody Nose, some Marine units lost more than half their men. The price tag for this unnecessary invasion was 6,265 Marine casualties.

The reoccupation of the Philippines began in October 1944, and 1,258 Marines, artillerymen from the V Amphibious Corps, were among the first to go ashore at Leyte. Someone put a sign on the beach, "By the grace of God and a few Marines, MacArthur's back in the Philippines." In the landings, the Japanese fleet threw everything it had at the invasion force in the Battle of Leyte Gulf, introducing the technique of suicidal kamikaze planes. When the battle was over, for all practical purposes the Japanese Imperial Navy had ceased to exist.

Iwo Jima has been described as "a bad-smelling pork chop, burned black, five miles long and two-and-a-half miles wide." This small, unattractive piece of real estate cost the Marines dearly. Of the 71,245 who fought there, 5,931 were killed and 17,372 were wounded. Three divisions were in action: the 4th and 5th went in early, and two regiments of the 3rd, in floating reserve, landed later. The invasion had been delayed for more than a month when the fleet was involved in the Philippines. D-Day was February 19, 1945, following a three-day bombardment. Aerial pho-

tography had shown 642 blockhouses, pillboxes, and gun positions; many more were dug into the coral.

The landing was tough, the Marines pinned down by interlocking machine-gun and mortar fields of fire. Japanese shelling kept the second wave from landing for hours. By the end of the day, a narrow beachhead was established, running from the base of Mount Suribachi to just beyond the initial landing area.

The next day the attack continued. The 28th Marines started up Suribachi; by sundown they had advanced two hundred yards. The Japanese counterattacked unsuccessfully that night. The Marines started up again in the morning. After a short but fierce fight, the top was taken. A small flag was raised. A few hours later another, larger flag was brought up from an LST by a patrol. As they worked, Associated Press photographer Joe Rosenthal took the photograph that would come to symbolize the Marine Corps.

Four days after landing on Iwo Jima, a company of the 26th Marines wait for tanks to blast Japanese pill boxes. The company already had suffered 40 percent casualties.

The flag-raising on Mount Suribachi didn't mark the end of the fighting. Five brutal weeks lay ahead. Not until March 16 did the Japanese commander commit ritual suicide, and the fighting sputter out.

One more island lay ahead, and it would be the scene of the biggest battle of the Pacific War. Okinawa is a large island, sixty miles long and an average of eight miles wide. It lay halfway between Formosa and Japan, an ideal staging area for the invasion of Japan. Attacking would be the 182,000 troops of the Tenth Army, of which 81,000 were Marines. They hit the beach on Easter Sunday, April 1, 1945. The 2nd Marine Division feinted a landing on the southern end of the island, while the main landing hit the middle. The plan was to cut the island in half, then send one corps north, the other south toward Shuri Castle and Naha, the island capital.

The 2nd Division lost a transport and an LST in a kamikaze attack. The 1st and the newly formed 6th Marine Divisions landed, and in four days of fighting reached the other side of the island and swung south. Some of the toughest fighting came when the 6th Division came to a complex of ridges dominated by a

Two amphibious tanks race toward the flaming shore of Anguar Island in the Palaus. These tanks land mere minutes after the naval bombardment is ended.

A wave of landing craft (LVTs) move past the bombardment line to hit the beach in the invasion of Okinawa in 1945. A battleship is in the background.

hill called Sugar Loaf. The Japanese were well dug in. Author William Manchester, who was with the 6th Division at Sugar Loaf, described the battle:

All greenery had vanished; as far as one could see, shellfire had denuded the scene of shrubbery. What was left resembled a cratered moonscape. But the craters were vanishing, because the rain had transformed the earth into a thin porridge—too thin even to dig foxholes. At night, you lay on a poncho as a precaution against drowning during the barrages. All night, every night, shells erupted close enough to shake the mud beneath you at the rate of five or six a minute. You could hear the cries of the dying but could do nothing. Japanese infiltration was always imminent, so the order was to stay put. Any man who stood up was cut in half by machine guns manned by fellow Marines. . . . We were there and deadlocked for a week in the relentless rain. During those weeks, we lost nearly 4,000 men.

The Marines broke the Sugar Loaf deadlock by landings behind the Japanese lines, but it wasn't until June 21 that the last pockets of resistance were silenced.

The statistics show the enormity of the battle for Okinawa. Some 110,000 Japanese and Okinawans had been killed, and 7,500 taken prisoner. The Japanese lost 7,830 planes; the U.S. 768. The Navy's loss exceeded that of Pearl Harbor: 36 ships sunk, 368 damaged, 4,907 Navy dead. Marine casualties were 2,899 dead, 11,677 wounded.

The Marines were on Okinawa getting ready to invade Japan when atomic bombs fell on Hiroshima and Nagasaki, hastening the end of the war. On September 2, 1945, Japan surrendered aboard the battleship *Missouri* in Tokyo Bay. The only senior Marine officer on deck when the documents of surrender were signed was General Roy Geiger, commander of the Fleet Marine Force, Pacific.

After the surrender, the first U.S. forces to land in Japan were the 1st and 3rd Battalions, 4th Marines, who went ashore at Tokyo. MacArthur and Nimitz joined them later in the day. A week later the survivors of the 4th Marines captured at Corregidor were released and honored at a formation.

In January, 1946 the Marine regimental headquarters left Japan for Tsingtao, China, to rejoin the 6th Division. The occupation of Japan was going smoothly, and the 5th Division sailed for home.

At the end of the war there were 458,000 in the Marine Corps, six divisions, and six air wings. Of the 16.3 million Americans who served in the wartime armed forces, some 5 percent had been Marines. Among Marine officers, 98 percent had served in the Pacific; 89 percent of the enlisted ranks served there. The total Marine casualty list recorded 19,733 dead and 67,207 wounded.

The Marines had made twenty-six successful invasions in the Pacific. The war that Pete Ellis had prophesied, and the amphibious techniques that he, Lejeune, and the others had developed had helped win it. And, island by island, battle by battle, the Marines had etched the memory of their courage into the American consciousness.

★

THE RULES CHANGE

A feeling of euphoria swept America after the surrender of Japan, and most servicemen were getting out of uniform as speedily as possible. The Marines, however, had a job to do in China. The official objective was to disarm the 630,000 Japanese soldiers there and supervise their return to Japan. Unofficially, the U.S. wanted a military presence in northern China to deter Russia, which had declared war on Japan in the closing days of the war, from moving troops into Manchuria. The U.S. also wanted to prevent Manchuria from falling to the Chinese Communists.

The 1st and 6th Divisions arrived in China in the fall of 1945, supported by the 1st Marine Air Wing. Russia didn't move into Manchuria, but there were numerous incidents with Chinese Communists. A motorized patrol was ambushed at An Ping, killing three Marines and wounding twelve. Five Marines were killed and

OPPOSITE PAGE: A mountain gale lashes Marines as they move from Koto-ri near the Chosin Reservoir in Korea to escape from the Red Chinese troops that suddenly struck south of the Yalu.

thirteen wounded when Chinese Communists raided an ammunition supply facility near Tanfku. Despite these provocations, there was public pressure to "bring the boys home," and the Marine force in China was cut in half by mid-1946.

The Chinese Communists were inexorably defeating the Nationalists. In December 1948 the Marines helped evacuate the last Americans from Shanghai, and the last Marines left China six months later. The Communists now ruled China, a fact that would have a profound effect on future U.S. policy in the Far East.

The peacetime strength of the Corps was set by Congress at 107,000, but its status was in doubt as President Truman pushed Congress to unify the armed forces. The National Security Act, passed in 1947, created the Department of Defense with subordinate Departments of the Army, Navy, and Air Force. Secretary of Defense James Forrestal announced in early 1948 that the Marines were not to constitute a second U.S. land army, nor would a Marine officer serve above the corps level.

The position of the Marines became more tenuous under Louis Johnson, Forrestal's successor. Sharp cuts were made in the Fleet Marine Force, and Johnson added insult to injury by doing away with the official observance of the Corps's birthday. Marines, however, responded by holding "private" parties.

Much of the trouble stemmed from Truman's dislike of the Marines. In replying to a congressman who urged that the Marines be represented on the Joint Chiefs of Staff, the former Army captain responded, "For your information, the Marine Corps is the Navy's police force, and as long as I am President, that is what it will remain. They have a propaganda machine that is almost the equal to Stalin's." Truman's sentiments caused a public uproar. He sent a contrite apology to the commandant, regretting his choice of words.

As the 1940s drew to a close, Marines were feeling pressure from all sides. The Corps was down to 75,000. The Army made it clear that it wanted to take over all land-based military forces, which would practically eliminate the Marines' role in amphibious warfare. The Army argued that the atomic bomb made amphibious warfare obsolete. The Air Force was coming at the Marines from another direction. Success in an atomic war hinged on absolute supremacy in the air, and all military aviation should be under the control of the Air Force, a move that would do away with the Navy's carrier-based planes as well as the Marine air wings. All the services were busily attempting to redefine their missions.

The National Security Act allowed the Navy to retain its air force, and the Marines would continue as a branch of the Navy. The services settled into an uneasy truce, not realizing how soon they would be tested.

Just before dawn on Sunday, June 25, 1950, seven infantry divisions and one armored division of the Communist North Korean People's Army (NKPA) crossed the 38th Parallel into South Korea, catching the free world off guard. The U.S. had only twelve active combat divisions, two of which were Marines. The four Army divisions in Japan had few combat veterans and were soft from occupation duty. Although the Army had several hundred troops in South Korea as advisers, the South Koreans still were poorly trained and poorly equipped. The NKPA had Soviet tanks, bombers, and jet fighters; many of its troops were Soviet-trained and had seen action in Manchuria.

An emergency session of the United Nations Security Council voted to intervene in Korea. (Russia could have vetoed intervention but was absent, protesting the presence of Nationalist China.) The following day, the General Assembly called on member nations to help repel the attack. Time was running out; NKPA troops had captured Seoul, the South Korean capital.

Korea was to be primarily an American war, but the U.S. military buildup was slow and chaotic. Commandant Clifton Cates offered immediate Marine support to General MacArthur, commander of the UN forces in Korea, with the 1st Provisional Marine Brigade. The brigade landed at Pusan and went into action August 7. Along with the 1st Cavalry and 24th Division Army troops, the Marines fought to stem the NKPA advance around Masan. The 5th Marines took "No-Name Ridge," tearing up the big Soviet tanks with rocket launchers, recoilless rifles, and 90mm fire. The NKPA divisions drew back, harried by Marine Corsairs.

With the NKPA drive blunted and the 1st Division soon to be in Korea, MacArthur began planning an amphibious landing at Inchon. It presented an array of problems. The access to Inchon was through the Flying Fish Channel, a narrow inlet where the outgoing tide ripped through at eight knots. The tide at Inchon was more than 31 feet, one of the highest in the world. The landing boats would have two hours to get in and out or be stranded. To make matters worse, there was no real beach; beyond the seawall was the city, leaving little opportunity to deploy the troops. The North Koreans thought an Inchon landing was impossible.

MacArthur formed X Corps for the invasion, consisting of the 1st Marine Division, some 3,000 Korean Marines, and 2,750 Army troops. The Army's 7th Infantry Division was held in reserve. Preparing for the landing, the Marines heard about President Truman calling them "the Navy's police force," and many of their tanks bore the hand-painted legend "Horrible Harry's Police Force."

The 260-ship invasion fleet steamed to Inchon, and an intense naval and air bombardment preceded the landing. The 3rd Battalion, 5th Marines, went in first and seized the harbor defense guns on Wolmi Island. The main landing hit at high tide with minimal opposition. MacArthur radioed the fleet, "The Navy and the Marines have never shone more brightly than this morning."

By the end of the day the beachhead was secure. Fighting became intense, however, when the Marines moved out of the city to drive toward Seoul some

Colonel Lewis "Chesty" Puller, left, commander of the 1st Marines, talks to Brigadier General E. A. Craig as the Marines drive toward Seoul after landing at Inchon.

twenty miles away. The first objective was Kimpo Airfield, west of Seoul. Its capture would permit a massive airlift of men and supplies from Japan.

MacArthur drove the Marines hard to recapture Seoul exactly three months after the start of the North Korean invasion, but the NKPA refused to cooperate. Marine casualties were high every step of the way. On September 26 MacArthur officially returned Seoul to Syngman Rhee, president of South Korea, while "Chesty" Puller's 1st Marines stood guard.

The North Koreans, MacArthur felt, were near defeat. He reported to the UN Security Council that his "decisive campaign" had stopped Communist expansion by force in Asia. He had asked for and received permission to send troops north of the 38th Parallel for a final mopping up.

The 1st Marine Division was sent to Wonsan in October, then was ordered to march north to the Yalu River where pockets of stubborn NKPA resistance were being encountered by other units. The terrain was rugged, mountain ridges running north and south isolating units from one another, and a bitter winter was setting in. None of this worried MacArthur, who was telling the press that the American troops might be home for Christmas. He discounted intelligence warnings that Red Chinese troops were massing near the Yalu.

On November 3 the 7th Marines ran into a Red Chinese division and, in a four-day battle, crippled it so badly that it never saw service again. Despite this bloody encounter, MacArthur went ahead with his battle plan: an offensive by the Eighth Army in western Korea and by the X Corps, including the Marines, in the northeast. The two-pronged drive was just under way when, on November 24, the Chinese struck in force. A disaster was in the making.

They came in overwhelming numbers, driving a wedge between the Eighth Army and X Corps. The Eighth Army was in full retreat. On the night of the 27th, the 5th and 7th Marines were attacked in force at Yudam-ni, west of the Chosin Reservoir, while other Chinese divisions cut the main supply route to the south. For five days the 1st Marine Division stood and slugged it out with eight Chinese divisions, some 100,000 Chinese to the Marines' 20,000. When the 1st Division was attacked, it was 20 degrees and snowing. The weather proved to be as formidable an enemy as the Chinese. The temperature often dipped below zero, freezing automatic weapons. Men on break collapsed in the snow, and officers had to cuff them awake to keep them from freezing to death.

A general withdrawal was ordered. Nearly sixty miles of mountains separated the Marines from the port of Hungnam, their one place to escape. To reach it they had to fight every step of the way. General O. P. Smith refused an order to abandon equipment and Marine dead. The breakout from the reservoir began.

The Chinese were attacking continually, and many Marine units suffered more than 50 percent casualties. Two emergency airstrips were built at Koto-Ri, and close air support helped the embattled Marines keep the Chinese from overrunning them. At Hagaru-ri the units of the division were reunited and supplies were air-dropped to them. Proceeding southward, they found a key bridge destroyed. Air Force C-119s dropped the components of a 24-ton temporary field bridge. Marine engineers installed it across the river.

The battered division limped into Hamhung on December 11 with its dead and wounded, equipment and vehicles. It had suffered more than 4,000 casualties and uncounted cases of frostbite and pneumonia.

The press was calling the retreat from the reservoir "America's worst military licking since Pearl Harbor." General MacArthur saw it differently: "This was undoubtedly one of the most successful strategic retreats in military history, comparable with, and markedly similar to, Wellington's great Peninsula withdrawal."

The passage of time has confirmed MacArthur's opinion of the Marine withdrawal. Army historian S.L.A. Marshall wrote, "No other operation in the American book of war quite compares with this show by the 1st Marine Division in the perfection of factual concepts precisely executed, in accuracy of estimate of situation by leadership at all levels, and in promptness of utilization of all supporting forces."

There never has been any equivocation in the mind of the Corps: the retreat from the Chosin Reservoir is a glorious chapter in Marine history. But the fact remained: the United Nations' forces had been ignominiously thrown out of North Korea.

By the end of the year, the Chinese had 21 divisions in Korea and the North Koreans 12, a total of more than a half million troops. An estimated million Chinese troops were in reserve north of the Yalu. The UN had 385,000 troops in Korea, many of them South Koreans. The Joint Chiefs of Staff decided it was now prudent to fight a defensive war.

MacArthur disagreed sharply with the Joint Chiefs. He wanted to bomb north of the Yalu, arm Chiang Kai-shek's Nationalists on Taiwan for an invasion of mainland China, and push forward to the victory that nearly had been his. His defiance became more open until he was dismissed by President Truman on April 11, 1951. The Communists greeted the arrival of his successor, General Matthew Ridgeway, by launching a spring offensive.

The attack came at the Hwachon Reservoir and peeled a South Korean division off the 1st Division's right flank. The Marines held. A later attack hit on the division's right, rolling back the Army's 2nd Infantry Division. The Marines closed the gap and blunted the enemy's drive. After the Chosin Reservoir, the division rarely was attacked frontally. The Chinese had learned to respect the Marines.

When the truce talks began at Panmunjom, the Marines were pulled back to the UN line in the Pyongyang-Seoul corridor. It was no respite, but rather fighting that resembled World War I trench warfare: patrols and raids, nasty localized action. This static war was to drag on from September 1951 to July 1953, when the truce finally was signed.

People remember Inchon and the Chosin Reservoir but forget that 40 percent of Marine casualties in Korea occurred *after* the truce talks began. In the beginning, the Marines would joke, "It's not much of a war, but it's better than no war at all." The joke was wounded at the reservoir and died on the Pyongyang-Seoul line.

The armistice was signed on July 27, 1953. The war had lasted three years, one month, and two days. The Marines had suffered 30,544 casualties: 4,262 killed, 244 non-battle deaths, and 26,038 wounded.

The performance of Marine prisoners of war in Korea gives an unusual insight into the importance of esprit de corps. There were 221 Marines captured, one out of 570 combat Marines. The Army rate was one out of 150. The Marine POW survival rate was 87 percent; the Army's 62 percent. And while America was shocked by Communist "brainwashing" of POWs, only one Marine POW was disciplined for cooperating with the enemy.

A chaplain who had served with both the Marines and the Army said he witnessed soldiers who "faked" injuries in order to be evacuated. Conversely, he saw Marines who concealed their injuries to be allowed to continue fighting.

The Corps was proud of its record in Korea but not pleased with its role there. The 1st Division had been used as one more division, albeit an elite one. Marine air wings were under the command of the Air Force, and close air support suffered. Marine ground units were accustomed to getting support from their wings in five to fifteen minutes; Air Force procedures and priorities had resulted in delays of thirty minutes to four hours.

An important victory during the final months of the war came in Washington, not Korea. Congress passed a law providing for a peacetime Marine strength of three divisions and three air wings, and, significantly, the commandant was given a seat on the Joint Chiefs of Staff, although he did not become a full-fledged member until 1976. The bill was shepherded through the Senate by two senators who were former Marines, Mike Mansfield and Paul Douglas.

During the Eisenhower years, the Marines were

kept busy. In the 1956 Suez crisis, Marines evacuated Americans from Alexandria and a UN truce team from Haifa. In Jerusalem, two Marines held off a mob attacking the U.S. consulate. A Marine helicopter rescued Ambassador Douglas MacArthur II and James Hagerty, Eisenhower's press secretary, from a Tokyo mob. And when a mob in Caracas, Venezuela, attacked the limousine carrying Vice President Nixon, a battalion of Marines was put on standby on a cruiser off the Venezuelan coast.

There were humanitarian missions. Marines helped rescue victims of earthquakes in Morocco, Turkey, and the Greek islands; flood victims in Spain, Ceylon, and Mexico; and hurricane victims in British Honduras.

And there were peacekeeping missions. In July 1958, after the coup d'état and assassination of pro-Western King Faisal of Iraq, revolt threatened the stability of Lebanon. President Camille Chamoun called for U.S. and British assistance. The 2nd Battalion, 2nd Marines, landed and established an armed perimeter around Beirut until order could be restored.

A U.S.-supported coup overthrew the Venezuelan dictator, Pérez Jiménez, in 1958. A battalion of Marines stood by to protect American lives and property.

When Fidel Castro seized power in Cuba in 1958, Marines stationed at Guantanamo Bay fanned out of the compound to protect the base's water supply. The Marines did not participate in the disastrous Bay of Pigs affair, but the entire Corps was put on alert during the October 1962 Cuban missile crisis.

Also in 1962, Marine Lieutenant Colonel John H. Glenn, Jr., became the first American to orbit the earth. Eight other Marine pilots also have served as astronauts.

All through these years the curtain was going up on the tragedy of Vietnam.

The issue of Indochina, as Vietnam was then called, got caught up in the Cold War. America repeatedly had urged France to grant Indochina independence, but several events made the U.S. reconsider: China had fallen to the Communists; Moscow and Peking both had recognized Ho Chi Minh's Viet Minh; and Charles de Gaulle had made U.S. support of the French position the price of French involvement in NATO. The U.S. also was talked into picking up much of the cost of the French effort in Indochina—close to a billion dollars a year.

In 1954 the French lost the Battle of Dien Bien Phu, and peace talks began in Geneva. The Viet Minh agreed to evacuate the south under the supervision of neutral nations. The U.S. disliked the treaty and organized the Southeast Asia Treaty Organization (SEATO) to halt the spread of communism in the area.

The U.S. now was supplying arms to South Vietnam, and the U.S. Military Assistance Advisory Group was training its army. The first Marine, Colonel Victor Croizat, joined the group in 1954.

U.S. assistance grew in size and scope. Ngo Dinh Diem had taken over South Vietnam after a questionable election and created a corrupt and repressive police state. By 1960 the North Vietnamese were supporting the South Vietnamese who were protesting Ngo Dinh Diem and his American supporters. These rebels, the National Liberation Front (NVA), known in the South as Viet Cong, launched a campaign

A Marine military adviser accompanies a South Vietnamese patrol in the early days of the war. The first Marine units to see combat landed at Da Nang on March 8, 1965.

of terrorism. President Kennedy sent in 100 more military advisers and 400 Special Forces troops.

For a decade the American military presence in Vietnam grew slowly. Marine drill instructors were training South Vietnamese marines. In 1962 Medium Helicopter Squadron 362 arrived to support Vietnamese troops, bringing the number of Marines in Vietnam to 600.

For the Marines, the Vietnam War began in 1965. The Air Force was bombing North Vietnam from its base at Da Nang, and the Viet Cong raided the base several times, to the indignation of the American government. On March 6, 1965, a decision was announced: two Marine battalions were being sent to protect the base at Da Nang, and they would fire if fired upon.

The Marines were responsible for the defense of Da Nang and the surrounding tactical zone—10,000 square miles of varying terrain, most of it controlled by the Viet Cong. Marine strength at Da Nang built to 5,000, but its role continued to be purely defensive. This became a sore point when an ARVN (Army of the Republic of Vietnam) battalion was ambushed by the Viet Cong and the Marines were not permitted to go to their assistance.

By 1965 four regiments of NVA were operating in South Vietnam. This was a factor behind launching Marine search-and-destroy missions. "We are countering an invasion of South Vietnam," said one Marine general.

The Marines were champing at the bit. On a Vietnam inspection tour, Commandant Wallace Greene, Jr., said his Marines were not in Vietnam "to sit on their ditty boxes, they were there to kill Viet Cong." They didn't have long to wait.

Secretary of Defense Robert McNamara toured Vietnam and found the situation deteriorating. This led President Johnson to increase the number of troops in Vietnam to 125,000. The number included four Marine regiments and four Marine aircraft groups.

The 1st Viet Cong Regiment was reported gathering for an attack at Chu Lai; the Marines struck first. A three-pronged attack, dubbed Operation Starlite, caught the Viet Cong off balance, killing 964 of the 2,000-man force. This was the first time the Marines had operated at regimental strength since Korea.

Operation followed operation: Blue Marlin, Golden

Mortarmen set up as a company of 5th Marines conducts a search-and-clear operation near An Hoa in 1969. After the 1968 Tet Offensive, the U.S. began withdrawing troops.

Fleece, Double Eagle; in eighteen months the Marines fought 150 battles, claiming 7,300 enemy dead. In thousands of small-unit actions, the Marines killed another 4,000 Viet Cong. Marine casualties: some 1,700 killed and more than 9,000 wounded.

What had this effort accomplished? Not that much. Of the 11,000 villages in South Vietnam, only 4,500 were considered friendly. And that estimate was to be proved far too high.

The operations continued: Tuscaloosa, Sierra, De-Soto, Independence, Stone, Beacon Hill—all inflicted heavy casualties on the Viet Cong, but the complexion of the war remained unchanged.

A demilitarized zone (DMZ) had been agreed upon at the Geneva peace talks, but North Vietnamese troops ignored it and poured into South Vietnam. Secretary McNamara ordered a "security wall" to be set up below the DMZ with barbed wire, electronic sensors, and land mines. Both the military and the press were skeptical of "McNamara's Wall." A Marine colonel commented, "With those bastards, you'd have to build the wall all the way to India, and it would take the whole Marine Corps and half the Army to guard it. Even then, they'd probably burrow under it."

A truce was customary at Tet, the Vietnamese celebration of the lunar new year, and 1968 was no exception. But this time the Viet Cong broke the truce to launch an all-out offensive. A force of 20,000 attacked Khe Sanh, and the battle settled into a siege that lasted seventy-one days. Simultaneous attacks hit

★ **IN THE FIELD**

Marines unload from an LCMS, LEFT, during a simulated amphibious landing. The equipment to land quickly on a variety of shorelines has improved greatly since World War II. BELOW, two CH–53 Sea Stallions land on the deck of a carrier after ferrying Marines ashore.

OVERLEAF, officers observe a tactical maneuver during a CAX (Combined Arms Exercise) at the huge Marine base at Twenty-nine Palms, California. INSET, an artillery officer shouts aiming coordinates to his battery. CAX permits the use of live ammunition to train troops.

A gunner mans the .30-caliber machine gun of an M-60
tank, LEFT. Tanks like these can be put ashore quickly
from modern Marine landing craft. The purpose of con-
tinual training is success in combat. The Marines have
the memory of Vietnam, ABOVE, by which to measure their
performance in the field. BELOW, an observer wearing a
white hat band for identification confers with a brigade
officer during the exercises.

OVERLEAF, a young Marine takes a breather as the sun
comes up during an exercise. Marines learn to take full
advantage of every lull in the simulated combat.

★

Quang Tri, Da Nang, Hoi An, Tam Ky, and Quang Ngai. A surprise attack captured the ancient city of Hue, once the capital of Indochina. Three Marine and thirteen ARVN battalions counterattacked, and after three weeks of house-to-house fighting, they recaptured Hue. Viet Cong guerrillas even infiltrated Saigon and briefly occupied the American embassy.

The Tet Offensive was the turning point in the Vietnam War. The irony of Tet is that it could have turned the war either way. The U.S. military felt that the Viet Cong had thrown everything they had into Tet, and failed. To the American media, though, the sheer ferocity of Tet seemed proof that the war was being lost.

Many thoughtful Americans were puzzled by the Vietnam War. They knew the logic of the so-called domino theory: if Vietnam fell, so would its neighbors, and where would Communist aggression finally end? Yet the South Vietnamese didn't seem eager to help themselves; indeed, many actively supported the Viet Cong. Even if we won, wouldn't we have to keep an occupying army there forever?

A growing segment of American youth actively opposed the war. Draft cards were burned to chants of "Hell no! We won't go!" Deferments came easily to the sons of the affluent, and, increasingly, Vietnam was being fought by blacks and the poor. Television was bringing the cruel realities of combat into American homes on the evening news, and Americans were deeply disturbed by what they saw.

America started to back away from Vietnam. President Johnson decided not to run for reelection. The bombing of Vietnam was cut back. Peace talks began in Paris. The American public became hopeful.

Peace talks have a perverse effect on the battlefield: both sides want victories to strengthen their negotiating positions. General Westmoreland launched Operation Pegasus to relieve Khe Sanh, and Operation Delaware Valley to clear the enemy from A Shau Valley, and both were successful. The Viet Cong struck hard at Da Nang, and made more than one hundred rocket strikes against a number of South Vietnam positions.

In 1969 the Marine Special Landing Force swept through the area south of Chu Lai in Operation Bold Mariner, and later landed at Hoi An. During the year,

A Marine sniper takes careful aim across a Vietnam rice paddy. Snipers are specially trained expert riflemen who are dead shots at ranges approaching 1,000 yards.

By dawn's early light Marines board a helicopter on the USS Tripoli *to be flown south of Da Nang for a battalion assault on Viet Cong units operating in the deep jungle.*

the I Corps, of which the Marines were a part, killed an estimated 10,000 Viet Cong. The Marines were slowly being pulled out. They began the year with 80,000 troops in Vietnam, ending it with 55,000.

The fighting ground to a halt, but it was mid-1972 before it was finally over. The Vietnam War was the longest and, in many ways, the hardest war the Marines had ever fought.

By war's end, 12,926 Marines had been killed and 88,542 wounded. (In World War II, 19,733 Marines were killed, 67,207 wounded.) In Vietnam, the Corps reached a total strength of 317,400, well below the 485,053 in World War II. Because of different personnel policies, more Marines actually served during the seven years of Vietnam (800,000) than did in the four years of World War II (600,000). It was that big a war.

Like Korea, Vietnam left the Corps with mixed emotions. Korea had ended in a stalemate, Vietnam in a defeat—South Vietnam collapsing after the American withdrawal. In both wars the Marines had fought with Army units under the command of Army generals. Neither was an amphibious war, and neither war had much popular support. And in both wars the troops often were hamstrung by political considerations.

Korea had been a conventional war with defined battle lines and a clear distinction between soldiers and civilians. Vietnam was a guerrilla war, a terrorist war. Death could be waiting in a "friendly" village; a native woman could rise up from a rice paddy with a submachine gun. Traditional tactics often were useless.

Before the dust had settled in Vietnam, minor crises around the world involved the Marines.

Syria and Egypt attacked Israel in 1973, in what became known as the Yom Kippur War. The Marine Amphibious Brigade of the Sixth Fleet stood by in the Mediterranean.

In 1974 Archbishop Makarios of Cyprus was overthrown and Turkey landed troops on the island. The Marines evacuated American citizens and other foreign nationals.

In Cambodia in March 1975 the Khmer Rouge was laying siege to Phnom Penh, the capital, when President Ford ordered Operation Eagle Pull. The 31st Marine Amphibious Unit sent in 300 Marines by helicopter and set up a defense perimeter. Two Marine helicopter squadrons evacuated a number of Americans, foreign nationals, and high-ranking Cambodians in two hours. The Marines from the embassy took down the U.S. flag and left on the last helicopter.

The Marines had a final mission in Vietnam. On April 21, 1975, President Thieu resigned with bitter words for the Americans, who, he said, had betrayed his country. The Viet Cong were at the gates of Saigon. Marines executed Operation Frequent Wind, the final evacuation of Saigon. Three platoons were sent in to assist the Marine Security Guard at the embassy, and nearly 5,000 Americans and Vietnamese were helicoptered out by midnight.

The next day the embassy was besieged with Vietnamese refugees. A mob used a fire truck in an attempt to force entry. Working around the clock, the Marines evacuated another 978 Americans and 1,120 foreign nationals. The helicopters were protected by fighters from the offshore carriers, but were still harassed by ground fire. Two helicopters went down, one killing the pilot and co-pilot.

Less than a month later, on May 12, 1975, a Khmer Rouge gunboat fired across the bow of the American container ship *Mayagüez* bound for Thailand. An armed boarding party took the 39-man American crew prisoner and landed them on Koh Tang, a small island off the coast of Cambodia.

President Ford ordered the Marines and other special units into action. Two assaults were planned: one to rescue the prisoners, the other to retake the ship. The 2nd Battalion, 9th Marines, was helicoptered in. One unit found the *Mayagüez* deserted. The other located the prisoners on a fishing boat. They were rescued without incident, but during the operation three helicopters were shot down and ten damaged. Eleven Marines were among the 15 U.S. servicemen killed; 41 were in the 50 injured.

Near the DMZ, young Marines set up a defensive position to protect a helicopter landing. North Vietnamese troops constantly violated the DMZ to get to South Vietnam.

In 1974 a mob of Greek Cypriots attacked the U.S. embassy in Nicosia. Marines held them off with tear gas grenades. Uganda dictator Idi Amin charged that the embassy Marines in Kampala were involved in subversion activity and ordered them out of the country. The U.S. closed the embassy instead. A similar charge was leveled against the Marines at the embassy in Peking, but it came to nothing. And when the U.S. recognized Red China, the embassy in Taiwan was attacked. The Marines again defended it with tear gas.

Tanks come ashore at Da Nang as the American buildup in Vietnam continues. Repeated attacks on the Da Nang air base prompted President Johnson to send in the Marines.

Evans Fordyce Carlson grew up in Vermont and served as an Army captain in World War I. Liking military life but not the Army, he enlisted in the Marines as a private in 1922. After receiving a commission, he was sent to Nicaragua to fight the rebels. Their basic tactics, he found, were to travel at night and ambush during the day. Carlson adopted their methods and improved on them—he traveled *and* ambushed at night. With a detachment of fifteen Marines on horseback, he once routed one hundred rebels and chased them across the border into Honduras. For this action he was awarded the Navy Cross.

Much of the time, Carlson was in China. Observing the Sino-Japanese war in 1937, Carlson was intrigued by the interrelationship of military and political war. He found the Red Army a tough, mobile, self-sustained force. Its officers took a real interest in the welfare of their men.

When he came home, he got in trouble by saying publicly that the Communists were the hope of China, and that the U.S. was undermining them by selling scrap metal and oil to Japan. He was officially censured and resigned from the Corps in 1939 after seventeen years of service. He went back to China as a civilian, and what he saw convinced him that Japan would attack the United States. He returned, reported what he saw, and was recommissioned a lieutenant colonel. He began to think of a force trained for long, swift marches, carrying automatic weapons and living on dehydrated foods for long periods. He and his operations officer, James Roosevelt, the president's son, drew up a plan for such a "raider" force and sold it to the Marine Corps.

Based on his guerrilla experience, he broke his Raider battalion units down into basic groups of three which he called fire teams. Each was equipped with a submachine gun, a rifle, and a Browning automatic rifle. Each company had two rifle platoons and a weapons platoon which carried light mortars and light machine guns. There was no weapon in the Raiders which could not be carried by one man.

Carlson invited suggestions and criticisms from his troops. He told them everything he was doing. He introduced the motto of the Chinese cooperatives, *Gung ho,* Chinese for "Work together—work in harmony." *Gung ho* became the watchword of the Raiders.

The Raiders first saw action in the abortive raid on Makin Island, for which Carlson received another Navy Cross. They then were sent to Guadalcanal to spearhead an Army landing. The Raiders were ordered to work north from the beach through the Japanese lines and go to Henderson Field, smashing enemy positions along the way. For fifty days the Raiders were in action. They ambushed the Japanese time and again. The Raiders hiked some 150 miles, killing 488 Japanese in a dozen skirmishes. Only 16 Raiders were killed and 18 wounded. Carlson was awarded his third Navy Cross.

After the Ayatollah Khomeini seized power in Iran in 1979, Marines evacuated 6,000 Americans. Before the evacuation could begin, a mob attacked the embassy in Teheran, injuring two Marines. Then an uneasy quiet settled on Teheran. Anti-U.S. demonstrations became a daily event, however, after President Jimmy Carter allowed the deposed Shah to enter the U.S. for cancer treatment. On November 4, 1979, the embassy was stormed and sixty-three Americans, including the Marine detachment, were taken prisoner. In a gesture to show that their quarrel was not with minorities, the Iranians released five women and eight blacks, including five Marines. The rest of the hostages were to spend 444 days in captivity.

A rescue attempt was made in April 1980, but it was aborted after mechanical failure forced the helicopters down in the desert. One helicopter exploded, killing eight servicemen, three of whom were Marines.

A Marxist government on the Caribbean island of Grenada was causing concern for the Reagan administration in the fall of 1983. Cubans on the island were building a jet airfield with, apparently, Russian support.

On October 19 the prime minister and one hundred of his followers were slain by a group of local radicals. More than a thousand Americans were in Grenada, most of them students in a local medical school.

President Reagan moved to occupy Grenada. Army Rangers and 400 Marines, along with troops from a six-nation Caribbean force, were put in. After short but brisk fighting, the island was secured. Eighteen U.S. troops had been killed and 67 wounded. The troops found stores of Russian-made arms and ammunition and twelve Soviet armored personnel carriers.

Another involvement ended in tragedy. Under an agreement negotiated by the U.S., the Israelis pulled their troops out of West Beirut, where they had been fighting the Palestine Liberation Organization. In August 1982, troops from France, Italy, and the U.S. moved into the area to assume "a carefully limited non-combat role." Eight hundred Marines from the Sixth Fleet helped oversee the withdrawal of PLO and Syrian troops without incident, then withdrew.

In September the Lebanese government, fearing renewed violence, asked that the peace-keeping force be returned. The Marines were assigned to guard the Beirut airport. The second day there, a Marine was killed in an explosion. Several more died from explosions and sniper fire. The Marine presence was increased to 1,200; another 2,000 were standing by offshore with the Sixth Fleet.

In Vietnam the Marines complained that they were asked to fight with one hand tied behind their backs. In Lebanon both hands were tied behind their backs. They were to be a "presence," not an effective force. Usually they stood guard and patrolled with unloaded weapons.

At dawn on October 23, 1983, a truck cleared several Lebanese checkpoints guarding the Marine compound and sped across an empty parking lot that the Lebanese Army had been using as a drill field. It crashed through the gate at the compound. The Marine sentry fired at the truck and is believed to have hit the driver, but the truck crashed into the building. An estimated six tons of explosives in the truck went off, killing 220 Marines and 21 Army and Navy Personnel.

More Marines were to die in Lebanon. Eight were killed in December 1983 in a Druze artillery barrage. When they were withdrawn early in 1984, the Marine death toll in Lebanon stood at 260.

The spotlight returned to the Marines in 1987 when a security scandal hit the U.S. embassy in Moscow. Four young Marine security guards were recalled. One was convicted and sent to prison.

Another Marine, Lieutenant Colonel Oliver North, serving with the National Security Council, was a key figure in the televised investigation into the use of monies obtained in a secret sale of arms to Iran to finance the contras in Nicaragua. North later retired from the Corps when he was indicted by a federal court.

The Marines, apparently, aren't destined to lead a quiet life, or to stray too far from the public eye.

This is the history the Marines have made. And, as we shall see, this is the history that helped make Marines what they are today.

A helicopter lands Marines on a Vietnam hilltop during Operation Oklahoma Hills, a multi-battalion drive at North Vietnamese army units infiltrating Happy Valley.

FIRST IN
THE FIGHT~

ALWAYS
FAITHFUL~

BE A U.S. MARINE!

CHAPTER 5★

A FEW GOOD MEN

To be young in America today is to be aggressively courted by the armed forces. Recruitment advertisements are everywhere: on television and radio, in newspapers and magazines, on billboards and posters, even on matchbook covers. Skywriters fill the air over crowded beaches with their slogans. Hundreds of thousands of slick, four-color booklets glamorizing service life are mailed to prospective recruits. Recruiters are at work at shopping malls, rodeos, stock car races, and county fairs. And if a youth should express interest, recruiters descend on his home with all the avidity of major league scouts wanting to sign a high school pitcher with a ninety-mile-an-hour fastball.

All this is a reflection of the tremendous manpower needs of the services. There is nearly a 50 percent annual attrition in the ranks, and those who leave must be replaced by volunteers. The draft ended shortly after the Vietnam War, leaving the services to their own devices. Military pay increases made the services more competitive with the civilian job market, but young people with the intelligence and drive to succeed in the service are the ones who can succeed in civilian life too, and make a lot more money along the way. It comes as no surprise to learn that recessions stimulate enlistments.

To solve their recruiting problems, the services have turned to Madison Avenue. Every modern marketing technique is employed in selling military careers, and the advertising and promotion budgets of the services rival those of major corporations.

Researchers interview high school students to find out what appeals to them about a particular branch of the service. New recruits are questioned about their reasons for enlisting. Copywriters and art directors mull over the findings to discover a way to tailor their message to real needs and desires. Top photographers and designers package the message into compelling commercials and advertisements. Meanwhile, media researchers are at work looking for the most cost-effective vehicles to carry the message. ("Does 'Monday Night Football' reach prospective recruits more efficiently than 'Miami Vice'?" "Is *Outdoor Life* a better buy than *Rolling Stone*?" "Parental approval is a factor in enlistments; how about reaching them on the 'Late News'?")

Before a new campaign is launched, it is tested. A commercial is shown to a carefully selected group of teen-agers, who are then questioned about what they saw. ("What do you think the commercial was trying to say?" "Was it believable?" "Did it make you think about enlisting?")

Testing is used at every step. Most magazine advertisements contain coupons to make it easy for a prospect to write in for more information, although no mention is made that the information will be hand-delivered by a recruiter. ("How many responses did this ad produce in this magazine?" "How many of the respondents actually enlisted?" "If it was cost-effective, let's move up from the coup-oned page to a spread with a bound-in return postcard.")

All of this effort, and the money and talent it represents, has a single purpose: to get qualified prospective recruits together with a recruiter. No one has ever enlisted by filling out a coupon. The services have recruiting offices around the country, and in foreign countries as well where there are military bases with a goodly number of young dependents. The agencies even supply field representatives to help the recruiters take advantage of the advertising, and to advise on local advertising and publicity.

To attract prospective recruits, the services use their advertising to project a distinctive image. These images speak volumes about how the services view themselves.

Join the Navy and see the world. The longest-running slogan of them all still sells the adventurous life at sea and the allure of foreign ports.

Aim high. Go Air Force. Lindbergh, Rickenbacker, and Wiley Post may be gone, but many young people respond to the romance of flight, and some of the Air Force commercials could be outtakes from the flight scenes in the movie *Top Gun.* The Air Force also has a strong appeal for the technically minded.

Go Army. Get a great start. Here is a curious case. The Army in effect winks at the prospect and says, "Come in for a while, get some good training at our expense, then go knock 'em dead as a civilian." A recent commercial shows a college student explaining to a coed how the GI Bill and other Army benefits are financing his education. It turns out she's ex-Army, too; even served in the Airborne! (The Army has a perennial problem getting volunteers for combat arms; the skills of an infantryman don't translate easily into civilian jobs.)

Then there are the Marines.

The few. The proud. The Marines. The message is really a challenge: "This is an elite outfit. If you think you've got the stuff to become a Marine, we'll let you try." A TV commercial likens becoming a Marine to being knighted by a medieval king. A poster illustrated with a photograph of a tough, grim drill instructor says, "If everybody could get in the Marines, it wouldn't be the Marines."

The Marines offer the toughest, most demanding life of any of the services, and instead of soft-pedaling this fact, they flaunt it. A Marine can visit as many interesting places as a sailor, choose from as many specialized training schools as a soldier, and if he likes airplanes, there's Marine aviation. But these are attractions to be discussed *after* the prospective recruit has bought the basic idea of the Marine Corps. To advertise these attractions, the Corps feels, is misleading, certainly undignified.

Call it truth in advertising or whatever, the Marines make no bones about what a recruit can expect from the Corps or what the Corps expects from a recruit.

A basic recruiting tool is a handsome, 48-page brochure, filled with beautiful color photographs and printed on quality paper, called *Life in the Marine Corps.* The introduction, "What you can expect of the Corps," begins, "*You will find it challenging.* Sure, the first few months at boot camp are hard work, and a lot of sweat." Other headings include: *You'll find it elite. You'll find it uncompromising. You'll find it proud. You'll find yourself.*

With only a passing nod to educational opportunities, the booklet presents the boot camp experience, complete with pictures of the close-to-the bone haircut, physical conditioning, and the omnipresent D.I.s.

Much is made of earning the right to be called a Marine. This concept of earning a title has no equivalent in the other U.S. services, and it is something all Marines take very seriously. And Marine is a precise term, properly capitalized; soldier, sailor, and airman are generic. A letter to *Leatherneck,* the unofficial magazine of the Corps, is illuminating.

> As a Marine recruiter, I stress the intangibles: pride, challenge, self-discipline, and the other factors which go into the making of a Marine. It was with great interest that I have read, over the years, the letters about what makes a Marine "different" than members of all the other services.
>
> There are many good letters, and many good points, but none satisfied me.
>
> Recently, I had an applicant from Lahoma, Oklahoma, and as I was driving her from Oklahoma City following her testing, I asked if she had noticed any difference between the Marines and other service members that she had come in contact with.
>
> She thought for a minute and said, "You can be *in* the Army, and you can be *in* the Navy, or you can be *in* the Air Force. But you *are* a Marine!"
>
> There it is. Sweet, simple and to the point.
>
> As the young woman explained, "You *are* a Marine," and the Corps is *you.* The pride, honor, and tradition rests on the shoulders of all of us who share the title, "Marine."

To one who knows the Marines, this letter, from Gunnery Sergeant Thomas Hill of Enid, Oklahoma, could just as well have come from any Marine recruiter. His feelings are shared by practically every Marine and former Marine. It's what the Corps is all about.

Marine recruiting advertising today is a true reflection of how the Corps views itself. Not that it always was that candid. A Marine who served more than a century ago wrote about old-time recruiting techniques in New York City:

> The drummer and I would put on our red full dress tunics, with swallow tails, form a procession and right

down the street we'd go. The captain bought some bright colored ribbons for the drummer and me, which we tied in bows on our arms and on the buttons on the sides of our shakoes, and when the wind blew, we certainly made a fine sight as we marched down Broadway to the Battery, then up the Bowery and back to the rendezvous on Chambers Street, ribbons flying and playing quick-steps all the way. Then the captain would get up on a dry goods box in front of the recruiting office and make a speech to the crowd, telling them what a fine place the Marine Corps was for a man and what a chance he'd have to visit foreign ports. That's how we got recruits in those days.

In those days a Marine private was paid six dollars a month, and discipline wasn't strict, it was brutal. Falling asleep on guard duty was punished by having the miscreant spend several months walking guard while wearing an iron collar and dragging a ball-and-chain. Disobeying an order brought twelve lashes with a cat-o'-nine-tails. And no infraction was too small to be overlooked.

Like the Corps itself, recruiting standards and practices have evolved through the years. Certain misconceptions about Marine enlistment still persist, though, and should be dispelled.

The Corps is not a last resort, or a haven for high school dropouts. Marine enlistment standards are as high as for any other branch of the service. Currently, more than 95 percent of its recruits are high school graduates; and the non-graduates have scored well on the intelligence tests. And unless a Marine finishes high school on his own time, he probably won't be permitted to reenlist.

Neither is the Corps a place where a bad actor can get himself straightened out. Gone are the days when a judge would offer a young offender the choice of the Marines or reform school. A police record, or evidence of drug or alcohol abuse, automatically disqualifies a potential recruit.

Finally, getting through boot camp is no guarantee of staying in the Corps. The right to be a Marine is earned, day by day. A Marine with a poor performance record, a bad attitude, a tendency to abuse alcohol or drugs, will be given an Undesirable Discharge, or, at best, turned down for reenlistment.

A platoon leader at Camp Lejeune summed up the current Marine attitude: "You've first got to prove to us that you've got the stuff to be a Marine. And you've got to prove that you've lost it. It works both ways, and we'll stick with you through a lot. But when you finally prove to us that you're a loser, you're history! There are too many good men out there who want to be Marines to waste good time on a loser."

In the old days, it was simple and quick to join the Marines. But what once was a whirlwind romance now is an involved courtship. Both parties have ample opportunity to get to know each other before they decide to make it legal.

First, a recruit's qualifications are checked. Is he between 17 and 29, and if he is 17, does he have written permission from his parents to enlist? Does he have any physical disqualifications: uncorrectable defective vision, asthma, epilepsy, abnormal height or weight, AIDS? Does he wet the bed? Does he have a drug or alcohol problem? A police record? Does he have any dependents? Is he a high school graduate?

If all his answers are acceptable, a date is set to send him to the nearest Military Processing Station (MEPS). Here he will be given a comprehensive physical examination, the Armed Forces Vocational Battery tests (ASVAB), and undergo a series of interviews.

MEPS weeds out a number of prospective Marines. On the ASVAB tests, which measure mental and me-chanical aptitudes, the Corps requires a score of 31, although other services will accept scores as low as 21. Nearly two-thirds of Marine recruits score 50 or above. One in twenty can't pass the physical. Others, reminded in the interviews that supplying false information in seeking enlistment is a felony, suddenly remember problems that slipped their minds in the recruiting office. They, too, fall by the wayside.

Those who score 50 or higher on the ASVAB tests have an attractive opportunity: the Qualified Enlistment Program (QEP). Under this new program, the recruit will be automatically promoted to private first class when he graduates from boot camp, and promoted again to lance corporal within eighteen months. He also is guaranteed the training field of his choice. Should he score 65 or higher, he can select a particular school from seventeen possible fields.

The Corps has an urgent need in some specialties. Should a QEP recruit select one of these, the Corps will pay him a cash bonus of $1,000 to $3,500. Instead of, say, aviation, he will be guaranteed Air Traffic Controller School, or Aerial Navigation School; if the Corps finds it can't fulfill its promise for any reason, he will be honorably discharged. Of course, there's a catch. To justify his specialized training, the QEP recruit must enlist for six years instead of the usual four.

The Marines have their share of recruits who are seeking to trade some time in the service for help in financing their college educations. Under the new GI Bill, a Marine veteran may receive from $300 to $1,300 a month for 36 months while attending college. To qualify, a Marine must set aside up to 10% of his pay each month; the amount he will receive in college depends on how much he saves, his length of service, and his service specialty. A Marine may attend college on his own time in the service, and the Corps will pay 75 percent of the cost.

The Corps also offers an apprenticeship program that includes on-the-job training for Marines who select certain occupational fields. Graduates become certified journeymen in their chosen trades.

Some recruits choose to join the Marine Reserve. One Reserve program is tailored to the school calendar. College students and high school students who have been accepted in college may spend one summer at boot camp, the following summer in specialized training. The remainder of their Marine obligation: weekend drills at a Reserve unit near their school or home.

The old service gripe "Hurry up and wait" now also applies to the enlistment process. After meeting all the qualifications, passing all the tests, and finding an enlistment program that satisfies both the recruit and the Corps, the recruit still must wait before going to boot camp, and his goodbyes postponed until the Corps is ready for him. Depending upon the time of year he enlists and the training he has chosen, the wait can be from two to six months.

The limbo between civilian life and the Marine Corps is called being "in the pool." The recruiter will stay in close touch while the recruit waits it out, and from time to time he and his fellow poolies will be invited to a Saturday get-together for fun, competitive games, refreshments, pep talks, and mutual support. Keeping poolies enthusiastic is a high-priority item for Marine recruiters. Even though they were sworn in at the processing station and, technically at least, are in the Marine Corps, they can change their minds and the Corps will let them go.

There was a time in the service when recruiting duty was a safe harbor for older noncoms who wanted to ease themselves into retirement. A pot-bellied sergeant would sit in the recruiting office, feet on the desk, waiting for someone to walk through the door. But no more. A Marine recruiter today is like a young, dedicated, hard-working salesman for a large corporation.

It takes special qualities to be a recruiter. He must be at least a lance corporal, have a spotless record, an impressive appearance, be recommended by his commanding officer, and volunteer. Those selected are sent to an intensive seven-week recruiters school. The Corps tries to place new recruiters near their home, or at least in the same part of the country. This is not so much to attract recruiters as to facilitate rapport between the recruiters and the prospective recruits. Recruiting stations in urban areas, for example, have a proportionally high percentage of black recruiters.

A recruiter's lot is not an easy one. The hours are long; often the only time he can talk to a prospective recruit is in the evening or on the weekend; sixty- and seventy-hour work weeks come with the territory. He has a quota to meet, usually three or four recruits each month. Once a recruiter dealt in warm bodies, and got credit for all the recruits he shipped off to boot camp. Recruiting and training now are under the same command, and one of the new rules gives a recruiter credit only for those who make it through. On an average, he loses one out of five.

To provide a carrot as well as a stick, the Corps gives a recruiter extra credit toward his quota if one of his recruits becomes one of the honor men of his platoon in boot camp. Quite often an honor man will have his boot camp leave extended for a few weeks so that he can accompany his recruiter on his rounds to be a living example of initial Marine success to his friends and peer group.

ACTORS

Don Adams
Nick Adams
Larry Blyden
Hugh Brannum
  (Mr. Green Jeans)
Macdonald Carey
Mike Connors
Brian Dennehy
Bradford Dillman
Glenn Ford
James Franciscus
Christopher George
Clu Gulager
Gene Hackman
Sterling Hayden
Louis Hayward
Charlton Heston
Bob Keeshan
  (Captain Kangaroo)
Brian Keith

Ask the man who was one!

Tyrone Power
MOTION PICTURE STAR

UNITED STATES MARINES

Tyrone Power

William Lundigan
Peter Lupis
George Maharis
Jack Mahoney
Lee Marvin
Steve McQueen
Martin Milner
Hugh O'Brian
Pat Paulson
George Peppard
Burt Reynolds
John Russell
Robert Ryan
George C. Scott
Jimmy Shigeta
Bo Svenson
Robert Wagner
James Whitmore
Larry Wilcox

ATHLETES

Paul Arizin	*Baseball*	William Marshall	*Baseball*
Carmen Basilio	*Boxing*	Bob Mathias	*Decathlon*
Hank Bauer	*Baseball*	Thomas Monaghan	*Baseball Team Owner*
Patty Berg	*Golf*	Ernie Nevers	*Football*
Angelo Bertelli	*Football*	Leo Nomellini	*Football*
Bernie Bierman	*Football Coach*	Ken Norton	*Boxing*
Jerry Coleman	*Baseball*	Charles Paddock	*Track*
Charley Conerly	*Football*	Bum Phillips	*Football Coach*
Alvin Dark	*Baseball*	Barney Ross	*Boxing*
Art Donovan	*Football*	Wes Santee	*Track*
Elroy Hirsch	*Football*	Frank Sinkwich	*Football*
Gil Hodges	*Baseball*	Leon Spinks	*Boxing*
Eddie LeBaron	*Football*	Dan Topping	*Baseball Team Owner*
Gene "Big Daddy"		Lee Trevino	*Golf*
Lipscomb	*Football*	Gene Tunney	*Boxing*
Tommy Loughran	*Boxing*	Bill Veeck	*Baseball Team Owner*
Ted Lyons	*Baseball*	Morton Waldstein	*Baseball*
Ken MacAfee	*Football*	Ray Wietecha	*Baseball*
Walter Mails	*Baseball*	Ted Williams	*Baseball*

COMMUNICATIONS

Art Buchwald	Josephus Daniels, Jr.	Jim Lehrer	Arthur Ochs Sulzberger
Hodding Carter	Rowland Evans	Dan Rather	Earl Wilson

ENTERTAINERS

Bob Burns	Mark Shields
Ed McMahon	Jonathan Winters
Mark Russell	Woody Woodbury

LITERATURE AND THE ARTS

David Douglas Duncan	William Styron
William Manchester	Leon Uris

MUSICIANS

Bob Crosby	Dick Jergens
Don and Phil Everly	Buddy Rich
Ray Heatherton	John Philip Sousa

PUBLIC SERVANTS

James Baker	*Secretary of the Treasury*
David Bell	*Director of the Budget*
Terrell H. Bell	*Secretary of Education*
Henry Bellmon	*Senator (Oklahoma)*
Daniel Brewster	*Senator (Maryland)*
Dale Bumpers	*Senator (Arkansas)*
Francis Case	*Senator (South Dakota)*
John Chaffee	*Senator (Rhode Island), Secretary of the Navy*
Paul Douglas	*Senator (Illinois)*
John East	*Senator (North Carolina)*
Robert Finch	*Secretary of Health, Education and Welfare*
Joseph Foss	*Governor of South Dakota, Commissioner of American Football League*
Orville Freeman	*Governor (Minnesota), Secretary of Agriculture*
John Glenn	*Senator (Ohio)*
Howell Heflin	*Senator (Alabama)*
Thomas Holcomb	*Ambassador to the Union of South Africa*
Edward Katzenbach, Jr.	*Attorney General*
Mike Mansfield	*Senator (Montana), Ambassador to Japan*
Joseph McCarthy	*Senator (Wisconsin)*
Donald Regan	*Secretary of the Treasury*
Charles Robb	*Governor (Virginia)*
James Roosevelt	*Representative (California)*
James Sasser	*Senator (Tennessee)*
George P. Shultz	*Secretary of State*
George Smathers	*Senator (Florida)*
Adlai Stevenson III	*Senator (Illinois)*
Stephen Symms	*Senator (Idaho)*
Alexander Trowbridge	*Secretary of Commerce*
Jack Hood Vaughn	*Director of the Peace Corps, Ambassador to Panama*
John Warner	*Senator (Virginia)*
James Webb	*Secretary of the Navy*
Pete Wilson	*Senator (California)*

MISCELLANEOUS

F. Lee Bailey	*Attorney*
Stephen Bowen, Jr.	*President, J. Walter Thompson, Inc.*
Walter Cunningham	*Astronaut*
Eric Johnston	*Head, Motion Picture Association of America*
Robert Kriendler	*Owner, "21" Club, New York City*
Fred Lasswell	*Creator of comic strip Snuffy Smith*
Vincent Sardi	*Owner, Sardi's Restaurant, New York City*

Like any salesman, a recruiter must learn to live with rejection and not let the ones who get away affect his performance. He also will get his share of disrespect, foolishness, and broken promises, from adults as well as prospects, and will have to turn the other cheek. This is not something Marines do gladly.

What sometimes is the hardest part of recruiting duty is being cut off from the psychological support of base life. Except for the three or four other Marines at the recruiting station, who have their own problems, he's a Marine living and working in a civilian world and he can't hide; every working day he's in Dress Blues. It can be lonely and confusing out there.

Being married is a help—sometimes. Wives also suffer the long hours, the emotional ups and downs, and miss having other Marine wives around to share their problems. The divorce rate among recruiters is substantially higher than it is for the rest of the Corps.

The Corps understands these things and provides perks to make recruiting duty more palatable. A recruiter receives $285 in extra pay each month. Recruiting duty has been designated by the Corps as "career enhancing," meaning that a three-year tour will earn an extra stripe or two, depending on how well the recruiter performs.

What about the recruits themselves? What are they like, these young men who voluntarily enlist in the Marines in peacetime? No two are exactly alike, of course, but a pattern does emerge.

Perhaps his father, older brother, or a friend was a Marine. He may remember a parade, the band playing the "Marines' Hymn," or *Sands of Iwo Jima* on TV late one night. Or he came home from school or work, bored and restless, half-watching TV and thinking about a future that seems to hold little promise, when a commercial caught his eye that ended with the words "The Marines are looking for a few good men." Maybe a recruiting sergeant, resplendent in Dress Blues and battle ribbons, had some interesting things to say at his school on career day. Whatever the stimulus, the idea of being a Marine began to intrigue him.

The Army captain in charge of a Military Processing Station in Georgia sometimes plays a little game with himself. "We get a steady flow of recruits for all the services through here," he said. "When I'm not busy, I like to try to guess which kids are going where. I'm usually right about the Marines. They're a bit more eager, and you sense some physical aggressiveness there. Not that they're rude or pushy, they're nice kids. It's more like seeing an athlete before a game.

"What I don't know," he continued, "is whether the Marines just attract kids like that, or do they get that way because they're going into the Marines? All I know is that I wish they were joining the Army."

The sergeant in charge of the Marine Recruiting Station in Atlanta laughed when he heard that story. "You tell that Army man the answer is 'both of the above.' We get the good ones, and the idea of being a

Marine gets inside them and they swell up just like pigeons. Hell, I was the same way myself when I signed up six years ago. I could not *wait* to get to Parris Island—changed my mind damned fast when I got there, mind you, but that's another story."

He pointed to a wall of his office. It was covered with the standard post-boot-camp portraits of new Marines: clad in Dress Blues in front of an American flag, looking stern, proud, and painfully young. "Those are our boys," he said. "All recruited here. Six honor men up there, you know. If I get a little down, I look at those pictures and get pumped up again.

"Seriously, I make it a point to ask everybody I recruit why they're enlisting," the sergeant said, "and you'd be surprised at how many different answers I get. A lot of them grew up as service brats and like the life.

One says he wants 'lectronics.' I say, 'Shoot! Everybody's got that.' He says, 'Did you ever look at those other guys? They don't look like *nothing!* Bunch of damn civilians dressed up in funny clothes!' That was his heart talking. He wants to be a Marine. That stuff about electronics is just something he thinks people want to hear. I'm betting—now, he's smart enough for electronics—but I'm betting he ends up a trigger-puller. That boy wants to be where the action is."

Threading through the reasons for enlisting in the Marines is a strand of seeming irrationality—a sense of adventure, the need to be challenged, a desire, as the sergeant put it, "to be where the action is." Whatever it's called, it will stand them in good stead in the Marines, beginning the moment they arrive at boot camp.

★

CHAPTER 6

THE MAKING OF A MARINE

*T*hey have been arriving since early afternoon and are beginning to fill up a corner of the waiting area in the Charleston, South Carolina, airport: young men, casually dressed, mostly in T-shirts, denim pants, and scuffed white running shoes. A few wear nylon high school letter jackets. Small groups form and re-form; hushed conversations are punctuated with nervous laughter. A Marine sergeant watches over them. He looks bored; he's done this many times before. Later he will load them on a bus to ride seventy miles through the warm summer night to Parris Island, where they will be initiated into the Corps.

It is after midnight when the bus arrives at the base and proceeds to the new, two-story receiving center. A sergeant climbs aboard. He is wearing the Smokey-the-Bear field hat of a drill instructor. The young men

---

OPPOSITE PAGE: The famous boot camp haircut convinces even the most skeptical that he is in the Marines. As long as he is in the Corps he will wear his hair "high and tight."

have been cautioned about drill instructors by their recruiters. All eyes are on him.

"On behalf of Brigadier General Hoar, commanding general of the recruit depot, I welcome you to Parris Island," he says, his voice devoid of expression. "Put out your cigarettes. Get rid of your gum. When I say get off the bus, you will hit the street running. You will see the yellow footprints painted on the street. You will put your feet on the yellow footprints. *Do you understand?*"

There is mumbled assent.

"When you are given an order here, you will shout, *'Yes Sir!' Do you understand?*

"Yes Sir!" the young men reply.

"I thought I heard something. I must be going deaf. DO YOU UNDERSTAND?"

"YES SIR!"

"Then *move* it!"

They pour off the bus, dash to the footprints, and stand at a semblance of attention. The D.I. looks them over. Several have neglected to bring their personal belongings and orders. They are sent running to retrieve them.

"Listen up," says the D.I. "My name is Sergeant

Standing in line at attention studying the next boot's haircut is an everyday occurrence at Parris Island. The phrase "hurry up and wait" may date from Caesar's legions.

Kelly. You will not call me Sergeant Kelly. You will not call any drill instructor by his name. You will call us 'sir.' You will call every Marine on this base 'sir.' Now listen up. Article 86 of the Uniform Code of Military Justice prohibits absence without leave. Article 91 prohibits disobedience to a lawful order. Article 93 prohibits disrespect to a senior officer. Get those through your head. Burn them into your brain. Obey them. *Understand?'*

"Yes sir."

"What was that?" He cups his hand to his ear.

"YES SIR!"

The D.I. then double-times the group into the reception center and orders them to sit in rows of school chairs. On the writing armrests are stacks of forms and Magic Markers. Three other D.I.s are in the large room. They regard the young men with expressions of disgust. One walks to the front.

"Listen up," he says. "You are Platoon 1210. Pick up the Magic Marker from the arm rest. Take the cap off the Magic Marker. With the Magic Marker, write the numbers one two one zero on the back of your hand. DO IT!"

For the next hour the young men fill out forms. When they are not writing or listening to instructions, they are ordered to put their heads on their folded arms like kindergartners. They are constantly commanded to work faster. They are tired and nervous, and some make mistakes. The ones who do are made to feel like fools, making the group more nervous, more prone to mistakes.

When they finish the forms, they are called forward, four at a time, to desks at the front of the room. They are ordered to empty their pockets and remove watches, rings, and other jewelry. Valuables are sealed in an envelope to be returned after boot camp. The remaining vestiges of civilian life—cigarettes, combs, condoms, whatever—are swept off the desk by the D.I.

It's now two in the morning. The group is double-timed into another room and ordered to stand at attention at a long table on which are individual piles of gear: shoe trees, shower clogs, toothbrushes and paste, deodorant, assorted brushes—some fifty items in all. On the table stands a small, middle-aged woman; her temperament, vocabulary, and tone of voice are identical to the D.I.'s. She holds a small canvas bag above her head. "This is a ditty bag. You all have ditty bags. Find your ditty bag. Hold it over your head. DO IT!" She proceeds to call out item after item until everything has been found and put in the ditty bags. Receipts for the items are signed, the cost to be deducted from the first pay check.

Next comes the infamous Marine haircut. The recruits line up in front of four barber chairs, their toes touching the heels of the person ahead of them. In the chairs, a few passes of an electric clipper and they are shorn to a point just short of total baldness.

In a shower room that can accommodate sixty, a lesson in personal hygiene is given. There is a Marine way to do practically everything, including taking a shower. A D.I. calls out, "Throw towel over the bar above you. Pull ring to turn on shower. Wet head. Soap head and face. Rinse. Soap right arm. Then left arm.

Rinse. Soap body. Rinse. Soap crotch and penis. Come on, nobody's looking at ya! Rinse. Soap left leg then right. Rinse. Rinse all over. Put on clogs. Take towel and dry. Put deodorant under left arm. Then right arm. Collect gear. *Move out!"*

Clad in towels and clogs, they march to be issued utility uniforms: "camies" (camouflage blouses, pants, and caps), skivvies (the Marine term for underwear), combat boots, and other miscellaneous items. They dress, store the excess in their new sea bags, and put their civilian clothes in brown paper bags. Underwear and socks will be discarded; the rest will be returned after boot camp.

The D.I. marches the new recruits to the mess hall. It is still dark outside, but they are starved. It's been a long time since burgers at the airport. Their first Marine meal, like the countless others they will eat, has been designed to provide a calculated portion of a daily total of 3,200 calories. And they will eat nothing else in boot camp: not candy, junk food, nor soft drinks. They will not smoke in boot camp, nor will anyone be allowed to smoke in their presence.

For the next few days, the sixty recruits of Platoon 1210 will live in the Receiving Barracks. They are marched there now to be issued linens and blankets, make their bunks, and stow their gear. Although they haven't slept in twenty-four hours, a new day is beginning for them.

At 0600 they are marched off to begin taking physical and mental examinations, fill out more forms, and undergo something known as the "moment of truth."

A four-hour battery of tests measure mathematical and mechanical aptitudes and verbal facility. The results will help determine the Military Occupational Specialty (MOS) for which the recruit is best suited.

The physical examination is particularly thorough. A special test is given to detect AIDS, and a urinalysis to determine if the recruit has used drugs during the past thirty days. Should either test prove positive, the recruit is automatically discharged. Correctible physical defects are handled now. Podiatrists prescribe special boot inserts; dentists remedy troublesome teeth. Defective vision is corrected with government-issue glasses, black-rimmed and shatterproof. Contact lenses are not allowed.

The Moment of Truth. Once more, each recruit is asked all the questions about his background that might affect his enlistment. He is warned that to give false information now will bring military punishment, but to reveal something that is disqualifying will only send him home at government expense.

The platoon will stay in the Receiving Barracks after processing has been completed until a company of four platoons is assembled. The recruits are introduced to close order drill, policing the barracks and the grounds, and other rudiments of Marine life. A mandatory postcard is sent home, called a "Momgram," to reassure the folks that their son is alive, well, and adapting to his new life. The recruits may not think so, but the days they spend in the Receiving Barracks are designed to be "low stress." When boot camp begins in earnest, the stress factor will soar.

Marines are bound together by the common experience of boot camp. It is longer, tougher, and more demanding than the basic training of any other service. No Marine is exempt. The Marine Officer Candidates School at Quantico, Virginia, is a version of boot camp. Young women recruits train separately at Parris Island; some exercises are modified, but are comparably arduous, and the curriculum and discipline are identical. A Marine takes comfort in knowing that every Marine has paid his boot camp dues.

Every Marine is trained and conditioned, mentally and physically, to acquit himself in combat. One of the tenets of the Corps is "Every Marine a rifleman."

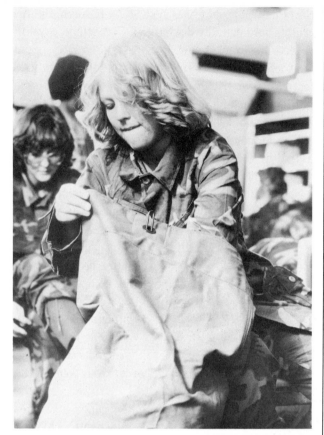

A brand-new female recruit packs her new gear into her sea bag. She has yet to get a Marine haircut—short, but nothing compared to what her male counterparts get.

Marines are expected to fire a rifle accurately at distances up to 500 yards. Marine cooks and bakers fought the Japanese on the beach at Wake Island. Aircraft mechanics at Da Nang fought Vietnamese infiltrators.

Combat training also helps a Marine define himself. He's a Marine, first and foremost; his service specialty may be clerk-typist or truck driver, but that's what he does, not what he is. He is a Marine.

The Corps fosters that sort of thinking. For example, there is nothing on a Marine uniform to indicate what the Marine does. The few exceptions to this rule are the wings of an aviator and the devices awarded to those who qualify in parachuting, scuba diving, and bomb disposal, and the Marine high command sometimes grumbles about those. Division and air wing patches were eliminated right after World War II for

the same reason: a homogeneous Corps. The specialty trappings that adorn the uniforms of the other services are scorned as "bells and whistles."

The Marines first came to Parris Island in the Civil War when it was a coaling station for the Union Navy. A Marine Officers School was established on the island in 1909, and the recruit depot began operation in 1915; most of the Marines who served in World War I were trained here.

The other boot camp is at San Diego, California. San Diego weather is better. Parris Island has boiling summers, and the damp cold of winter can cut to the bone. Hurricanes have swept the island. All four of America's poisonous snakes can be found here: the coral, water moccasin, copperhead, and rattler. There are alligators and sharks. It is impossible to avoid being bitten constantly by sand fleas. At the mention of Parris Island, many Marines instinctively start to scratch.

Recruit life hasn't changed that much over the years. The oldest veteran and the youngest private can still enjoy swapping stories. There has been one major change, though, and it came about because of a scandal at Parris Island.

On April 6, 1956, a drill instructor decided to punish his platoon with a night march. He led his seventy-four

A sturdy specimen is examined by a Navy Corpsman. All training is monitored by doctors to prevent injury and heat exhaustion. Corpsmen accompany Marines in combat.

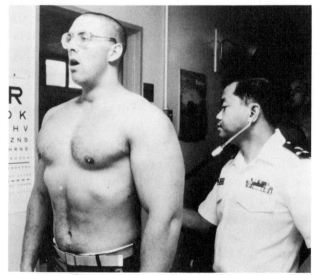

recruits into a tidal swamp called Ribbon Creek, and six drowned. He was court-martialed, the commanding general was relieved of duty, and Congress ordered a board set up to reform recruit training.

Within a year, 197 D.I.s were relieved of training duties and a number of reforms were instituted. Night marches were forbidden in swamps, marshes, or streams; D.I.s no longer could bury recruits in sand up to their neck, punch or kick them, or lock them in wall lockers.

Trouble came again to the boot camps in the middle 1970s. A recruit at San Diego was beaten to death in pugil-stick training; a Parris Island recruit was shot by a D.I. Both the House and Senate Armed Forces Committees ordered full investigations. The *New York Times* editorialized, "A few [Marine] training officers seem to have difficulty in distinguishing between the tough, but human, discipline that builds men and a perverted sadism that degrades and destroys them." Most people believed that either the Corps was looking the other way at training abuses or was unable to control its own handpicked D.I.s.

One who saw the problem clearly was Commandant Robert Barrow, a D.I. himself in his early career and a former commanding general at Parris Island.

"We had more abuses at Parris Island and San Diego than the Marine Corps was willing to admit. The odd thing about this was that almost without exception, the individual who experienced it believed it was good for him. That is why it never came out.

"A lot of D.I.s don't raise their voices, don't raise their hands. They don't engage in any form of hazing, and they get the same good results. But they are powerful people, of strong character, who have great confidence in themselves and don't need to engage in that kind of nonsense.

"I've gotten a lot of 'hate' mail from Marines and former Marines, saying, 'You are ruining recruit training.' Now, recruit training is at once the most precious thing we have in the Marine Corps, and the most fragile. We can't let the D.I.s screw that up; it is the guts of the Marine Corps."

Commandant Barrow then described the young men who join the Marines:

A sentry patrols the barracks while the rest of company drills. Under the eye of the D.I., recruits clean, polish, and stow gear in a way their mothers wouldn't believe.

"Many, if not all, want desperately to believe in something. Most of us want one or more strong personal commitments—religion, home, community, or some other institution which would extract from us involvement and strong beliefs. In today's world, the opportunity for such strong commitment has waned significantly, and many young people look around them in vain for such opportunities. For many, the search ends with the Marine Corps.

"Second, there is an inherent need in all males of the animal world to prove their masculinity or maleness. In the past, it has accounted for such decisions as the opening of the new frontier, 'going to sea' and other forms of adventure. The opportunity for such legitimate proving of one's manliness is shrinking. A notable exception is the Marine Corps.

"The Marine Corps reputation, richly deserved, for physical toughness, courage and its demands on mind and body, attracts those who want to prove their manliness. Here the search ends.

"Perhaps unwittingly," the commandant concluded, "the Marine Corps exploits and builds on these two basic desires: to believe in something, and to prove one's manliness, and, in the process, the Marine Corps gains two of its most important virtues—spirit and discipline. These virtues are the mark of excellence in any military organization, and are absolutely essential to success in combat."

Today the Marine Corps bends over backward to make sure that D.I.s don't abuse recruits. Swearing is out. A D.I. must refrain from using obscene, profane, ethnically or racially degrading language to recruits; he can't even curse to himself in their presence. Physical abuse is out too; about the only time it is safe for a D.I. to touch a recruit is in administering first aid.

The only form of physical punishment still permitted is what is euphemistically called Incentive Physical Training (IPT), which recruits call "intensive physical torture." An offending recruit is called out by his D.I. and put through a punishing series of calisthenics. But IPT has clearly defined limits. It may be administered to a particular recruit only five minutes in any given hour, and each dose must be broken by a thirty-minute breather.

A D.I. charged with abusing a recruit is immediately relieved of duty; if found guilty, he may be fined, transferred to other duty, demoted, or discharged if the offense is egregious.

Gone are the days when a recruit was given an offensive nickname by his D.I. and punishment came in a variety of imaginative ways: duckwalking around the drill field, quacking all the way; running up and down barracks stairs with a full sea bag; standing in front of your platoon with arms waving, shouting, "I'm a shitbird!" To drop a rifle was to sleep with it. To neglect personal hygiene was to be scrubbed with sand. Old-time D.I.s were known for the creativity of both their language and the punishment they handed out.

Many Marines and former Marines deplore the current constraints on the D.I.'s authority. Through the years Marines have emerged from the brutality of boot camp to acquit themselves brilliantly in combat. Will the new Marines perform as well? It is a fair question.

The linchpin in Marine training continues to be the drill instructor, and it is important to look closely at the man under the field hat.

A prospective D.I. must have an exemplary record, be a sergeant, have a commanding presence and leadership qualities, be recommended by his commanding officer, and volunteer. Like recruiting duty, the billet calls for extra pay and is "career enhancing" to compensate for the hardships of the job. The hours are murderous: D.I.s are with the boots every waking hour of every day, and one D.I. sleeps in the D.I. shack in their barracks at night. D.I.s have more than their share of marital problems.

The Drill Instructor School at Parris Island packs a lot into a ten-week course, and it is every bit as demanding as boot camp itself. There are courses on Standard Operating Practice, which governs how D.I.s handle recruits; recreational supervision and evaluation; leadership; weapons and marksmanship training; and evaluation. A lot of time is spent in physical activity, including close order drill, individual combat training, and PT. There is plenty of homework, with frequent tests.

In their free time, novitiate D.I.s walk around on the lawn opposite the school with their small book of marching commands, practicing how to bark out orders.

Each recruit platoon is assigned three D.I.s, or "hats" in boot parlance. The senior drill instructor wears a black patent leather belt as a symbol of authority; recruits speak of him as the "Black Belt" or "Big Dad." He is assisted by the "Second Hat" or

Leland "Lou" Diamond enlisted in 1917 and fought with the 6th Marines from Château-Thierry to the Argonne and stayed on for the Occupation. He was older than most of his fellow Marines. His service record gave his birthday as May 30, 1890, but his friends said the date came off a tombstone. In 1921 he went to China for a tour of duty. He later saw action in the Caribbean. By World War II, Lou Diamond already was a Marine legend. His booming voice earned him the sobriquet "The Honker," and stories of his amazing accuracy with a mortar spread throughout the Corps. In a peacetime maneuver, he reputedly put a mortar round down the chimney of a house 1,900 yards away.

In 1942 Lou learned that his outfit was headed for the Pacific and he was being left behind because of his age. He talked a naval doctor friend into certifying him "fit for active duty anywhere," and pleaded his case with his battalion commander. "Where would my boys be without me?" he said.

The first day on Guadalcanal, he won the praise of the commanding general for the accuracy of his unit's mortar fire. With the Marines pinned on a ridge, Diamond's mortar platoon was called on to blast the Japanese. The target area was more than a mile away, narrow and bordered on two sides by Marines. Working under sniper fire, the platoon poured shells on the Japanese position. General Vandegrift called the mortar barrage "a decisive factor in halting an enemy attack." When Edson's Raiders were held up for several days at Matanikau Ridge, Edson sent for Lou.

Diamond delivered what eyewitnesses called the fiercest mortar concentration in Marine history.

On Guadalcanal Diamond was so famous that whenever a mortar was fired, someone would say, "There goes Old Lou." Once Japanese destroyers were streaming in close to the island and shelling at will. To bolster morale, Lou decided to take a shot at a fast-moving destroyer, missing by 1,200 yards, but a reporter caught up in the Diamond mystique wrote, "He almost sank a Jap destroyer. He kept firing away and almost had the range when the Jap commander fled." Fiction embellished fact throughout Lou's career to the annoyance of his fellow Marines.

After two months on Guadalcanal, Lou Diamond had two broken ribs, malaria, kidney trouble, and rheumatism. His weight was down from 220 to 162. He was evacuated, the Marines lining up as he passed in a jeep on the way to Henderson Field.

Recuperating in New Zealand, he persuaded a friend to give him orders to board a supply ship bound for New Caledonia. From there he conned his way to Guadalcanal, only to learn that his outfit was in Australia. He somehow rejoined his platoon in Australia, walking the last few miles to the camp. Reportedly he was complaining to his commanding officer a few hours later that his men "weren't getting their beer like they should."

"Heavy 'A'," who is in charge of instruction, and by the "Third Hat," who handles disciplinary matters. Both wear the wide web belt the Marines call a "war belt."

These are the supporting players in the drama that will star Platoon 1210. The curtain is about to rise.

The platoon moves now to a training barracks. As soon as it is squared away, the senior D.I. introduces himself and his assistants. He gives a short speech, one he memorized as part of his training.

"Our mission is to teach each and every one of you to be a Marine. A Marine is one who possesses the highest military virtues. He obeys orders, respects his seniors, and he constantly strives to be the best in everything he does. The hallmark of a Marine is disci-

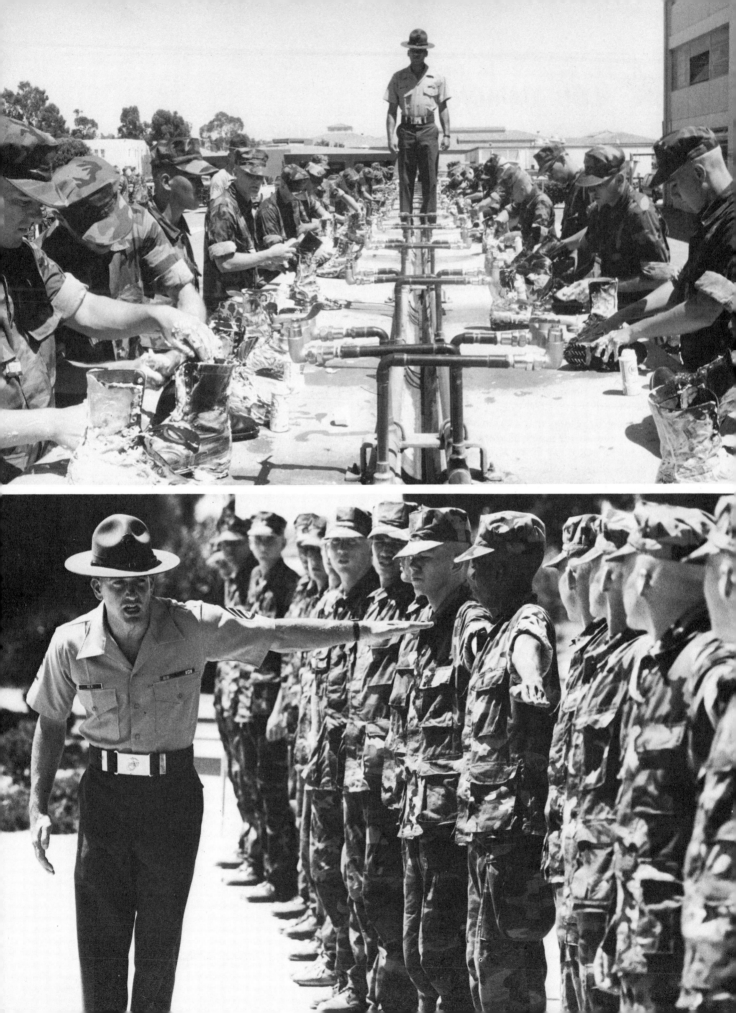

OPPOSITE PAGE, ABOVE: Recruits scrub their boots and the D.I. makes sure they do it the Marine way— by hand. A lesson in self-reliance, and a useful skill when operating in the field. OPPOSITE PAGE, BELOW: Dressing a formation isn't easy at first and the D.I. shows his charges how. The days of physically abusing recruits are over, and the D.I. must communicate in subtler ways.

pline and spirit, and these are the goals of your training. Every recruit in this platoon can become a Marine —*if* you can develop self-satisfaction and spirit. We will give every effort to train you, even after some of you have given up on yourself.

"Starting right now, you will treat me and all other Marines with the highest respect, and you will obey all orders without question. You will be treated with firmness, fairness, dignity, and compassion. You will not be threatened with bodily harm, abused, or mistreated by me, any other Marine, or fellow recruit. If this should happen, you will report the incident to me. If I abuse or mistreat you, I expect you to report it to the company commander. My drill instructors and I will be with you every day, everywhere you go.

"This is what I and my drill instructors will do. We expect you to give 100 percent of yourself at all times. Specifically:

"You *will* do everything you are told to do, quickly and willingly.

"You *will* treat all Marines and recruits with courtesy and respect.

"You *will* be completely honest in everything you do. A Marine never lies, cheats, or compromises.

"You *will* respect the rights and property of all other persons. A Marine never steals.

"You *will* be proud of yourself and the uniform you wear.

"You *will* learn the things you are taught. Everything we teach you is important.

"You *will* work hard to strengthen your body.

"Most important of all, you will *never* give up. You will *never* quit. We cannot train you unless you have made up your mind that you are going to be a Marine. This is the challenge of recruit training—the opportunity to be a Marine."

Platoon 1210 settles into the training regimen. Reveille is before daybreak, at 0500, and they hit the deck running. Taps comes at 2100, before dark in summer, after the recruits have been running most of the long day. Getting in shape is primary; they do two one-hour sessions of calisthenics daily. A warm-up consists of straddle hops, shoulder rotations, toe touches, bends and thrusts. They form a line for pull-ups, each does as many as he can, goes to the end of the line, and waits to try again. Leg lifts. Push-ups. Sit-ups. Ten repetitions each. In a week, they'll be doing twenty. Later on, thirty. The session winds up with a mile-and-a-half run, once around the field. They will work up to three miles and more.

Medical corpsmen stand by at PT sessions. Recruits who have a potential health problem or are badly overweight wear shirts with two red bars on the back, and are watched closely. In the summer the temperature-humidity index is monitored and training is cut back or suspended when the index gets dangerously high.

An Initial Training Test is given at the end of the first training week. To pass, a recruit must do at least two pull-ups, 35 sit-ups in two minutes, and a mile-and-a-half run in 13½ minutes. Those who fail are transferred to a Physical Conditioning Platoon for even more intensive workouts, including weightlifting. In the special platoon, overweight recruits receive an 1,800-calorie diet; underweight recruits, a 4,500-

Sounding off, boots at Parris Island answer the D.I.'s commands loudly and clearly. The secret of surviving the ordeal of boot camp is enthusiasm and hard work.

★ A MARINE LEXICON

Silhouetted against the sky, recruits at San Diego scale a barrier on the confidence course. Racing the clock, recruits also build strength and agility.

aboard	on base
ALICE	individual field pack (All-purpose, Lightweight, Individual Carrying Equipment)
all hands	everybody
As you were!	resume what you were doing
Aye, aye, Sir!	acknowledgment of an order
BCD	Bad Conduct Discharge
BDR	Basic Daily Routine
billet	assignment or job
blouse	jacket of the uniform
Blues	Dress Blues formal uniform
boondocks	swamps, small towns (also *boonies*)
boot	recruit
boss	Senior Drill Instructor
brass	officers
brig	jail
bulkhead	wall
bunk	bed (also *rack*)
camies	camouflage field uniforms
Carry on!	same as *As you were!*
Casual Company	unit of men awaiting reassignment
catch a hit	to receive a dressing down by a superior (also *chewed out*)
CG	Commanding General
chit	authorization or receipt
chow	food
chow down	to eat
click	one notch of rifle sight adjustment
CMC	Marine Corps Commandant
colors	the American flag; also the ceremonies of raising and lowering the flag
com rats	commuted rations: payments for meals away from the mess hall
corpsmen	Navy medics who serve with the Marines
cover	hat or cap
cover ass	to take precautions to avoid blame
cruise	period of enlistment
dark green	black Marine
deck	floor (also can mean to knock down)
deuce gear	782 gear, equipment carried by an individual Marine
D.I.	drill instructor
ditty bag	canvas bag for toilet articles, etc.
dog and pony show	a special drill, etc., performed for visiting dignitaries
double time	marching cadence of 180 36-inch steps a minute
dry run	practice exercise
EST	Essential Subject Test given each year to lower enlisted grades
field day	barracks cleanup
field scarf	necktie
fleet	Fleet Marine Force (FMF)
float	sea deployment of a unit
galley	kitchen

Gangway!	Move out of the way!	*police*	to clean or tidy up
gear	equipment	*PX*	Post Exchange, a base department store
gizmo	gadget; any object that defies description	*quarters*	living space
go-to-hell hat	cloth overseas hat	*rack out*	to go to bed
grinder	parade ground	*rappel*	to descend from a helicopter or cliff by rope
grunt	Marine infantryman	*ready box*	wooden ammunition box
guidon	small flag bearing unit's number	*reconn*	reconnaissance
gung ho	highly motivated (Chinese for "work together")	*round*	a bullet or shell
		sack out	to go to bed (also *rack out*)
gunny	gunnery sergeant, a rank unique to the Marines, equivalent to Army technical sergeant	*scuttlebutt*	water fountain; also gossip exchanged around same
		scuz rag	cloth for cleaning up
hat	drill instructor	*seabag*	sausage-shaped canvas bag for personal gear
hatch	door	*Second Hat*	Assistant D.I. in charge of instruction
head	toilet (a visit to the toilet is a *head call*)	*secure*	to stop, lock, or put away
high-and-tight	standard Marine haircut: close on the sides, a quarter-inch or so on top	*sick bay*	base hospital
		six, six and a kick	six months in the brig, six months loss of pay, and a Bad Conduct Discharge
hooch	two-man field tent		
hump	march (verb and noun)	*skipper*	commanding officer
ICT	Individual Combat Training	*skivvies*	underwear
in hack	under arrest	*slopchute*	bar, saloon
IG	Inspector General	*smoking lamp*	permission to smoke, if it's lit
Joe	coffee (*Joe-pot,* coffee pot)	*snap in*	to practice firing; also to give, or get, instruction in a new task
klick	kilometer		
ladder	stairway	*SOP*	Standing Operating Procedure
leave	vacation	*sound off*	to complain; also to shout
liberty	authorized absence up to 72 hours	*squared away*	neat; everything in order
		SRB	Service Record Book: personal file on a Marine
light green	white Marine		
LP	listening post	*survey*	to turn in old equipment for new
Maggie's drawers	a red disc on a pole waved in front of a rifle target to signal a miss	*swab*	a mop, or to mop (a sailor is a *swabbie*)
		TD	training day
Moment of Truth	last opportunity to correct false information on personal records before recruit training begins	*Third Hat*	Assistant D.I. in charge of discipline
		T/O	Table of Organization
		topside	upstairs
momgram	postcard sent home on arrival at boot camp	*turn to*	to begin work
		UA	unauthorized absence (once called AWOL)
mustang	an enlisted man who becomes an officer		
		in hack	under arrest
overhead	ceiling	*unk*	unqualified
over the hill	absent without authorization	*unsat*	unsatisfactory
over the hump	more than halfway through an enlistment	*war belt*	web belt worn in the field, from which hang canteens, etc.
passageway	corridor	*Willie Peter*	white phosphorous round fired by artillery or mortar to identify where the round landed
pencil whip	to make up a story for the record		
PFT	Physical Fitness Training		
piece	rifle		
pogey bait	candy	*the word*	confirmed information

calorie diet. As soon as they are up to the standard, they are returned to regular training.

Close order drill takes up many hours during the initial training weeks. Recruits get acquainted with the M16A2 rifle, committing its characteristics to memory: "The M16A2 is a 5.56 millimeter, lightweight, air-cooled, gas-operated, magazine fed, shoulder weapon . . ."

There is a close relationship between a Marine and his rifle. Recruits must memorize "My Rifle: The Creed of a United States Marine," written by a general in World War II.

> This is my rifle. There are many like it but this one is mine.
>
> My rifle is my best friend. It is my life. I must master it as I must master my life.
>
> My rifle without me is useless. Without my rifle, I am useless. I must fire my rifle true. I must shoot straighter than my enemy who is trying to kill me. I must shoot him before he shoots me. I will.
>
> My rifle and I know that what counts in this war is not the rounds we fire, the noise of our burst, nor the smoke we make. We know that it is the hits that count. We will hit.
>
> My rifle is human, even as I am human, because it is my life. Thus, I will learn it like a brother. I will learn its weaknesses, its strengths, its parts, its accessories, its sights, and its barrel. I will ever guard it against the ravages of weather and damage. I will keep my rifle clean and ready, even as I am clean and ready. We will become part of each other. We will.
>
> Before God I swear this creed. My rifle and I are the defenders of our country. We are the saviors of my life.
>
> So be it, until victory is America's and there is no enemy, but Peace!

At this stage of training, however, a recruit's mystical union with his rifle consists of carrying it while marching and learning the tedious process of cleaning it.

Classroom work begins. Recruits learn Marine history; not military history per se, but a concoction of history, tradition, and symbolism. More history is tucked into the leadership course. Medal of Honor citations are read, the point made that these heroes were once boots themselves and went on to glory by never letting the Corps down.

In Interior Guard class, they learn the General Orders of a Sentry. Putting theory to practice, they walk post outside their barracks, stand fire watch in-side, and take turns being sentries while the rest of the platoon trains. Other classes introduce the mysteries of the Marine Corps Promotion System, Lifesaving, and the Tailoring, Maintenance, and Laundering of Uniforms. A recruit does all his own laundry during boot camp.

In the Code of Conduct, the treatment of prisoners of war is explained, both for captors and captives. Other military do's and don'ts come in the Law of Land Warfare. First Aid teaches how to avoid heat exhaustion, shock, and infection, and how to transport the wounded.

As they learn how to avoid injuries, they are learning how to inflict them.

There are five killing blows with the bayonet, and assorted defensive techniques including the high block, low block, and parry. Recruits practice them over and over, shouting at the top of their lungs. After achieving some proficiency, they test their skill with the bayonet over a course that simulates battlefield conditions: shell holes, tunnels, and barbed wire. Working in three-man fire teams, they search out and bayonet "enemy" dummies along the course.

Disciplinary problems crop up during the early weeks of training. The offending recruits are brought to Office Hours, an informal but official court conducted by the company commander. He can levy fines, order a recruit to repeat training in another platoon, or, in extreme cases, have him discharged. Nearly one in five recruits is either moved back or discharged during the early training weeks. With the trouble-makers gone, the morale of the platoon improves.

A time of testing comes at the end of the third week: tests to determine their progress in physical conditioning, tests on classroom work, an inspection of their quarters, rifles, and equipment, followed by a parade review.

The four platoons march off to the parade deck, where the judges hand the D.I.s a list of thirty commands to be given and executed. The judges note both individual recruit's and the overall platoon performance. The D.I.s also are graded.

The platoon with the highest cumulative score in the tests and parade review will receive a trophy; the lowest-scoring will march and drill with its guidon furled, its ineptitude there for all to see. All the platoons will work extra hard to better their performance.

Hand-to-hand combat is essential to Marines. Recruits take turns throwing one another. Upper-body strength increases an average of 30 percent during boot camp.

"Nobody ever drowned in sweat," the Marine saying goes. The platoon is taught that no Marine ever need drown in water either, if he knows what he's doing. The key is the mnemonic word FUSE: Full-lung inflation; Utilizing the water itself for support by leaning forward and keeping your face down; Slow, easy movements; and Extreme relaxation. But easy to forget, though, while jumping from a catwalk to hit the water twenty-two feet below, wearing camies, boots, helmet, and a heavy flak jacket, and carrying a rifle. Before boot camp is over, every recruit must be a qualified swimmer.

By now, Platoon 1210 regularly takes to the field to learn the craft of combat. There they have tasted the curious contents of the dark-brown plastic package known as MRE (Meal-Ready-to-Eat). Inside are a number of small packages, containing such things as dehydrated potatoes, meatballs with a sauce of sorts, cocoa mix, crackers, a packet of jelly, instant coffee, matches, salt, chewing gum, a square of a cakelike substance, and toilet paper. All that's needed is to add hot water.

Recruits look forward to rifle training, which begins in the fourth week. The first phase is called Grass Week.

At the Weapons Battalion Area, a ninety-minute march from the barracks, the D.I.s turn the platoon over to the P.M.I.s, the Primary Marksmanship Instructors, who are also permitted to wear the campaign hat. The P.M.I.s explain each step involved in correctly firing a rifle, demonstrate it, then drill the recruits until they can do the steps perfectly every time. Marine marksmanship is as codified and precise as Euclidian geometry. Learn the technique, practice it diligently, and you will be a dead shot. A very dead shot indeed.

There are many steps to master: sighting and aiming, including sight alignment; the aiming point, and the proper position of the eye; the shooting positions —prone, sitting, kneeling, and standing; sling adjustment; the stock weld, where the stock meets the cheek; trigger control; the techniques of rapid fire; sight adjustment; how to compensate for the trajectory of the bullet at various distances; and finally, the data book.

In his data book, a recruit notes everything about

A recruit is fitted for his first set of Dress Blues—a big moment in becoming a Marine. More than halfway through boot camp, their hair is starting to grow back.

Two D.I.s watch their charges practice for the graduation parade. Many hours are devoted in boot camp to close order drill. Marines are proud of their marching ability.

every shot he fires on the range: date, time, distance, range and target number, weather conditions, windage and elevation used, where he thought his shot would hit, and where it did hit. A good marksman knows where his shot is going to hit the split second he fires; there are no surprises.

Beyond the basics, there are shooting techniques to master. The sighting eye must focus on the front sight, not the target. The shooter must relax and be peaceful. This slows the heartbeat so that it will not affect the accuracy of his shot. He must find a natural respiratory pause in his breathing where he can easily hold his breath for a second or two while squeezing off his shot.

There are constant dry-firing practices, and the recruit memorizes the commands: "Snap in. Load and lock. Weapon on shoulder. Unlock. Sight alignment. Sight picture. Aim in. Breath control. FIRE! Take weapon from shoulder. Put rifle on safe. Lock bolt to rear. Sit down on ready box, rifle on lap, muzzle pointed downrange. Call your shot. Mark it with a dot in the book. Reload. Let bolt go home. Tap bottom of magazine. Push forward assist." This activity is called "Snapping In."

After the platoon has finished dry firing, it moves to one of the five identical ranges for the real thing.

There are firing lines at 200, 300, and 500 yards; each line has fifty firing positions. An instructor with a loudspeaker controls the firing from a movable tower in the center of the line. There is a coach for every four shooters on the line. A long mound of earth called a berm runs just below the elevated targets. Behind the berm are the pits where recruits raise, lower, and score the targets. They also signal the shooter where he hit by means of a long pole with a disk at the end, red on one side and white on the other. A miss is signaled by swinging the pole back and forth, red side out. A miss is called "Maggie's Drawers," from the days when a red flag was used.

Qualification Day arrives and the recruits are anxious; a lot rides on their scores. To fail to qualify is to be an "unk" and be transferred to the Marksmanship Training Platoon. And there is more at stake than simply qualifying. They all want to earn the Expert badge, worn with pride by privates and generals alike.

They fire slow and rapid fire, using the various shooting positions, from the 200, 300, and 500-yard lines. Fifty shots are fired, each scoring from zero, a miss, to five, a bull's-eye. A perfect score is 250. To qualify and receive a Marksman badge requires a score of 190; Sharpshooter, 210; and Expert, 220.

When the smoke finally clears, the average platoon

will have ten Experts, fifteen Sharpshooters, twenty-five Marksmen, and ten "unks." Marines must requalify on the rifle range annually. If their score improves sufficiently, they can earn a higher rating; conversely, they can move to a lower level.

Qualification Day marks the halfway point in boot camp. The recruits have come a long way since they hit the yellow footprints. Perhaps it is just as well that they have no idea how far they still have to go.

Every marine remembers standing on the yellow footprints, TOP, the first act on arrival at boot camp. The numbers, CENTER, identify the recruits' platoon. Beyond individual training, a recruit must learn to function as part of a unit. A D.I., BOTTOM, makes sure the platoon is properly lined up. Platoons spend several hours each day on close order drill.

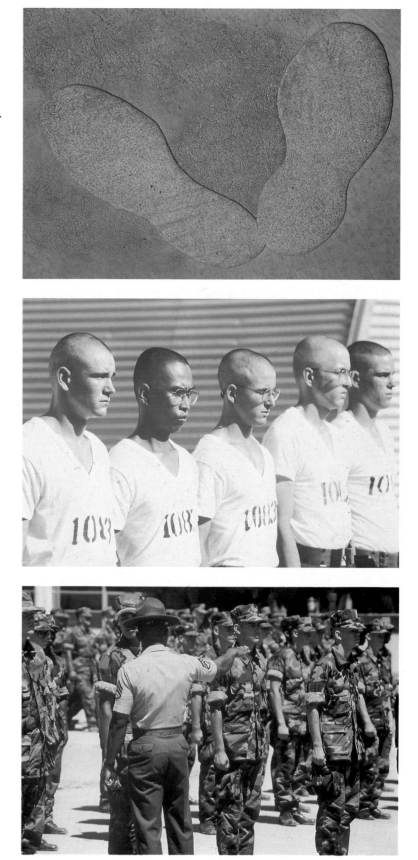

The drill instructor, OPPOSITE, is the most important person in the life of a Marine recruit. Wearing a field hat as the symbol of his nearly absolute authority, he drives his platoon all day, every day, demanding instant obedience and the perfection of military skills.

"Every Marine a rifleman" is the watchword of the Corps. An instructor, ABOVE, watches closely as a recruit practice fires on the rifle range. Soon the recruits will be putting their new skills to work in the field, TOP. All recruits learn to fire the pistol, and some specialties require advanced skills. A new military policeman, RIGHT, squeezes off shots at the pistol range.

A recruit, OPPOSITE, guards his platoon mates' rifles while they are in a classroom. A recruit rarely goes anywhere without his rifle and spends much of his time keeping it in top shape.

The procedure never varies, OPPOSITE. The D.I.s demonstrate a new skill in the field, then the recruits try it themselves. Recruit haircuts never vary either. Here the recruits are being indoctrinated in hand-to-hand combat. The subject is the bayonet, ABOVE, how to defend with it, how to kill with it. Recruits must constantly shout their enthusiasm: "Hoo-rah! Hoo-rah!"

Taking a break in the field, RIGHT, a D.I. lunches on an MRE (Meal Ready to Eat). Combat rations are designed to give Marines proper nutrition and an adequate calorie intake.

★

In simulated combat training, recruits storm out of a mock-up of an AMTRAC (Amphibious Tractor landing vehicle), LEFT. Field exercises take up much of the final weeks of boot camp. A D.I., BELOW, watches as his platoon charges an "enemy" position. The combat skills the recruit learns in boot camp will be refined when he reaches the School of Infantry.

Crawling under barbed wire, TOP, *is tough, dirty work
but a necessary combat skill. On the confidence course at
OCS,* ABOVE *and* OPPOSITE, *the rigors of the obstacle
course are combined with the solving of typical battlefield
problems.*

OVERLEAF. *Every PT session in boot camp includes a run, increasing from a mile and a half to three miles as the
recruits' stamina builds. The guidon is carried furled when the platoon fails to meet the standards of the D.I. or does
poorly in competition.*

CHAPTER 7

THE SKILLS OF A WARRIOR

Boot camp giveth, and boot camp taketh away. Qualifying at the rifle range is an emotional high. The recruit has demonstrated his ability to master the skill the Corps prizes most highly. He is halfway through boot camp, over the hump, convinced now that he can make it all the way. But a week of unglamorous work lies ahead: Mess and Maintenance; M&M as it's called, and it seems like a step backward.

Recruits assigned to the mess hall report for work at 0300 and change into working clothes: white pants and skivvy shirts, topped off with white paper hats. A cook, grouchy and as hard to please as a D.I., holds a hygiene inspection before the recruits are allowed to touch food. They make coffee, fill the juice dispensers, set up the chow line, and serve breakfast. When the meal is over, they clean and scrub up, empty the GI

OPPOSITE PAGE: A M199 155-millimeter self-pro-pelled cannon can get into position quickly and send a lot of steel down-range. Armament has become heavier and more agile in recent years.

cans, swab the decks, then are given a twenty-minute break. After the break, they change into fresh whites and start all over again. By the time they finish for the day and march back to the barracks, it will be dark. They work seventeen-hour days.

Four recruits, chosen by rotation, are left in the barracks each morning. They take care of the platoon's housekeeping chores—clean the barracks, make bunks, do the laundry—so that the rest can come back and collapse on their bunks.

Other platoons are assigned maintenance chores. They cut grass, paint, rake leaves, polish brasswork, police the grounds, and keep the base shining.

The chow is surprisingly good. Nutritionists prepare menus for well-balanced meals on a forty-two-day cycle, the fare varying with the weather. In the winter, high-carbohydrate foods are served at every meal; in the summer, they are replaced with foods with a high liquid content: salads, soups, fruit, jello and puddings. The nutritionists also take into account the likes and dislikes of the average recruit, and go heavy on beef and chicken, light on fish and liver.

Special meals are served on holidays, including the

Marine Corps's birthday: usually steak or turkey with all the trimmings, an appetizer, and cake. Gone, however, are the once traditional free cigars.

At the end of the chow line, a D.I. waits to inspect each recruit's tray. The recruit stops, snaps to attention, holding his tray in front of him, and shouts, "Good morning, sir!" and his name. The D.I. checks the tray for nutritional content, then barks, "Go!" The recruit goes to the section set aside for his platoon. He has twenty minutes to eat and chat with his buddies. He probably won't notice the inspirational messages displayed around the mess hall. A typical one reads "To err is human, to forgive divine—neither of which is Marine Corps policy."

As M&M week wears on, the recruits grow more tired, and less tolerant of anything or anyone who makes their life harder. A recruit who isn't doing his full share is quickly brought into line by the rest of his platoon. One reason for M&M week is to give the platoon a taste of self-discipline.

With M&M behind them, the recruits prepare for a week in the field. They are issued ALICE packs (All-purpose, Lightweight, Individual Carrying Equipment), a modern version of the knapsack weighing close to fifty pounds when loaded with all the gear needed on bivouac. This field work is called Individual Combat Training (ICT).

Before ICT begins, the platoon is marched again to the Weapons Training Area for pistol indoctrination, three hours of firing, field stripping, and cleaning.

In the field the recruits concentrate on defending and attacking positions. They learn that firing a rifle in combat is not the same as firing on the range: they learn to react quickly, sense the distance to the target, and fire in short bursts, often from the hip.

There is a lot to learn. They practice throwing grenades, crawling under barbed wire, putting on gas masks. A gas chamber gives them one fifteen-second exposure to riot gas, an improved version of tear gas, and they emerge coughing and choking, tears streaming from reddened eyes. They thread their way through simulated mine fields, puffs of smoke marking their missteps. They practice observing and reporting by following the acronym SALUTE: the Size of the

Attacking "enemy" troops are fired on by a gun crew with an M-60E3 light machine gun. The barrel of the gun gets very hot in use and must be changed frequently.

enemy's force, its Activity, Location, the Unit involved, Time of spotting, and its Equipment. War has become a business of acronyms.

Training in individual combat skills is followed by small-unit drills, the emphasis on making the recruits work and think together. They practice setting up for action, selecting defensive positions that allow criss-crossing fields of fire. They charge out of mock landing craft and helicopters, carrying full equipment, and deploy. The D.I. breaks them up into attackers and defenders, and they stage sham firefights. They learn to move through the woods silently and use the terrain for concealment. They make a night march. It is hard, exhausting work, and they learn why a rifleman is called a ''grunt.''

On the final day in the field, the platoon is awakened at 0400 and marched the ten miles back to the barracks. There they draw their first monthly pay: $620.40 before deductions, nearly ten times the pay of forty years ago. They are paid by check. The Old Corps paid cash on the barrelhead.

The recruits are measured and fitted for the blouse, trousers, and barracks cap of the green service uniform ''A,'' then get a Marine ''high-and-tight'' haircut, the sides clipped short so that no hair shows when a cover is worn, but the hair on top is allowed to be as much as a half-inch long.

Pugil-stick training begins the next day. A pugil stick is a four-foot pole with a padded, sausage-shaped appendage over both ends. Recruits put on football helmets with face masks, rubber neck rolls, and crotch cups. Pairing off, they start banging away at one another with the sticks; the first to strike a clean blow to the head or neck is the winner. Bouts are fought for first the platoon, then the company, championship. Fighting with pugil sticks, the Corps believes, fosters aggressiveness and fighting spirit.

Both are good qualities to bring to the obstacle course. Among the more challenging of its eleven obstacles: the Monkey Bridge, which involves climbing a twelve-foot rope to a platform, then inching along a footrope over a thirty-foot stretch of water, all the while hanging on to an overhead rope for balance; and the final obstacle, the Slide for Life.

On the Slide for Life, a recruit goes up a cargo net to a thirty-foot-high platform, shimmies out on a rope, suspending himself by his arms and legs above shallow water. He pulls himself along backward, looking up at the sky. Halfway down the rope, he must stop and reverse direction, a feat of upper-body strength and agility. Some recruits can't handle the turnaround and fall into the water.

A good platoon can negotiate all eleven obstacles in forty-five minutes.

Another test of nerve and agility is the forty-five-foot rappelling tower. Each recruit must make two descents, one simulating a drop from a helicopter, the other going down a cliff. First the recruit is strapped into a seat harness which is linked to a rope, from which he fashions a sling. He yells, ''Marine Corps!'' as he steps off the platform backward, controlling his fall by putting tension on the sling by squeezing the rope. In the cliff descent, he also steps off backward, bouncing off the tower wall with his feet once or twice on the way down.

The recruits feel cocky after their rappels, but an instructor takes them down a peg by demonstrating what is called an Australian rappel. He dives off the tower head first, only breaking his fall a few feet from the ground.

The rappelling tower is one of several places where a recruit may freeze. If an instructor can't talk him out of his panic, he is allowed off the tower, but his Marine days are over.

In the ninth week of training, Platoon 1210 takes another battery of tests. One covers all the academic material taught in boot camp, eleven categories in all. There's also another IPT test, and the requirements have gone up: a minimum of five pull-ups, fifty sit-ups in two minutes, and a three-mile run in 24.5 minutes. A recruit's IST score will be taken into consideration for certain physically demanding military specialties, and is also one factor that his D.I.s weigh when they select the recruit to be the platoon honor man.

Winding up the week is training in hand-to-hand combat, techniques adapted from the ancient martial act of kendo. The recruits pair off and take turns throwing each other to the ground. Each throw is accompanied by a feigned chop to the windpipe, a kick to the groin, or some equally disabling blow.

Training now centers on preparing for graduation, close order drill to ensure a smart appearance at the final review, and cleaning and polishing barracks, rifles, and equipment to perfection.

The battalion commander conducts the final inspection, and it is as thorough as the D.I.s have predicted.

Wearing white gloves and followed by a note-taking junior officer, the commander goes up and down the rows of recruits. He stops before each one, the recruit presents arms, and his rifle is examined minutely for any trace of dirt or gun oil. He checks the recruit's uniform, occasionally using a ruler to make sure a rifle badge is precisely one-eighth of an inch above the left pocket of the blouse. Windowsills and the tops of doors are checked for dust, toilet bowls and the bottoms of sinks for dirt.

In the relief that follows the final inspection, no one pauses to think of the recruits who have fallen by the wayside. Nearly one out of four who hit the yellow footprints are gone. Whatever the reason for their failure, all are now civilians. Nor does the platoon wish to be reminded that some of its surviving number won't make it through their first year, either. This is a time to savor accomplishment, to feel good.

The platoon turns in its rifles and gets ready for the first day of liberty since they arrived. They can't leave the base, but they can strut in their brand-new uniforms, shop at the post exchange, and taste the first junk food they've had in eleven weeks. Many will spend the day with their families who have come to see them graduate tomorrow and take them home for their two-week leave.

On Graduation Day, the platoon forms and marches with the company to the parade deck. The base band leads them on to the strains of "Semper Fidelis." The company comes to a halt in front of the reviewing stand and crowded bleachers. The chaplain says a prayer. The honor men of each platoon are announced. (They are the only graduating recruits wearing Dress Blues, gifts from the Marine Corps Association.) The band plays the national anthem, then the graduates pass in review. The band plays the "Marines' Hymn," which is expected, and "Auld Lang Syne," which isn't, and there's a catch in one's throat. One remembers a boot camp graduation photograph from a war past, young faces circled to note those killed in action. The graduates stop again before the reviewing stand, and

are dismissed. A great roar goes up. The recruits of Platoon 1210 are officially Marines.

D.I.s push forward, wanting to be the first to shake the hands of their platoon members and call them "Marines." Everyone is either embracing or taking pictures. There's a refreshment table, but it is largely ignored. General Joseph Hoar, the base commander, is there, shaking hands with parents, and saying, yes, there has indeed been a remarkable change in their son. Slowly they drift off to their cars; a few, perhaps, notice the sign that arcs over the road by the parade deck. It says, "It all begins here."

Graduation from boot camp is not the end of a Marine's school days in the Corps. Every member of Platoon 1210 will report to one school or another after his two-week leave. Going to school is an important part of life in the Marines, particularly in peacetime.

There are some 225 schools for enlisted personnel, ranging in length from two weeks (Advanced Mark IV File Management System) to fifty weeks (Electronic Maintenance in Improved Hawk Missile Fire Control Repair).

It is a comment on the complexity of modern warfare to learn that there are thirty-five specialties open to enlisted Marines, and only three—Infantry, Field Artillery, and Tank and Assault Amphibian Vehicle—are off limits to women Marines. Together, these specialties form a picture of the inner workings of the Corps.

All recruits now first attend the four-week School of Infantry at either Camp Lejeune, North Carolina, or Camp Pendleton, California. It takes over where boot camp leaves off. The curriculum includes tactics, the techniques of camouflage, map reading, and survival. In the *Infantry* some graduates go on to other schools to learn to be machine gunners, mortar men, and Anti-Tank/Assault Guided Missile men. Others go to school at Quantico to learn the deadly business of being a sniper. And still others are assigned to the crack reconnaissance battalions and will have the opportunity to become a parachutist and a scuba diver.

Marines going to *Field Artillery* battalions train at Navy schools in shore fire control, or with the Army at Fort Sill, Oklahoma, as a fire controlman, a scout observer, or in the more involved techniques of a radar or meteorological crewman.

OPPOSITE PAGE: An instructor rappels from a rock at the Pickel Meadow mountain warfare center in the Sierras. NATO depends on Marines to help defend Europe's rugged northern frontier.

MARINE ACRONYMS

AAV	Assault Amphibian Vehicle
ACE	Aviation Combat Element
AE	Assault Echelon
AFOE	Assault Follow-on Echelon
ASRT	Air Support Radar Team
ATCC	Air Traffic Control Center
BLT	Battalion Landing Team
BSSG	Brigade Service Support Group
CATF	Commander Amphibious Task Force
CE	Command Element
CMC	Commandant of the Marine Corps
CSS	Combat Service Support
CSSE	Combat Service Support Element
DASC	Direct Air Support Center
DOA	Days of Ammunition
DOS	Days of Supply
DRAGON	Man-Portable Anti-Tank Missile System (Medium)
FAAD BTRY	Forward Area Air Defense Battery
FSCC	Fire Support Coordination Center
GCE	Ground Combat Element
H&HS	Headquarters and Headquarters Squadron
HAWK	Anti-Aircraft Missile
HOW	Howitzer
JCS	Joint Chiefs of Staff
LAAMBN	Light Anti-Aircraft Missile Battalion
LAV	Light Armored Vehicle
MACCS	Marine Air Command and Control System
MACG	Marine Air Control Group
MACS	Marine Air Control Squadron
MAG	Marine Aircraft Group
MAGTF	Marine Air-Ground Task Force
MASS	Marine Air Support Squadron
MATCS	Marine Air Traffic Control Squadron
MAW	Marine Aircraft Wing
MEB	Marine Expeditionary Brigade
MEF	Marine Expeditionary Force
MEU	Marine Expeditionary Unit
MPS	Maritime Prepositioning Ships
MSC	Military Sealift Command
MSSG	Marine Expeditionary Unit Service Support Group
MWCS	Marine Wing Control Squadron
MWSG	Marine Wing Support Group
NCA	National Command Authorities
NSE	Navy Support Element
RLT	Regimental Landing Team
(SP)	Self-Propelled
TACC	Tactical Air Command Center
TADC	Tactical Air Direction Center
TAOC	Tactical Air Operations Center
TOW	Tube-Launched, Optically Tracked, Wire-Guided Missile
VMA	Marine Attack Squadron
V/STOL	Vertical/Short-Takeoff and Landing Aircraft

In *Tank and Assault Amphibian Vehicle,* crewmen for the M-60 A-1 tank are trained by the Army at Fort Knox, Kentucky, in the operation of tracked vehicles, tactical employment, and the loading, handling, and firing of the tank's big gun. At Camp Pendleton, a five-week school trains assault amphibian vehicle crewmen. They learn to navigate the craft to shore and deliver infantrymen to action.

Success in battle depends heavily on *Communications,* and the largest formal school complex in the Corps is the Communication-Electronics School at Twenty-nine Palms, California. (When the school was founded in 1932, it was called the Pigeon and Flag Handler Platoon.) The school graduates 6,400 Marines annually and conducts forty-three separate courses of instruction. The basic courses include instruction for radio operators, communication center operators, microwave equipment operators, and high-frequency communications operators. Subjects include voice and radio procedures, how to encode and decode classified material, transmitting and receiving radio messages, and monitoring emergency frequencies.

Army and Air Force schools train Marines to detect and neutralize the dangers of *Nuclear, Biological and Chemical Warfare.* NBC specialists operate the highly technical and delicately calibrated detection instruments, and operate and maintain nuclear and chemical detection equipment. These specialists also train other Marines in the use of field detection equipment.

An important specialty is *Intelligence,* which covers such subjects as the preparation of terrain models, the interpretation of aerial photographs, and the analysis of enemy tactical data. An allied field is signal intelligence, which is part of ground intelligence warfare. Among the skills taught are International Morse Code teletype operations, communications and radar analysis, even proficiency in foreign languages. These specialists are responsible for knowing what the enemy is doing.

In World War II the field construction needs of the Marines were handled by the Seabees, the Navy's construction battalions. Now the Marines are do-it-yourselfers. Their combat engineers operate heavy equipment, put up temporary buildings, build roads, and even carve runways out of the jungle. At the engineer school complex at Camp Lejeune, students learn carpentry, welding, metalworking, and the other field engineering skills, including demolition. This specialty is called *Engineer Construction Equipment and Shore Party.*

At the Army's Fort Belvoir in Virginia, other Marines are learning to be draftsmen. They will assist in the preliminary planning of construction projects, pre-paring scale drawings of roads, airfields, barracks, and other construction sites. The Army trains Marines here in *Drafting, Surveying and Mapmaking;* necessary skills for these future civil engineers.

Weapons must be kept in top working order, and that's the job of *Ordnance.* At the Army arsenal at Aberdeen, Maryland, Marines spend from five to fifteen weeks learning how to repair small arms, tracked vehicles, optical instruments, turrets, and artillery. They study hydraulics, shop mathematics, electrical systems, welding, and the heat treatment of metals. It's not quite the same as working in a machine shop, though. Among the jobs of ordnance is the defusing of unexploded bombs.

Ammunition and Explosive Ordnance Disposal goes steady-hand-in-steady-hand with ordnance to maintain combat firepower. At Redstone Arsenal in Alabama, Marines study ammunition storage, including the characteristics of projectiles, bombs, mines, and fuses. The techniques of disposing of high-explosive ammunition and nuclear weapons are taught in a fourteen-week course at the Army facility in Indianhead Gap, Maryland. It's tough, dangerous work but essential to the Corps's mission.

A squad in battle dress—camies, helmets, boots, and flak jackets—move it out. New arms enable Marines to get greater firepower from fewer men in a squad.

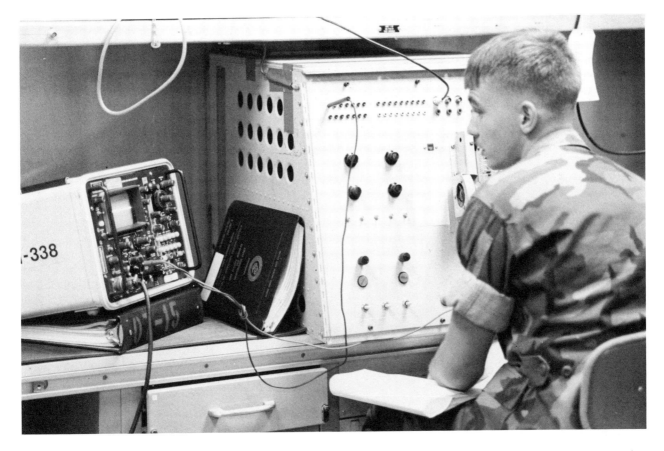

OPPOSITE PAGE, ABOVE: *Riflemen in gas masks prepare to advance in a training exercise. Knowing how to defend against chemical warfare techniques is an important skill of the modern warrior. OPPOSITE PAGE, BELOW: A sniper and his spotter in camouflage "gullie suits" at work during maneuvers. The spotter notes where shots are landing, suggests changes, and looks for new targets. THIS PAGE: Special equipment is used to teach a Marine how to spot problems in sophisticated electronic equipment. There are some 225 schools, with an enrollment which lasts from two to fifty weeks in length.*

To keep its troops on the move, the Marines have one of the largest fleets of field vehicles in the world. *Motor Transport* drives the vehicles and repairs them. Mechanics study the theory of the internal combustion engine, carburetion, and the electrical system before trying their skills in the field.

Combat Marines require a steady flow of supplies every step of the way. *Logistics* is there to see that ammunition and other essentials are where they're needed when they're needed. Logistics clerks study troop movements, supply and equipment planning, and embarkation procedures.

Computers are as important to the Corps as they are to the world of business. *Data Systems* technicians operate digital computers, run programs, and process business and scientific data. They are trained at Quantico in the principles of computer language, programming methods, and the processing of tape and punch cards.

Computers and other communications equipment sometimes malfunction, and there are Marines trained to get them working again. That's the task of *Data/Communications Maintenance*. The schools are long and highly technical, whether the equipment is a computer teletype machine, radio, or radar. Students study electronic theory, schematic wiring, Boolean algebra, and circuitry. They use special testing equipment, voltage meters, and circuit analyzers. Not only can the Marines operate all their sophisticated equipment, they can install, maintain, and repair it as well.

Nowhere in the Corps is there as high a concentration of technicians as in Marine Aviation. One big job is

Lewis Puller left Virginia Military Institute after his first year to join the Marines. It was 1918 and he wanted to get into the war. Still in training when the war ended, he was placed on the inactive list ten days after receiving his reserve commission. He rejoined the Corps a few days later as a private, and for the next thirty-six years he didn't miss any more wars.

Although Puller was only a Marine sergeant, he served as an officer in the Gendarmerie d'Haiti, a quasi-military force set up under a treaty with the United States. He returned after nearly five years in Haiti with a Navy Cross for valor and the nickname "Chesty"; he was commissioned a second lieutenant. He became an aviation cadet but was washed out as "not suitable aviator material" after botching his first two solo flights. Sent to Nicaragua to fight the Coco rebels, Puller earned his second Navy Cross. After Nicaragua, he was a "Horse Marine" in China.

"Chesty" Puller loved being in the field and would serve more than twenty years overseas during his long career, amassing more than fifty medals and decorations.

When World War II began he was a forty-four-year-old lieutenant colonel. He won his third Navy Cross in the defense of Henderson Field. On Cape Gloucester, he took over two other battalions after their commanders were wounded, moving through heavy fire to reorganize them, then led them in taking a strongly fortified enemy position. He was awarded a fourth Navy Cross.

When the Korean War broke out Puller was in a desk job in Hawaii. He pulled every string available and got command of his old outfit, the 1st Marines. The 1st Marines made the landing at Inchon and helped recapture Seoul, and then continued to advance northward. They were at the Chosin Reservoir in late November 1950 when the Chinese Communists struck. The Marines were surrounded by enemy forces in the rugged mountains and the bitter cold. When Puller learned his regiment was surrounded he said, "Those poor bastards. They've got us right where we want them. We can shoot in every direction now." Slowly, painfully, the Marines fought their way out of the trap. They inflicted awesome casualties on the Chinese as they slowly made their way back over sixty miles of icy, twisting mountainous road. "For superb courage commanding the division's rear guard," Chesty Puller became the only Marine ever to be awarded a fifth Navy Crosses.

Throughout his career, there was an unbreakable bond of mutual respect between Puller and his men. However, he did not always hold his superiors in the same high regard. If he had something to say, he said it and damn the rank or consequences. This probably contributed to the fact that he became a general only after thirty-three years in the Corps.

Serving under "Chesty" Puller was considered a high honor. His Marines knew they would be ready when they went into combat. He was tough, on himself as well as his Marines. In training or in battle, he led from the front. He never neglected the welfare of his men. He would fight the Marine establishment for them just as fiercely as he would fight the enemy.

Aircraft Maintenance, a specialty involving hydraulics, welding, the ins and outs of jet propulsion—all the things necessary to keep planes and helicopters in the air. Other Marines become specialists in *Air Control/Air Support, and Anti-Air Warfare.* They work with the pilots to ensure that aircraft hit targets accurately and intercept hostile aircraft. In school they study electronic countermeasures and the operation of tactical data system equipment.

Navigational controls, meteorological instruments, photographic equipment, and electrical simulators are cared for in *Electronics Maintenance,* by such specialists as Aviation Radar Repairers, Air Traffic Control Communications Repairers, and Tactical Data Communications Center Repairers. There are thirty-three schools in this specialty alone, at various Marine and Air Force bases.

Air Traffic Control requires nineteen weeks of study at a Navy school in Memphis, Tennessee, to learn to monitor the sky for air traffic and to issue takeoff, flight, and landing instructions to pilots. Controllers operate sophisticated radar equipment that computes the exact speed, altitude, and direction of aircraft. Among the subjects that controllers must master are aerology, en route traffic control, navigation, and radio. Similar training is given to Marines who will be part of flight crews as aerial navigators or airborne radio operators.

The Marines in *Aircraft Services* have the responsibility of dealing with airplane crashes. They study the theory of fires and fire fighting, and how to rescue crew members from burning aircraft. Aircraft operation specialists, also part of air services, prepare strip charts for pilots making cross-country flights.

Aviation Ordnance personnel are trained by the Navy in Memphis to maintain the complex weapon systems employed in Marine aircraft. They study shop practices, the principles of hydraulics, and the techniques of gunsight alignment. Ordnance specialists arm the planes before a mission.

Airborne radios, radar, navigational systems, and the like are referred to as *Avionics* and are maintained and repaired by Marines trained under the Navy at Memphis in schools ranging in length from eleven to twenty-nine weeks.

An important element of Marine Aviation is the *Weather Service;* its forecasts determine whether a squadron flies or stays on the ground. The Air Force trains Marines in aerography at Chanute Field in Illinois, covering subjects like aerological mathematics and physics, weather observations and analysis, and radar wind determination.

There is a need in the Corps for many skills that do not relate directly to combat. All Marines eat, for example, and there are schools for cooks and bakers. The responsibility of *Food Services* also includes menu planning for good nutrition and special dietary requirements. There even is a special school for the management of Marine clubs.

The clerks in *Supply Administration and Opera-tions* control inventories of millions of dollars' worth of Corps material, everything from peanut butter to tank treads and jet fuel. Other specialists handle the preparation of equipment for storage and shipment.

Like supplies, Marines, their families, and their personal and household goods are constantly on the move. The Army at Fort Eustis, Virginia, trains Marines to be specialists in *Transportation,* freight operation clerks or passenger transportation clerks, and to help thousands of Marines move across the country and overseas.

A small army of clerks in *Personnel and Administration* organize written and automated records on equipment, funds, personnel, supplies, and all the other aspects of the Corps. Both Camp Pendleton and Camp Lejeune have eight-week courses to train administrative, unit diary, and personnel clerks.

The Marine Corps is, among other things, a big business, and *Auditing, Finance and Accounting* takes care of paying salaries and allowances, keeping and auditing financial records, and estimating and administrating budgets. Camp Lejeune has schools for the various specialties and indoctrinates the students in the elements of accounting and auditing.

In the *Utilities* career field, Marines train to be hygiene equipment operators, plumbing and water supply specialists, refrigerator mechanics, and electricians at schools at Camp Lejeune. (Office machine repair specialists and, of all things, fabric repair specialists are trained by the Army at Fort Belvoir, Virginia.) They maintain large heating and cooling systems; install and repair furnaces, boilers, and refrigeration equipment.

Like any other community, a Marine base needs a police force, and one is provided by *Military Police and Corrections.* MPs keep order on the base and protect it from civil disorder. They take part in military investigations, work with crime laboratories, and administer court orders. In wartime, MPs administer prisoner-of-war operations. Military Police officers and correction specialists train with the Air Force at Lackland, Texas.

Where there are police, there are lawyers, and the Marine Corps is no exception. In *Legal Services,* enlisted personnel process legal claims, research court decisions, conduct interviews, and take statements. The Marines train their own legal specialists at Camp Pendleton.

The Marines even train Marines to train, or at least to supply training essentials. In *Training and Audiovisual Support* are still photographers, movie makers, graphic specialists, and audiovisual technicians, all trained by the Air Force at the Lowry Technical Training Center in Colorado. The Marines in *Printing and Reproduction* are also involved in the training process, printing brochures, posters, and pamphlets. Process camera operators and offset press operators learn their skills at Fort Belvoir.

Budding journalists are attracted to *Public Affairs.* Every base has its own newspaper, and reporters and photographers cover the varied activities of Marines on and off duty. Radio broadcasters also cover special events for both service and civilian stations. Public affairs specialists work with the media to help the Marine Corps's story reach the public. Print and broadcast journalists go on maneuvers and exercises with combat troops, and in wartime serve as combat correspondents. Journalists attend the Defense Information School, Fort Benjamin Harrison at Indianapolis.

Musicians have their own occupational specialty in the Corps—*Band*—and they are trained at the Navy base at Little Creek, Virginia. It takes forty weeks of training to become a member of the Drum and Bugle Corps, twenty-four weeks to complete the basic music course and, later, another twenty-three weeks to complete the intermediate music course. There's even a forty-week advanced course to train musicians to become assistant band leaders.

Finally, there are schools that aren't linked to a particular occupational specialty; the schools for re-

During amphibious exercises at Camp Pendleton, an LVT-P7 landing vehicle lumbers ashore. New equipment can land Marines in places thought inaccessible not too long ago.

cruiters and drill instructors are examples. This category is called *Special Field Training*. Marines selected for embassy guard duty attend a six-week school at Quantico; Marines who will join security units guarding nuclear weapons aboard Navy ships and installations are trained at Norfolk or Mare Island near San Francisco. Some Marines go to the Air Force base at Keesler, Mississippi, to learn the protocol of memorial services and chapel management.

Important schools for Marines as they progress through the ranks are the NCO Academy and the Staff NCO Academy, both six weeks of intense preparation for additional leadership responsibilities. At the staff academy, sergeants receive their unique NCO swords and learn to use them in drills and ceremonies.

For Marines unable to attend school for one reason or another, the Marine Corps Institute offers correspondence courses in most of the subjects. The Institute has helped many Marines and Marine reservists, over the years, qualify for promotion.

A school that affects every enlisted Marine is *Career Information and Counseling,* a four-week course at San Diego. For all sorts of reasons, some Marines find themselves to be round pegs in square holes, and every unit has a trained career counselor to help find the specialty for which they are best suited. A surprising number of Marines have switched specialties during their career. A major at Quantico explained the rationale behind this seemingly lenient policy:

"The Corps is small, and in a small outfit, the more things a Marine can do well, the better, whether officer or enlisted man. The other services can afford people who can do one thing and one thing only. We can't. One of the great things about the Corps is if you really want to do something—and doing it makes sense to the Corps—it usually can be worked out."

There is one caveat: new opportunities usually involve reenlistment. One of a career planner's primary goals is to make good Marines into career Marines.

A number of enlisted Marines have their heart set on a particular school: Officer Candidates School. It is not an unrealistic goal; the Marines have a tradition of officers rising from the ranks. They even have a word for it, "mustang." To be a real mustang, an officer must have served four years in the ranks or have been a sergeant.

The prevalence of mustangs at all levels in the Officer Corps is one reason why Marine officers themselves are a special breed. There are other reasons too, and all of them are part of the Marine Corps story.

★

CHAPTER 8

THE OFFICER CORPS

*T*he Marines do not subscribe to the theory that leaders are born, not made. Nor do they believe that leadership is something that can be taught in a classroom. In the Corps, leadership is an art, the influence and direction of people in a manner that inspires obedience, respect, confidence, and loyal cooperation. The Marines believe that leadership evolves in the crucible of necessity, formed from the basic elements of observation, experience, and emulation. It is made clear to every officer candidate that above and beyond all the firm, concrete things the Marine Corps can offer, the most valuable commodity is merely an opportunity: the chance to grasp, understand, and hold dear the meaning of leadership. From that base all else follows.

This concept of leadership has served the Marine Corps well through the years. Consider some of the

OPPOSITE PAGE: A decorated Marine officer gives a sword salute. Throughout the long history of the Marines, one of the keys to success in battle is a superbly trained officer corps.

remarkable officers who emerged in World War II: Alexander A. Vandegrift, whose 1st Marine Division at Guadalcanal gave the Allies the first decisive land victory over the Japanese; Holland M. "Howlin' Mad" Smith, considered the father of modern amphibious warfare, who masterminded the invasions of Saipan and Tinian; David M. Shoup, who as a colonel at Tarawa earned the Medal of Honor; Merritt A. "Red Mike" Edson of Marine Raider fame; Lewis B. "Chesty" Puller, who was to receive a record five Navy Crosses during his long and distinguished career.

Exceptional officers weren't confined to the senior ranks. A sergeant commissioned during the battle for Tulagi, William Deane "Hawk" Hawkins, was posthumously awarded the Medal of Honor for heroism at Tarawa. The assault commander later said, "It's not often that you can credit a lieutenant with winning a battle, but Hawkins came as near to it as any man could."

Since the Medal of Honor was first authorized during the Civil War, it has been awarded to 71 Marine officers, twice to Smedley D. Butler, a quintessential Marine leader if there ever was one. This is not to

Smedley Butler was the son of a Quaker congressman from West Chester, Pennsylvania, who lied about his age to enlist in the Marine Corps at the outbreak of the Spanish-American War. After only six weeks of training, he was commissioned a second lieutenant, but by the time he reached Cuba, the war was almost over.

In 1900 he joined a Marine force being sent to China to protect the U.S. legation in Peking. The Boxers were attacking foreigners whose governments controlled much of China's economy. Butler's unit saw plenty of action. After one engagement, he, another lieutenant, and four enlisted men carried a wounded man seventeen miles, most of the distance under enemy fire.

Butler next saw action in Honduras in 1902. American interests were threatened by a revolution and the Marines were sent in. "It wasn't exactly clear to me what all the fighting was about," he later recalled. He developed an amused disdain for Central American politics and politicians. He also developed a growing reputation as a tough fighter with a flair for inspiring small detachments to attack with élan.

Butler served three times in Nicaragua between 1909 and 1914. In 1914, now a major, he was sent to Mexico with a Marine force to protect U.S. interests. He went in civilian clothes to Mexico City to spy on the city's defenses in case the Marines should have to evacuate U.S. citizens. Fighting erupted when it was learned that a shipment of arms was on the way to Mexico from Germany. Butler commanded a battalion at Veracruz, and earned his first Medal of Honor, directing Marine fire at snipers by pointing them out with his swagger stick.

Sent to Haiti in 1915, Butler was put in charge of organizing a constabulary. A band of Haitian rebels made a last stand at a mountaintop fort. Butler, leading a twenty-four-man party, found a drainage ditch leading to the fort's main courtyard. Under fire, Butler and three Marines managed to get inside the fort and kill the rebel leaders. The disorganized natives surrendered. Butler was awarded a second Medal of Honor.

Butler's rough manner had made him enemies in the higher echelons of the Corps. They considered him a brilliant fighter but unreliable. As a consequence, he didn't get to France until September 1918 and was placed in command of a debarkation depot.

Butler commanded a force sent to Shanghai in 1927 to protect Americans during the Chinese civil war. He was there until Chiang Kai-shek emerged as the new ruler of China in 1929. He was promoted to major general at the age of forty-eight. Tired of service politics, he retired, dying in 1940.

---

suggest that the quality of an officer corps can be measured solely by its medals, but bravery is a critical dimension, for bravery is contagious; weak officers, no matter what their professional skills may be, can't inspire their men to be brave.

During World War II, America had a love affair with its heroes; they were household names. Where are the heroes of the Korean War and Vietnam? people ask. Medals of Honor were awarded to 42 Marines in the Korean War, 57 in Vietnam, including 12 officers. Who besides relatives, friends, and fellow Marines can name one of them? In an age of nasty little wars, heroes are out of fashion.

To maintain its Officer Corps of 20,000, the Marines recruit and train some 1,800 officer candidates each year from several sources. A major source of regular officers is the Naval Reserve Officers Training Corps (NROTC) Marine Option. Candidates for this program must score high on a stiff competitive intelligence test, pass the physical examination for Marine

Two ground crewmen, TOP, ready an F-18 Hornet. The twin jets of the Hornet can drive the plane at supersonic speeds. Another crewman, ABOVE, does maintenance work on a CH-53 Sea Stallion. RIGHT, a UH-1M Huey kicks up dust from the desert as it comes in for a landing during a combined arms exercise. OVERLEAF, Marines rappel from a helicopter on an SPIE (Special Personnel Insertion/Extraction) rig. This technique is used when a small Marine unit needs to get in and out of a combat area fast.

★

A flight of AV-8B Harriers, LEFT, come in low over the water to support attacking Marine ground troops. An F-18 Hornet, TOP, is serviced before a flight. Two Marine pilots, RIGHT, share a smile after a successful mission. Marine Aviation is dedicated to giving ground troops close air support in combat, a hallmark of the Corps.

On the opening page of this section, pilots scramble to their AV-8B Harriers. A Marine A-6 Intruder and an RF-4D Phantom, FAR LEFT and FAR RIGHT ABOVE, join Navy and Egyptian planes in a flight over the pyramids. A young Harrier pilot, RIGHT, relaxes before a training mission.

officers, and gain admission to one of the sixty-six colleges and universities that have an NROTC unit. While attending college, the candidate receives tuition, textbooks, fees, and an allowance of $100 per month. NROTC training goes on throughout the school year. After the freshman year, there is a six-week training cruise aboard a Navy ship or indoctrination at a major shore installation. Sophomores get four weeks of warfare specialties training. Juniors attend a pre-commissioning training period at the Officer Candidate School (OCS) at Quantico; men for six weeks, women ten. Other students who have completed their sophomore year can join what is called the College Program. They receive the $100 a month allowance but not the tuition benefits, and attend OCS.

There are other ways a college student can work toward a Marine Corps commission. The Platoon Leaders Class, the single largest source of Marine officers, is popular on campuses that do not have an NROTC unit. Training consists of two summer six-week sessions at Quantico, or one ten-week session for those who join the program in their junior year. By agreeing to an additional active duty obligation, Platoon Leaders Class candidates receive the $100-per-month allowance during the school year, provided they maintain an overall "C" average.

The Platoon Leaders Class has two interesting options. PLC-Aviation gives members the opportunity to graduate with a commission and actual flying experience. After completing all the pre-commissioning training, students receive FAA-approved flight instruction at the Corps's expense. In PLC-Law, active duty is postponed until the student has finished law school and been admitted to the bar.

College seniors and graduates can apply for Officer Candidate Class even if they did not participate in any of the programs while in college. Aviation and Law are also open to them.

Midshipmen at the Naval Academy can elect to be part of the quota of the graduating class each year that receive commissions in the Marine Corps. Of each graduating class at the Academy, only 16⅔ percent, about 170, can elect service in the Marine Corps. For some years now, there has been a waiting list for Marine duty. And although it happens less frequently, graduates of West Point also can opt for service in the Marines. They initially lack a background in naval service and traditions, but they bring a compensatory sound training in military tactics and skills.

A Woman Officer Candidate Program is open to college juniors, seniors, and graduates. At Quantico, women candidates participate in much the same rigorous screening programs as do their male counterparts. They may train after their junior year or after graduation. Those who train after their junior year are eligible for financial assistance as seniors. Like their enlisted counterparts, women officers may go into any of the Marine occupational fields that do not put them into a combat situation. The exceptions are pilot, infantry, artillery, combat engineer, and armor.

The Marine Corps always has encouraged qualified enlisted men to become officers. There is a long tradition of "mustangs," officers who have served at least four years in the ranks or made sergeant before becoming commissioned. Each year 170 appointments to the Naval Academy are made by the Secretary of the Navy, 85 from the regular Marine Corps and the Navy, 85 from the Marine and Navy Reserves. An enlisted man, or woman, is appointed to Annapolis based on his score on an examination. And if the appointee's secondary school background is shaky, he will be sent to the Naval Academy Preparatory School at Newport, Rhode Island, for an academic year.

Enlisted Marines are eligible for a program that will send them to a four-year civilian college and result in a regular commission. It is the Marine Commissioning Education Program (MECEP), and can involve either technical or liberal arts studies. A Marine continues on active duty and is paid accordingly, using his accumulated Veterans Administration benefits and various grants to pay for tuition.

In the Enlisted Commissioning Program (ECP), a Marine finishes college in his free time at an institution near where he is stationed, the Corps paying the tuition, and is sent to OCS on graduation.

Another route from the ranks to the Officer Corps is the Warrant Officer Program. It is designed to provide officers who are true specialists in one military occupation. The applicants usually have served at least ten years and are staff sergeants. When a Marine in this program is appointed, he is a warrant officer but, curiously, not a commissioned officer, although he wears an officer's uniform. A commission will come after two years of satisfactory service when he moves up to the second of four warrant officer grades. If there is an opening in his specialty, a Chief Warrant Officer can become a limited duty officer and progress to the rank of lieutenant colonel; unlike regular officers, a limited duty officer will be assigned duty only in his specialty.

"I may be prejudiced, but I think warrant officer is the best rank in the Marine Corps," says a Chief Warrant Officer in the New York City Marine public affairs office. "Other officers respect you because you are a specialist, and enlisted men respect you because you've come up the hard way. They know you've done your share of cleaning heads, too."

There are many routes to an officer's bars but they all lead to Quantico. This big Virginia base is called the "Crossroads of the Marine Corps" because of the concentration of schools there. Sometime in his career, practically every Marine has trained for something or other at Quantico. With the exception of the graduates of the service academies and warrant officers, the first stop for the would-be officer is OCS. The Officer Candidate School's mission is to evaluate and screen candidates and make sure they meet the standards required of a Marine officer. Some 3,200 candidates enter OCS each year, but not all make the grade. As in boot camp, about one-quarter of each class is eliminated. The most common reasons are physical deficiencies identified during the initial examination and debilitating injuries incurred during training. Some candidates don't measure up to the standards for academics, or leadership, and are brought before an evaluation board. Finally, the OCS commanding officer will determine if the candidate stays or goes.

In simplest terms, OCS is a total immersion course in being a Marine. Outwardly, OCS resembles boot camp: the drills and exercises are the same, and omnipresent D.I.s keep a relentless pressure on the candidates throughout the program. Sixteen hours of hard work are crammed into each training day; there is no free time. A typical day mixes physical training, academic classes, field training, drill, policing the barracks, and caring for equipment. In the Officer Candidate School, all the bases are covered.

What makes OCS different from boot camp is the strong emphasis on being a leader. In the field, the candidates practice practical applications of leadership. This is augmented by leadership discussions led by OCS instructors.

The academic instruction includes the history and traditions of the Corps, customs and courtesies, land navigation, and a number of general military subjects. Most subjects are confined to the basic level; the exception is tactics. The Corps insists that every new officer acquire a sound foundation of individual combat skills and squad tactics. Without being knowledgeable in these fundamental areas, an officer cannot effectively lead Marines. Instruction includes offensive and defensive tactics, combat formations, fire team and squad level tactics.

The candidate's progress is constantly monitored. There are written tests on academic subjects, and instructors evaluate field work. The leadership evaluation comprises 50 percent of the candidate's final grade. The training schedule calls for a minimum of one full day of field work a week and four overnight bivouacs during the course.

The part of OCS that officers usually remember most vividly is physical conditioning. At least four days a week there are grueling two-hour sessions divided into four parts. First is a twenty-minute warm-up, designed to keep muscular injuries to a minimum. The main event of the session is made up of a combination of events: the obstacle course, the Fartlek course, distance running, and the run circuit.

The obstacle course stresses upper-body development and builds self-confidence. It's a graded event, and as training progresses, the candidate must negotiate it in shorter and shorter times. On the Fartlek course, the candidate runs a 3.5-mile course over undulating terrain, stopping at exercise stations along the way. There are both individual and platoon distance runs, starting at a mile and a half and working up to 6.2 miles. After completing the Fartlek course or a distance run, the candidate will hit the run circuit. There are eight exercise stations along a one-mile run on flat terrain: leg lifts, dips, sit-ups, wind sprints, and other forms of torture.

The third phase is twenty minutes of upper-body development (UBD). There are seven exercises, including tricep dips, rope heaves, and pull-ups. Finally, a short session of exercise shakes out any kinks or stiffness. The purpose of physical training in OCS is to develop within the candidate the stamina and endurance to sustain him in combat. It also gives the staff an opportunity to evaluate the candidate's performance under physically stressful conditions.

The Marines point out that classroom work and test

The braid on top of a Marine officer's hat is called quatre foil *and dates from the Revolution when it identified officers to snipers in the ship's rigging.*

performance cannot give a true indication of leadership potential. That is why the leadership program at OCS is designed to place the maximum physical and mental stress on a candidate through the simulation of combat situations. Nine practical application problems test the unit leader's ability to rapidly make a decision based on limited information, formulate a plan, issue the plan to his men, and lead them in the accomplishment of the mission. The most demanding of these is Small Unit Leadership Evaluation II (SULE II). Candidates are in almost constant motion under controlled stress for forty-eight hours.

SULE II begins with reveille at midnight. Within thirty minutes, the candidates are off on a fifteen-mile march. At first light, the candidates form into squad units and begin a series of navigation and tactical exercises, interspersed with reaction course problems. The squads move at a forced-march pace against set time limits between the tactical problem area and the reaction course.

The reaction course is a training method picked up from Hitler's Germany where it was used to train Waffen SS troops. Physically, the confidence course consists of eight three-sided compartments, each containing a combat problem and the material with which to solve it. The team is briefed on the problem by the instructor, and a team leader is appointed. At the instructor's command, the team has eight minutes to solve the problem.

Here is a typical situation: "These pilings represent the remains of a bridge which has been blown up by the enemy nuclear artillery. Portions of the pilings and the stream have been contaminated and cannot be touched. You are part of a squad operating in enemy territory. One of your party has been critically wounded in the back. You know that in an abandoned ambulance on the other side of the stream there is a stretcher which you will need to transport your wounded across the stream. Your task is to cross the stream, return with the stretcher, and transport your wounded across the stream.

"You have brought these six planks from the basement of a nearby house. Use what you need and be careful not to touch either the contaminated pilings or the stream with any piece of equipment or any part of your body."

During the problem-solving, evaluators are checking the performance of every member of the team. Does the leader quickly come up with the right solution? Is he able to properly communicate it to the other members? If he's wrong, do the others offer suggestions? And do they do it in a way that doesn't upset team discipline? How does the leader take advice? The confidence course is as revealing of character as a psychiatrist's couch.

The squads do all eight confidence course problems, alternating leaders as they go. All candidates have been through the course before, but in training, problems rarely were solved in the allotted time. It is the rare candidate who knows how to solve more than a few of the problems by the time SULE II rolls around.

By the end of SULE II, the candidates will have marched about sixty miles. Throughout the forty-eight hours, their endurance, motivation, and leadership have been tested to the fullest. An OCS instructor commented, "The young men and women who graduate from Officer Candidate School must prize their commission above all else. We see to it that they earn every ounce of their gold bars."

Graduation from OCS is an impressive and festive occasion, as the bars of a second lieutenant are pinned on the graduate's Dress Blues and he accepts the certificate of commission that begins "Know ye, that reposing special trust and confidence . . ."

At the graduation ceremony, the new officers will be wearing their Dress Blues for the first time. An officer must buy his own uniforms from either the PX or civilian suppliers; the initial outlay can range from $2,000 to $3,000 and more, depending on the level of quality he selects.

The candidate has proven he has the stuff to be a Marine officer, but he has a long way to go before he will get a taste of command. After a brief leave, he reports back to Quantico to attend The Basic School (TBS). Every Marine officer, regardless of sex, the

circumstances of his commission, or potential assignment in the Corps, goes through The Basic School, and has done so since it was first established in 1891. Why are Marine officers different? The answer begins at The Basic School.

No other branch of the armed forces has formal training for officers equivalent to TBS. TBS has three objectives: first, it provides a foundation of professional education; second, it teaches a basic knowledge of ground combat operations; finally, it gives each new lieutenant a real appreciation of the physical demands of leaders in combat.

TBS lasts twenty-three weeks and consists of more than 1,300 hours of instruction. To put this into perspective, the average college student, if he attends every class over the four years, will accumulate 1,440 academic hours. And the 1,300 hours at TBS does not include time to study or complete homework assignments, drill, do physical training, or accomplish a host of other tasks.

The home of The Basic School is Camp Barrett, a self-contained and self-sufficient part of the naval base at Quantico. It was located here in 1958 and has evolved from a collection of tents and temporary buildings into a modern facility. There are quarters for 1,250 officer students and 385 support personnel, modern multimedia classrooms, an auditorium, a gym with an indoor swimming pool, a PX and uniform shop, even its own medical and dental clinic. Camp Barrett also has the largest and most diversified small-arms armory in the Corps.

At Camp Barrett, a training company has a strength of 200 to 250 officer students, organized into five platoons. Each platoon is headed by a staff platoon commander, a captain or a senior first lieutenant. Each company is commanded by a major. The company staff make a lasting impression on the officer students, all chosen carefully and thoroughly screened. The first step in teaching an officer student to be a leader is to set a good example, and the staff officers represent the qualities the Corps prizes most highly. They are assisted by enlisted D.I.s who, if anything, push their charges a little harder than do their boot camp counterparts simply because they are officers.

Of the officers attending TBS each year, between fifty and eighty are women. They undergo the same discipline and course of instruction as do male officers, with minor modifications. Some twenty foreign military officers also attend each year. Recent countries

Newly commissioned second lieutenants chat after the ceremony at Quantico, Virginia. The road to a gold bar is the same for men and women candidates: OCS and The Basic School.

represented have included South Korea, Colombia, El Salvador, Ecuador, Senegal, Gabon, Tunisia, Morocco, Saudi Arabia, and Thailand. Marine training and standards of excellence have helped shape the military in many countries.

The professional education of officers at TBS is divided into three categories of instruction and evaluation: leadership, academics, and military skills. The final standing of an officer is based on a compilation of his performance in these areas. And this will affect both his assignment after graduation and his future promotions. This gives TBS an intensely competitive atmosphere.

How exactly is the art of leadership taught? One way is by something called the student billet holder concept. Throughout the course, each officer is given the chance to fill positions of leadership, ranging from company commander to fire team leader, both in garrison and in the field. When a student officer completes

a leadership assignment, his performance is evaluated by his platoon and company commanders and he is counseled about what he did wrong.

Leadership is also taught in the classroom at TBS. In fact, leadership and tactics and command are the two main areas of instruction. Tactics instruction culminates in a three-day exercise, reminiscent of SULE II, that is carefully structured to pull together all the aspects of the previous instruction and test the student officer's grasp of the principles and demands of ground combat leadership.

The other half of the academic instruction, command and leadership, involves problem-solving exercises. A scenario is presented to the student officers. They must identify and prioritize problems, and describe possible solutions. The academic portion of the lieutenant's final grade is based on his grades on a series of thirteen written examinations.

One-third of the final overall grade is based on mili-

Officers and enlisted Marines alike must keep their marksmanship up to demanding standards. A colonel checks his weapon at the Quantico, Virginia, range.

tary skills: marksmanship, land navigation, and physical fitness. By the time a lieutenant graduates from The Basic School, he will have fired 700 rounds of 5.56 ammunition from the M16A2, 250 rounds of 9mm pistol ammunition, 600 rounds of machine-gun ammunition from both the M-249 Squad Automatic Weapon (SAW) and the M-60E3, two Light Anti-Armor Rockets (LAAW), and ten rounds of 40mm from both the M203 rifle-mounted grenade launcher and the MK19 heavy machine gun.

Each officer also has fired nearly 2,000 rounds of blank ammunition, utilizing the Multiple Integrated Laser, or MILES System. As a round is fired, a short, low-intensity laser beam is emitted. If the officer student has aimed accurately, the beam will set off a loud buzzer on the "enemy," signaling that he has been killed or wounded and is out of the simulated combat exercise.

During the year's series of exercises at TBS, more than 7,000 rounds of artillery ammunition, 175 rounds of tank main-gun ammunition, 12,000 rounds of mortar ammunition, 18 wire-guided antitank missiles, and several hundred tons of air-delivered ordnance are expended in support of training.

During the year at TBS, there are eight BASCO-LEX (amphibious training exercises at the nearby facility at Little Creek, Virginia); eight "three-day war" field exercises; four live-fire, combined arms demonstration exercises; 144 squad live-fire exercises; and countless other field exercises.

An officer must also be a gentleman, and the social graces are not neglected. To expose the lieutenants to the social traditions of the Corps, TBS in a typical year will host nine company mess nights and nine commanding general's receptions. There also are social events connected with the numerous orientation visits by various organizations. One of the visits is by 1,200 Naval Academy midshipmen during the "Marine Week" of their second-class-year summer cruise.

Attention to the social side of an officer's life doesn't detract from the real purpose of TBS. One company commander summed it up this way: "Let me tell you what TBS is all about: We prepare new officers to lead our most precious asset—the enlisted Marine. And as long as we do that, we firmly believe that the continued success of the Corps depends, in large part, on the continued success of TBS."

Upon graduation from The Basic School, the lieutenants proceed to what are termed "follow-on schools" to attain the skills peculiar to their military occupation specialty. These schools vary in length from six weeks to sixteen months. Officers are assigned military occupational specialties based on performance, the needs of the Corps, and their own desires, and about 90 percent get one of the three specialties they have chosen. Prospective aviators go to flight training at Pensacola, Florida; artillery officers to the Army Field Artillery School at Fort Sill, Oklahoma; tracked vehicle officers to armor school at Fort Knox, Kentucky. Lieutenants assigned to the infantry, however, stay at Camp Barrett to attend the Infantry Officer Course.

In addition to these primary specialty areas, a new

lieutenant may be sent to a follow-on school in communications, data systems, engineering, legal, air control, or supply. In the special support area, the schools include military police, motor transport, public affairs, intelligence, personnel and administration, logistics, signal intelligence/ground electronics warfare, and auditing/finance/accounting.

Officers are trained at the Infantry Officer Course to command a platoon: rifle, weapons, mortar, antiarmor, heavy machine gun, or reconnaissance. The course includes seven hundred training hours, of which only eighty are in the classroom. The stress is on practical application. Tactical proficiency is gained by participating in extensive field exercises. This is backed up by war-gaming and sand-table exercises. Weapons instruction focuses on developing proficiency in the operation of automatic and crew-served weapons, as well as a mastery of fire direction and forward observation procedures. The finale of the nine-week course is an exercise in which the students must locate and destroy a mobile radar installation, reaching the objective in small rubber boats.

All officers have a specialty, but they don't spend all their time in the Corps performing it. One of the functions of Headquarters Marine Corps is to make sure that career officers get a variety of assignments. This allows officers to develop to their full potential, and to qualify themselves for command responsibility. The relatively small size of the Corps is conducive to this diversity of officer assignment. Chances are that a Marine officer will have done more things and assumed more responsibility than an officer of comparable rank in any of the other services.

There are a great number of possible assignments, but every Marine career officer, either ground or aviation, can reasonably expect to participate in five basic types of duty: student, instructor of other Marines, the command of tactical units, staff assignments with major Marine units or with other services, and such special assignments as sea duty, naval attaché, or recruiting.

Every Marine officer follows a career pattern keyed to his particular occupational field, undertaking a progression of new responsibilities that provide the rounded experience required by the Corps.

During his first five or six years, a typical officer will complete an entry-level military occupational school and complete a tour of duty. This may be with the Fleet Marine Force, which consists of the three Marine divisions and three aircraft wings, or such non-FMF duty as assignment to a major headquarters.

If his performance level is high, he will have acquired a regular commission, been promoted to first lieutenant, and selected for captain. Being selected for the next higher rank means an officer has met all the necessary qualifications, been recommended, and placed on the waiting list. (A Marine Corps riddle: What's the difference between A private first class and a second lieutenant? Answer: A private first class has been promoted once.)

By the end of ten to twelve years, a highly qualified officer can expect to be a major. He's probably been back to school for more professional training, and as a captain, he commanded a company. As a major, he is executive officer of a battalion or squadron. If all has gone well, the Corps is grooming him for bigger things.

An officer will complete several tours of duty in his second decade in the Corps. He might be a staff officer at Marine Headquarters or an inspector-instructor in a Reserves unit. He may command a company or a squadron. He can look forward to being selected to attend a top-level service school, a significant step to further advancement.

It's a hard climb up the promotional ladder in the officer corps. At every rung the requirements are stiffer, the competition more intense, the vacancies fewer. The size of the Corps limits upper-level officer promotions.

Nor are career advancement problems confined to the upper ranks. In the officer corps, as in civilian life, there are predictable crises. The first comes early. Every OCS graduate receives what is, in effect, a temporary commission and has a fixed time to serve in the Corps, usually four years. If he wants to make the Marines a career, he must apply for a regular commission. This process is called augmentation and usually takes place when he is a captain. An officer rarely is permitted to stay in the Corps after his term of duty is up if he hasn't been augmented.

Other crises involve three advanced service schools. If a captain wants to command a battalion, he should attend the year-long Amphibious Warfare School at Quantico. But a lot more captains apply than there are places in a class; being accepted is the Marine equivalent to a college graduate being accepted in a top business school. If a captain doesn't make Amphibious Warfare School, he can complete the course of study by correspondence through the Marine Corps Institute.

Majors who want regimental staff assignments need to attend the Command and Staff College, also at Quantico. Lieutenant colonels and colonels know that the Naval War College at Newport, Rhode Island, is an important step toward a general's stars. The level of competition for these schools is brutal.

Even for less ambitious officers there are career crises. If a lieutenant or captain is passed over for promotion twice, he is out of the Corps; and with his gold bars come a wealth of opportunities to foul up, and enough foul-ups will cost him his commission. His commanding officer files detailed fitness reports on him each year, and these become part of his permanent service record. He must keep his weight within a prescribed limit and pass regular fitness tests and medical examinations. A messy divorce can hurt his chances for promotion; a drunk-driving conviction can destroy them.

Sins of omission can be as bad as those of commission. "Sometimes when a man makes major," a 2nd Division staff colonel said, "you can hear his pack hit the ground—thunk!—and he's stopped trying. He may have been a hard-charger once, now he's only going through the motions. The sad part of it is that he may not even be aware of what's happening to him, that he's on his way out."

For the exceptional officers, the Corps spreads a rich educational feast. At the first level, beyond the schools already mentioned, qualified officers may attend: Communications Officer School, Quantico; The Engineer School, Fort Belvoir, Virginia; the Signal School, Fort Monmouth, New Jersey; Judge Advocate School, Charlottesville, Virginia; Military Police School, Fort McClellan, Alabama; Transportation Officers School, Fort Eustis, Virginia; Post Graduate Intelligence Course, Washington, D.C.; and the Test Pilot School, Patuxent River, Maryland.

At the next level, field-grade officers are presented with these possibilities: U.S. Army Command and General Staff College, Fort Leavenworth, Kansas; Air Command Staff College, Maxwell Field, Alabama; Armed Forces Staff College, Norfolk, Virginia; Canadian Forces Staff College, Toronto; Spanish Naval War College, Madrid; and the Staff and Command College of the Federal German Armed Forces, Hamburg.

These are only some of the possibilities. Under the Marine Graduate Education Program, for instance, a field-grade officer (major or above) may have the opportunity to pursue an advanced degree at a civilian college. This program is designed to give professional expertise in such fields as aeronautical engineering, statistics, communications, engineering, computer sciences, and defense system analysis. Officers have attended the School of Journalism at Columbia University in New York City and the Harvard Business School. The Marine Corps Institute and the Extension School offer a dazzling array of correspondence courses to broaden the professional background of an officer throughout his career.

At the top of the officer corps pyramid are colonels being groomed for important commands. They may be sent to the National War College, Washington, D.C.; Army War College, Carlisle Barracks, Pennsylvania; Air War College, Maxwell Field, Alabama; Armed Forces Industrial College, Washington; British Imperial Defense College, London; NATO Defense College, Rome, Italy; Norwegian National Defense College, Oslo; Australian Joint Service Staff College, Canberra; and the National College of Canada, Kingston, Ontario.

Some senior officers see this wealth of educational opportunity as a mixed blessing. In the Corps, after all, advanced education is not an end unto itself; its sole purpose is to make good officers better.

"Many junior officers are yuppies, as strange as that may sound," a staff officer of the 1st Division said. "They approach the Corps as they would IBM— they're either going to the top and get some stars, or they're going to grab all the educational goodies they can and cut and run. And damn it, we're not in the business of training civilian executives here; we're training officers to lead Marines in battle. Period.

"Perhaps I'm too Old Corps. Maybe Vietnam is too much with me. I don't know. There's nothing really wrong about a captain driving a BMW, or jogging in a designer running suit with a Walkman on his head, or never wearing his uniform off the base, or drinking wine coolers or whatever—*if* he performs in the field. But that's one damn big if."

What does the Corps expect of its officers in an age

of changing values? Just what it always expected: leadership, leadership in combat, leadership in every aspect and phase of their professional life. In a booklet prepared by the Corps for prospective officer candidates, *As an Officer of Marines,* the very first page quotes General Lejune, who talks to the heart of the matter:

The relation between officers and men should in no sense be that of superior and inferior nor that of master and servant, but rather that of teacher and scholar. In fact, it should partake of the nature of the relationship between father and son to the extent that officers . . . are responsible for the physical, mental and moral welfare as well as the discipline and military training of the young men under their command.

A range officer draws a bead on a target with the Corps's new Browning automatic pistol, which replaces the old Colt .45. Smaller caliber conforms to NATO standards.

CHAPTER 9

SUPPORT FROM THE AIR

The Marines have sufficient planes and helicopters to be ranked as the eighth largest air force in the world. But the Corps feels the statistic has no meaning, for it compares apples with oranges. In fact, the Corps insists it doesn't have an air force at all, in name or in function. This isn't mere semantics or a quirky tradition. It has to do with the mission of the Corps and the role aviation plays in it.

To Marines, an air force is huge bombers speeding to faraway targets protected by fighter planes. The job of Marine Aviation is quite different: to make the Marine ground troops more effective in combat. Helicopters fly Marines into battle. Planes destroy enemy emplacements, strafe troops, spot for artillery, and protect the Marines from enemy aircraft.

"In the Navy or Air Force, the hot shot is the fighter pilot," explained a pilot at the Cherry Point, North Carolina, Marine Air Station. "Our hot shot is the grunt, the Marine with the rifle trying to get up that hill. Our only purpose—the only reason the Marines have planes at all—is to help him.

"All Marine squadrons have an infantry or artillery officer as liaison, and pilots do tours of duty attached to ground units. We work with the ground officers who call in and direct air support. We each know the other guy's problems and how he works under fire. It pays off.

"It's crazy," he continued. "No other outfit works air-ground the way Marines do. They try, sure, but it's always two different things, the fly boys and the grunts, and when things get hot, they both look out for their own. And that's when air-ground falls apart."

This Marine unity was underlined by the captain's uniform. Only the wings above his campaign ribbons identified him as an aviator, and below the ribbons were the badges that showed he had demonstrated basic combat skills by firing Expert with the rifle and pistol. Squadrons do have distinctive patches, but they are only worn on flight suits.

The Marines look askance on anything that sets one

OPPOSITE PAGE: A pilot poses in front of his Harrier, a plane that can land and take off like a helicopter, then perform like a fighter. Perfect for use on small forward bases.

Marine apart from another. There is no equivalent to "Off we go into the wild blue yonder . . ."; the "Marines' Hymn" is for all Marines, pilots and mechanics included.

No aviator has ever been commandant, but in recent years the Marines have had an assistant commandant, also a four-star general, and usually he has been an aviator.

The low profile of Marine Aviation has not kept colorful characters away. In World War II, Colonel Gregory "Pappy" Boyington shot down twenty-eight Japanese planes while setting an equally memorable record for flamboyant behavior. Colonel John Glenn, the first astronaut to orbit the earth, was called "Magnet Ass" when he flew fighters in Korea because of his apparently uncanny ability to attract antiaircraft fire. The legendary Red Sox slugger Ted Williams was a decorated fighter pilot in World War II and Korea. Their successors, colorful but not yet famous, fly for the Marines today.

Marines learn their aviation skills from the Navy, and are trained to operate off carriers. Every Marine fighter and attack squadron performs tours of duty aboard carriers. The techniques of close air ground support are learned and honed to perfection in countless exercises and maneuvers with Marine ground troops. Each of the three Marine divisions has an air wing counterpart, and the wings are only minutes away from the division bases.

The Marines now are equipped with state-of-the-art planes and helicopters, sophisticated electronic gear, and missile systems. The Marines, for example, are the only U.S. service to use the AV-8B Harrier. This remarkable plane, which caught the fancy of the world during the Falklands War, is an attack plane that can stop dead in the air, hover, and land and take off vertically, just as a helicopter can. It is ideal for the Marines because it can operate out of a postage-stamp-sized forward area, getting to where it is needed faster and staying there longer.

To see Marine Aviation today, to sense its interior logic and feisty combat readiness, makes it difficult to comprehend the vexing problems it encountered over the years. Like the Corps itself, Marine Aviation spent years of making do with skimpy appropriations and hand-me-down equipment, operating unwillingly under the command of the Air Force, and weathering repeated attempts to either do away with it or fold it into another branch of the services.

Like so many worthy enterprises, Marine Aviation began with a salesman, a demonstration, a free offer, and the irresistible attraction of something new.

Marine airmen form up to spell the Corps's initials in Haiti in 1919. The plane in the background is a Curtiss-Burgess N-9 seaplane powered by a 150-horsepower engine.

The salesman was Glen Curtiss, and his product was his new biplane. He demonstrated it at Norfolk, Virginia, on November 10, 1910. He offered to train a pilot at no cost, and the Navy accepted, later purchasing three of his planes. An aviation training camp was set up at Annapolis near the Naval Academy.

The Marines thought aviation might fit into a new concept they were developing for operating out of advanced bases, and sent Lieutenant Alfred A. Cunningham off for pilot training. He arrived on May 22, 1912, now celebrated as the birthday of Marine Aviation, and became Marine Aviator Number 1.

In the 1913 fleet exercises, senior officers were given airplane rides. One of them was Colonel John Lejeune, who would rise to commandant and become a strong advocate of aviation. The next year Europe went to war and Congress voted a million dollars to fund a Naval Aeronautic Service. A training base was set up at Pensacola, Florida, and Marines were allowed to attend. At the 1914 fleet exercises, two Marine pilots flew in support of Marines on maneuvers in Puerto Rico, the first Marine air-ground operation.

The Navy acquired a new seaplane in 1916. While testing it, Marine Lieutenant "Cocky" Evans was attempting a loop when the plane went into a spin; a spin at that time meant a crash. Evans instinctively pushed the wheel forward to pick up speed, applying rudder to stop the plane from turning. The plane came out of the spin, and Evans's new technique was made part of pilot training. Years later, he was awarded the Distinguished Flying Cross for his contribution to air safety.

America began a rapid buildup of its armed forces in response to Germany's unrestricted submarine warfare. The Marine Corps Aviation Company was created with two missions: to fly seaplanes to hunt and attack submarines, and to fly land planes for reconnaissance and artillery spotting. Captain Cunningham arranged with the Army to train Marines in land planes.

When America entered the war, Cunningham went to France. He visited French and British air bases flying several combat missions, which made him the first Marine to see combat in World War I. But the American Army, seething at being forced to accept a Marine infantry brigade, told him that if a Marine squadron got to France, it would never see action.

The British offered a way out. The undermanned RAF was looking for a way to bomb German subma-

The first Marine to become a naval aviator was Alfred A. Cunningham. In World War I he led the 1st Marine Aviation Force, credited with downing twelve German planes.

rine bases. Cunningham proposed using Marine and Navy pilots in British planes. A Northern Bombing Group was formed. The British supplied planes again when the three squadrons of the 1st Marine Aviation Force arrived in July 1918, and soon they were in action over the Western Front.

Lieutenant E. S. Brewer and his gunner, Sergeant H. B. Wersheiner, on September 28 became the first Marines to shoot down an enemy plane. Both were wounded but managed to land safely. A week later three Marine planes delivered 2,600 pounds of food and ammunition to a surrounded French regiment.

In mid-October five Marine planes returning from bombing a railroad yard were attacked by a squadron of Fokker D-VIIs. Lieutenant Ralph Talbot and his gunner, Corporal Robert Robinson, shot one down, but both were severely injured by machine-gun fire. Fokkers swarmed around the plane; Robinson was hit again and collapsed. Talbot swung the plane around, shot down another German, and escaped in a steep dive. Talbot landed the plane near a hospital; having safely delivered Robinson, he returned to his base. Talbot was killed in a training crash two or three weeks later. Both men were awarded the Medal of Honor.

By the end of the war, Marines had flown forty-three missions with the RAF and another fourteen on their own, shooting down four German planes with eight probables. In 1919, Marine Aviation was cut back to 1,020 men from a wartime high of 2,362. Air bases were established at Quantico, Parris Island, and San Diego.

The Corps was in action during the 1920s and 1930s in Central America and the Caribbean, and Marines were flying in support of ground troops. Most of the senior Marine aviators in World War II had seen action in Nicaragua, Haiti, and the Dominican Republic.

Marine Aviation was cut back again in the Depression. Squadrons were eliminated, units stationed overseas were recalled. Despite the budget cuts, the role of Marine Aviation was being hammered out: support amphibious landings, and support troops once they passed the beachhead.

The biplane reached its zenith in the 1930s, and designers competed to come up with single-wing planes acceptable to the Navy and the Marines. Two winners: the remarkable Grumman F4F Wildcat, a tough fighter with retractable landing gear which could fly rings around the old Brewster Buffalo it replaced; and the Douglas SBD Dauntless, a light bomber that carried its payload beneath its fuselage, below the radius of the propeller, making possible steep diving runs. But there never were enough of the new planes to go around, and in 1941 many Marine squadrons still were flying the old biplanes.

When the Japanese bombed Pearl Harbor, the fighters and bombers of Marine Air Group 21 were put out of action on the ground. VMF-211 with twelve new Wildcats, at sea aboard the carrier *Enterprise* when the Japanese struck, arrived at Wake Island four days before the Japanese struck. Seven planes were destroyed by Japanese bombs; the others fought on until the garrison was overwhelmed.

Marine squadrons also were in action with the Navy. VMF-221 engaged a force of 108 Japanese carrier-based planes heading for Midway on June 4, 1942, losing fifteen planes. Eight SBD dive bombers from VMSB-241 made an unescorted attack on two Japa-

Major Alfred A. Cunningham, father of Marine aviation, at the controls of a DH-4B observation plane over Santo Domingo in 1922. Curiously there is no Marine insignia.

nese carriers, but all were shot down. By the end of the day, only two fighters and eleven dive bombers of the Marine squadrons flying out of Midway were operational. The U.S. fleet arrived, and by June 6 four Japanese carriers had been sunk. The Battle of Midway had been won.

Marine planes helped turn the tide at Guadalcanal. The Marines landed on August 7, and five days later, Wildcats and Dauntless dive bombers were able to operate out of Henderson Field. VMF-223 shot down sixteen out of twenty-seven Japanese bombers on the 24th; thirteen of sixteen bombers fell two days later. Marine dive bombers from Henderson Field attacked four destroyer-transports coming down the Slot, damaging three. The Wildcats weren't as fast or as agile as the Zeros, but they could take more punishment; a burst into a Zero usually sent it down in flames.

As the battle for the island raged, the Cactus air force—"Cactus" was the code name for Guadalcanal —patched its damaged planes together and fought on. VMF-121 arrived in relief in October. One new pilot, Captain Joe Foss, got his first kill his second day in the air. He would have twenty-six before the war was over. Marines were soon flying the new F4U Chance Vought Corsair, faster than the Zero, with twice the range.

After Guadalcanal, the Marines took Bougainville, and their Corsairs were making fighter sweeps on the big Japanese base at Rabaul. Major "Pappy" Boyington's VMF-214, called the "Black Sheep" Squadron because it had been put together with replacement pilots, was blasting the Japanese out of the sky. Boyington ran his personal string of kills to twenty-eight before being shot down and captured. Marine SBD dive bombers and TBF Grumman Avenger torpedo bombers sank or drove off the warships at Rabaul, putting the key Japanese base out of action.

The Navy refused the Marine squadrons carrier space for the invasion of Tarawa, and the lack of close air support was one of the reasons the invasion was so costly. After the Eniwetok invasion, ten Marine fighter and four bomber squadrons based there helped neutralize the Japanese forces on the other islands in the Marshalls.

Marine squadrons were back in business in the bloody battle for Peleliu. Operating from a captured air strip, the Corsairs were less than a mile from the front line. Using rockets and napalm for the first time, VMF-14 and VMF-22 blasted the dug-in Japanese. Another innovation at Peleliu was a squadron of night-fighters: Grumman's new F6F Hellcats equipped with special radar. After the island was secure, the squadrons neutralized the nearby islands of Palau and Yap.

At the end of June 1944, Marine Aviation consisted of five wings, 28 groups, 126 squadrons, and 112,626 personnel, of whom 10,457 were pilots. General Vandegrift persuaded Admiral Nimitz to put Marine squadrons back on carriers. There would be eight carrier air groups, each with eighteen fighters and twelve torpedo bombers. The Marines also were now flying B-25 Mitchell bombers, and eventually there would be five squadrons of them operating in the Pacific.

The reoccupation of the Philippines involved Marine air support. A nightfighter squadron, VMF(N)-14, moved to Leyte. MAG-12's four squadrons of Corsairs provided air support when the Army's 77th Division landed on the west side of Leyte. When the 6th Army hit Luzon, both MAG-12 and MAG-14 were in action. More squadrons arrived in the Philippines and supported the 1st Cavalry on its drive to Manila.

Back on carriers, Marine squadrons participated in Navy battles as the war drew to a close. VMF-124 and VMF-213, aboard the *Essex,* were in the raids against ports and airfields in Indochina, and on the Japanese home islands. During the invasion of Iwo Jima there were eight Marine squadrons on the four supporting carriers. VMF-214 and VMF-452 were aboard the *Franklin* when two bombs struck her flight deck and put her out of the war.

At Okinawa, the last great Pacific invasion, Marine planes were on the carriers of Task Force 58. Marine General Francis Mulcahy was tactical air commander of all the land-based air support. The III Amphibious Corps had four Marine Light Observation Squadrons flying Grasshoppers, the Consolidated OY-1, for artillery spotting. Ten days after landing, two hundred Marine planes, most of them Corsairs, were operating on shore.

At the end of the battle for Okinawa there were twenty-two Marine squadrons ashore, ten more on carriers. The two most active squadrons, VMF-112 and VMF-113, aboard the *Bennington,* were in almost continuous combat from February 16 to June 8. They shot down 82 enemy planes, destroyed another 149 on the ground, dropped over 100 tons of bombs, and fired more than 4,000 rockets. The squadrons lost 18 pilots and 48 planes.

The war ended on August 14, 1945. Two battalions of the 4th Marines were in the early occupation of Japan, and MAG-31 was moved up from Okinawa to support them. MAG-22 came to Japan when the 2nd Marine Division arrived. Other Marine units were sent to China to support the Marines there, including the 1st Marine Aircraft Wing, with squadrons at Peiping, Tientsin, and Tsingtao.

Marine Aviation was shaped after the war by the coming of jets and helicopters. The Army had the Lockheed P-80, and the Navy had its own jet, the McDonnell FH-1 Phantom, which was capable of operating off carriers. VMF-122 was the first squadron to receive a few FH-1's in 1947, but years were to pass before jets became Marine standard equipment. By that time, the Douglas F3D-2 Skynight, the McDonnell F2H Banshee, and the Grumman F9F-1 Panther were the jets being supplied.

The Marines had experimented with rotary-wing aircraft as far back as 1932 when the Pitcairn Autogyro was used in Nicaragua, but it didn't have a large enough payload to be useful. Igor Sikorsky's helicopter was another matter. The Marines sensed the role that helicopters could play in amphibious warfare, and in late 1948 set up an experimental helicopter squadron, HMX-1. The Marines weren't satisfied with their helicopters. They wanted a craft that would carry 5,000 pounds of payload for 200 or 300 miles at 100 knots.

Gregory Boyington was born lucky. He grew up in a comfortable home in Tacoma and was able to go to the University of Washington during the Depression. He majored in a new science, aeronautical engineering, and was a member of the ROTC. Quick, strong, and aggressive, he was on the swimming and wrestling teams, and held the Pacific Northwest Intercollegiate Middleweight Wrestling title. He enlisted in the Volunteer Marine Corps Reserve in 1936 and was appointed an aviation cadet. After he won his wings, he was a flight instructor.

Craving action, he resigned his commission and went to China to join the American Volunteer Group, the legendary Flying Tigers. Before the group was disbanded, he logged 300 combat hours and shot down six planes. By the time of Pearl Harbor, he was an old hand at killing Japanese.

In 1942 he was recommissioned a first lieutenant, sent to the Pacific, and given command of VMF-214, a new squadron of pilots so green that it was known as the Black Sheep Squadron. Boyington, then thirty-one years old, was nicknamed "Pappy."

On Guadalcanal, in its first month in combat, the squadron shot down 57 enemy planes. Before they were through, its pilots would account for 127. Pappy personally shot down 22 of them. This made him one of the leading Marine aces of the war.

On a fighter sweep over Rabaul, he shot down three planes, then spotted more enemy planes below him. Boyington's plane was hit and his main fuel tank exploded. He bailed out and landed in the water. He had been seriously wounded. Pieces of his scalp were hanging in front of his face, his left ear was almost torn off, there was shrapnel in his arms and shoulders, his left ankle was shattered, and he had two bullet wounds in his legs.

After eight hours he was picked up by a Japanese submarine, and later was sent to a prison camp in Japan. The camp held Allied pilots and submariners whom the Japanese believed could provide valuable information. They were held as captives, rather than POWs, and the Japanese never reported their existence to the International Red Cross. Boyington's family didn't know he was still alive until he was liberated at the end of the war, twenty months after he was imprisoned. On his return, Boyington was promoted to lieutenant colonel and was presented the Medal of Honor by President Truman. The accompanying citation included a description of one of Boyington's most daring exploits. "Resolute in his efforts to inflict crippling damage on the enemy, Major Boyington led a formation of twenty-six fighters over Kahili on 17 October (1943) and personally circled the airdrome where 60 hostile planes were grounded, boldly challenged the Japanese to send up planes. Under his brilliant command, our fighters shot down twenty enemy aircraft without the loss of a single ship."

It would be the eve of the Korean War before such helicopters were available.

South Korea was invaded by North Korea in 1950, and a Marine brigade was on its way there in three weeks. It included three fighter-bomber squadrons equipped with Corsairs, a light observation squadron, and two HO3S-1 Sikorsky helicopter squadrons. One of them was VMO-6, the first helicopter squadron in history to be trained for combat.

Off Korea, on the carriers *Sicily* and *Badoeng Strait,* were VMF-214 and VMF-323. A nightfighter squadron, VMF(N)-513, was at Itazuke in Japan. By September the rest of the squadrons that would make up the 1st Marine Aircraft Wing were on their way.

Carrier-based Marine aircraft supported the invasion at Inchon, and when the troops captured Kimpo Airfield, two squadrons operated out of there. In the first month after the invasion, Marine aircraft flew 2,736 missions.

After landing at the port of Wonsan, the 1st Marine

Division headed for the Chosin Reservoir, near the Yalu River. As winter came, the Red Chinese crossed the Yalu and attacked. The Marines were surrounded. They were supplied by Marine transport planes, R4Q-1's, the Flying Boxcars, which air-dropped nearly two million pounds of supplies. Corsairs from Wonsan, Yonpo, and carriers harassed the Chinese troops as the division fought its way out of the trap. One anonymous rifleman composed a ditty that began:

Up in Korea, midst rocks, ice, and snow,
The poor Chinese Commie is feeling so low.
As our Corsairs roar by overhead,
He knows his buddies soon will be dead.

Jet fighters were being supplied to Marine squadrons in 1951, mostly F9F-2 Panthers. Marine pilots were itching to tangle with the Chinese MIGs, but they were kept busy flying support for the infantry.

Helicopter rescue operations were an almost daily occurrence in Korea, and quick evacuation and medical attention was credited for the high percentage of injured Marines who were able to fight again. For sheer theatricality, one such rescue took place when Major David Cleeland's Corsair was hit by ground fire and he crash-landed on the frozen Annyong Reservoir. The other three Corsairs circled overhead to give him protection. As he climbed out of the cockpit, Mongolian cavalrymen came charging across the ice. Cleeland ran, and the Corsairs bombed and strafed the horsemen. Their bombs broke the ice, plunging the horsemen into the water. While they floundered, a helicopter swooped in and rescued Cleeland.

A few Marine pilots got their share of aerial combat, mostly those flying off carriers or as part of Air Force units. Flying off the *Bataan,* Captain Philip DeLong and Lieutenant Harold Daigh were jumped by four YAK jet fighters. DeLong, a World War II ace with eleven kills, shot down two YAKs; Daigh shot down one and damaged another.

The only Marine who became an ace in Korea by shooting down five or more planes was Major John Bolt, who was on exchange duty with the Air Force. Bolt shot down six MIGs in his ninety-day tour of duty. (He had shot down six Zeros while flying on Guadalcanal with "Pappy" Boyington.) Major John Glenn was credited with three MIGs while on exchange duty with the Air Force.

Lieutenant Colonel John H. Glenn, Jr., Marine ace in Korea, the first man to orbit the earth, and now a senator from Ohio. Several Marine aviators were in space program.

A few Marine enlisted pilots flew in Korea, as they had in both World Wars. Sergeant Robert "Bulletproof" Hill flew seventy-six combat missions, winning the Distinguished Flying Cross for evacuating wounded Marines under heavy fire.

Captain Ted Williams, thirty-four years old when recalled to duty, flew thirty-eight missions in Korea. Another baseball star, Yankee second-baseman Jerry Coleman, also was recalled to active duty and flew sixty-three combat missions.

When the armistice came, the 1st Marine Air Wing had flown 127,496 combat missions; the wing's helicopters had evacuated nearly 10,000 wounded; and 436 Marine aircraft had been lost.

Over the next decade, the Marines worked on getting the aircraft they needed to perform their mission. The A-4 Skyhawk, the F-8 Crusader, and the F-4 Phantom were in service in most fighter squadrons by 1960. The Navy and the Marines worked together in the development of the F8U-1P, a photo-reconnaissance version of the Crusader. John Glenn set a new transcontinental speed record in the Crusader, averaging 726 miles per hour.

The Marines paid particular attention to helicopters, and three were developed: the Kaman HOK, a twin-engine, twin-rotor design; the HRS, which was modified to double its horsepower and capacity; and the HR2S, the largest military helicopter in service. In the 1960s these were replaced by the helicopters that would perform so well in Vietnam: the little Bell UH-1E Huey; the Vertol CH-46 Sea Knight, a turbine-powered medium transport; the CH-34D and the big Sikorsky CH-53A Sea Stallion.

To utilize these helicopters, three vintage carriers —the *Valley Forge,* the *Boxer,* and the *Princeton*— were modified to handle only helicopters, and new helicopter carriers, LPHs, were ordered built.

The first Marine unit to see action in Vietnam was a helicopter squadron, an omen of the developing conflict. The combat experience of the squadron helped develop the concept and tactics of the helicopter gunship. HMM-362 flew 4,439 sorties before being relieved.

The center of action in Vietnam shifted to the airfield at Da Nang. (The officers' club sign read "Far Eastern Indochina Jungle Fighters & Combat Pilots Association Ltd.") HMM-163 and HMM-261 were now flying daily missions in support of the South Vietnamese ground forces. But as the buildup continued, Da Nang and the airfield became targets for the Viet Cong. To protect Da Nang, the 9th Marine Expeditionary Brigade was sent in. The year was 1965, and the Vietnam War had begun for the Marines.

A second airfield was urgently needed. Marines landed at Chu Lai and an airfield was built there in a matter of weeks. Four Marine squadrons flying Douglas A-4 Skyhawks and several helicopter squadrons moved in.

During the bloody fighting at Khe Sanh, A-4s from Chu Lai flew support for the embattled Marines, and several were shot down during the fighting.

Two new types of planes went into operation in 1966: the McDonnell RF-4B Phantom and the Grumman A-6A Intruder. The big, two-engined RF-4B carried two crewmen and an array of sophisticated electronic imagery equipment, especially useful at night. The A-6A could carry a greater bomb load than the A-4 and had a highly advanced bombing computer, increasing its accuracy.

During the early days of the Vietnam War, the Air Force directed all air operations, which limited Marine pilots in supporting their ground troops. Marine squadrons aboard carriers also were being used in operations that took them away from their primary mission. More and more, helicopters were filling the void. They were an integral part of the daily existence of the Marine infantryman in Vietnam.

In August 1965 the Marines made the first night assault of the war when the 2nd Battalion, 3rd Ma-

MARINE AIRCRAFT

A-4 Skyhawk	Light Attack Aircraft	EA-6B Prowler	Electronic Warfare Aircraft
A-6 Intruder	All-Weather, Attack Aircraft		
		F-4 Phantom	Fighter/Attack Aircraft
AH-1 Sea Cobra	Attack Helicopter	F/A-18 Hornet	Fighter/Attack Aircraft
AV-8 Harrier	V/STOL Light Attack Aircraft	KC-130 Hercules	Aerial Refueling Aircraft
		OA-4 Skyhawk	Observation/Light Attack Aircraft
CH-46 Sea Knight	Medium Assault Transport Helicopter		
		OV-10 Bronco	Observation Aircraft
CH-53D Sea Stallion	Heavy Assault Transport Helicopter	RF-4B Phantom	Tactical Air Reconnaissance Aircraft
CH-53E Super Stallion	Heavy Assault Transport Helicopter	TA-4 Skyhawk	Light Attack Trainer
		UH-1 Huey	Assault Utility Helicopter

Two CH-53 Sea Stallions sweep toward simulated combat in maneuvers carrying full loads of Marines and equipment. Helicopters are the workhorses of modern warfare.

rines, was helicoptered into the Elephant Valley north of Da Nang. Soon helicopter assaults were a daily occurrence. By the end of the year, Marine helicopters, operating out of their main bases at Ky Ha and Marble Mountain, were lifting an average of 40,000 passengers and more than 2,000 tons of cargo a month.

Many Marines wounded in the war owed their lives to the helicopters that swooped in to evacuate them to a field hospital or hospital ship. During 1968 alone, more than 60,000 Marines were evacuated in over 40,000 sorties. It was dangerous duty. Often helicopter crewmen were themselves among the casualties.

In 1967, Captain Stephen Pless, a UH-1 Huey pilot, responded to a rescue call from four Marines pinned down on a beach by the Viet Cong. He made repeated strafing runs, firing rockets and machine guns, before he could land. His helicopter had been damaged by Viet Cong fire, and when he got the Marines aboard, it

took four attempts before he could get airborne, all the while under heavy enemy fire. For this action, Captain Pless became the only pilot among the fifty-seven Marines awarded the Medal of Honor in Vietnam.

During the 1968 Tet Offensive, the North Vietnamese Army (NVA) isolated and besieged the important Marine base at Khe Sanh, a stumbling block to reinforcements coming into South Vietnam from Laos. A massive airlift kept the 6,000 Marines supplied. VMGR-152 and two helicopter groups, MAG-16 and MAG-36, were rushed into action. Continuing bad weather and heavy NVA ground fire, however, curtailed the effectiveness of the C-130s. The Marines adopted an Air Force trick to keep the transports in operation. The C-130s would come in low, drop their tail ramps, and when they were over the landing area, electrically operated parachutes would pull out the pallet-mounted cargo. The planes then would fly back to their base without landing at Khe Sanh. During the

A pilot relies on his ground crew to see him onto the runway and bring him off the runway when he returns. For many aviation skills Marines are trained by the Navy.

airlift, transport helicopters were flying day and night, bringing in supplies and evacuating the wounded.

Helicopter crews also learned new tactics during the siege. One was called the Super Gaggle, and it involved both helicopters and fixed-wing planes. A TF-4F would first scout the landing area to determine the weather conditions. If the ceiling was high enough, the TF-4F would call in A-4 Skyhawks and, simultaneously, CH-46s would launch from their bases. The slower speed of the helicopters would allow time for the A-4s to shoot up enemy positions in the area. During the landing and unloading, helicopter gunships flew cover. Super Gaggles were able to keep the Marine outposts at Khe Sanh supplied during the seventy-seven day battle.

Operation Niagara was the code word given to the aerial operations at Khe Sanh. Besides the airlift, there were thousands of close air support missions, radar-directed bombing runs, and strikes by Air Force B-52s. So many planes were converging on the area that air traffic control became a problem. Often planes were stacked up over the area, waiting to be called in for their bombing runs. At the height of the battle, more

than three hundred sorties were being flown daily—one every five minutes.

On October 31, 1968, President Lyndon Johnson announced a unilateral halt to the bombing of North Vietnam, and the North Vietnamese responded by agreeing to the Paris peace talks. One result of the bombing halt was to allow the Marine squadrons to return to close air support. During the year, 47,436 combat sorties were flown by fixed-wing aircraft, 639,194 by helicopters. But the tide had turned in Vietnam. America was backing away from an unpopular war.

First to feel the effect of the new American policy toward Vietnam was the 1st Marine Air Wing. Some of its squadrons were redeployed to Japan and the remainder were consolidated. By the fall of 1971, the number of Marine squadrons in Vietnam was down to sixteen from a pre-Tet high of twenty-six. Those that remained were kept busy. South Vietnamese troops launched Lam Son 719 to rout out Viet Cong staging areas in Laos. The Marines were to supply security en route, and HMH-463 airlifted in troops and equipment. VMA-311 flew hundreds of sorties during the operation, hitting Communist trails and supply routes. Before the costly operation was over, it was abundantly clear that the ARVN could not function effectively in the field without heavy American air support.

The last Marine squadron in Vietnam, HML-167, went home in May 1971, and without air support South Vietnam was a sitting duck. The NVA struck on Good Friday 1972, pouring across the DMZ supported by tanks and heavy artillery. The ARVN fell back, stunned. Squadrons were rapidly mobilized and sent back to Vietnam. VMFA-115, 212, and 232 returned to Da Nang, VMA-211 and 311 to Bien Hoa near Saigon. VMA(AW)-224 was in action from the carrier *Coral Sea,* soon losing four Intruders in combat. Three Marine A-6As helped mine the Haiphong harbor, the main North Vietnamese port.

Heavy air action continued to the very end. VMFA-115 and VMFA-232 operated out of the remote air base at Nam Phong, nicknamed the "Rose Garden"

because of its barren appearance. Many missions were flown into Laos and Cambodia after the action stopped in South Vietnam. An accord was signed in Paris for a cease-fire to take effect on January 27, 1973. Part of the agreement called for the mines to be swept out of the Haiphong harbor, and HMH-463 flew CH-53As in the operation. The last American combat aviation unit in South Vietnam, MAG-12, left on January 29, although Navy and Marine carrier-based planes continued to bomb targets in Laos and Cambodia until the end of the summer.

In March 1975 the North Vietnamese army surrounded Saigon. The South Vietnamese retreat turned into a route, and the U.S. Seventh Fleet prepared to support an evacuation from Saigon. On April 25 orders were given to execute Frequent Wind, the evacuation of American personnel from the beleaguered South Vietnamese capital. HMH-462 and HMH-463 shuttled back and forth from offshore ships under the protec-

In a huge wooden hangar at El Toro, California, Marines do preventive maintenance on a helicopter. Hangar was built in World War II to house antisubmarine blimps.

tion of Navy and Air Force jets. During "The Night of the Helicopters," the Marines brought out more than 2,000 people. As the last helicopter carrying the American ambassador lifted off, the Communist troops were pouring into the city. The long war was finally over.

The role of the Marine Corps came under Congressional scrutiny in the years following Vietnam, and no area was more controversial than Marine Aviation. Aircraft increased the firepower and mobility of the Marines, true, but during Vietnam it had reached a point where Marines were employing thirteen types and twenty-two models of combat aircraft and helicopters. Didn't this constitute a wasteful duplication with aircraft of the Navy and the Air Force? In particular, was the Corps justified in keeping its fighter/attack squadrons?

Questions even were raised about one of the Corps's most sacred precepts: close air support. When the Marines were used in land campaigns with the Army, as was the case in Vietnam, was there a valid reason for separate Marine air support? The Marines contended that they had developed the coordination of air support far beyond anything the Air Force could provide. Some Army officers agreed. "The Air Force tactical squadrons should spend a few months with the Marines," said one Army captain. "I don't know what causes the difference, but it is there. The Marine pilots give us the impression that they are breaking their hearts to help us out."

Marine Aviation weathered the investigations and has been gradually updating its aircraft ever since. The Marines take great pains in selecting aircraft, insisting on long service life, ease of maintenance, and a high degree of combat survivability.

All the current Marine planes are impressive, and collectively they represent a formidable offensive force. But only when the aircraft is in action supporting Marines on the ground can one sense the symbiotic relationship that is the essence of their mission.

F4P Phantom reconnaissance planes display impressive tails at the air base at Cherry Point, North Carolina. Planes like this are designed to fool enemy radar.

Air and ground coordinate to a degree that suggests they are simply two parts of the same organism, which, of course, they are.

A correspondent in Vietnam was interviewing some off-duty officers in Saigon. He turned to one and asked, "What do you do?" "Well," he said, "I'm a Marine platoon leader, but right now the Corps has me flying a jet plane."

A ground crew member takes a breather on an F-18 fighter. Eyes and ears must be protected working around planes. F-18 squadrons take turns operating off Navy carriers.

CHAPTER 10

THE CUTTING EDGE

One of the unique characteristics of the Marine Corps throughout its history has been its ability to adapt its form to the changing dynamics of warfare. Usually these changes haven't been readily apparent to the layman, and they have evolved slowly, but they were significant nonetheless. Since the end of the Vietnam War, this process of quiet change has accelerated. As a result, there now is a new state-of-the-art model of the Corps.

To appreciate the recent changes and their significance, a bit of historical perspective is in order. For the first hundred years, the Marine Corps never numbered more than 4,800, roughly the size of a modern reinforced regiment. In those days, the only permanent Marine units were the detachments aboard ships and at Navy yards.

In 1836, when the Marines were called out to fight the Indians in the South, Commandant Henderson formed a provisional regiment composed of two battalions, small units by today's standards but representing nearly half of the Corps. It was disbanded after a year of service. A similarly small regiment was formed for the Mexican War in 1847, and also soon disbanded.

At the turn of the century, several events prompted a change in the composition of the Corps. The Philippine Insurrection in 1899, the Boxer Rebellion in 1900, and political unrest in the Caribbean prompted the government to increase the responsibility and size of the Corps. Regiments were formed, but they were temporary and have only a sentimental connection to current regiments with similar designations.

In the large standing armies of Europe, the regiment traditionally has been the largest standing body of troops, and officers and men usually stayed with the same regiment throughout their service. The regiments would vary in strength, and could be made up of any number of companies or battalions.

In the early 1900s the Navy began thinking of a well-organized force of Marines to go with the fleet and have the capability to seize and hold advance

---

OPPOSITE PAGE: A parachutist hits the silk. A number of Marines are jump qualified, but few have jumped in combat. Helicopters now land troops in areas inaccessible by land.

bases. This led to the creation of the 1st and 2nd Advance Base Regiments in 1913, and they are considered the first permanent regiments in the Corps. U.S. interventions in Haiti, Mexico, and the Dominican Republic made more regiments necessary, and the 3rd and 4th were formed.

There were four Marine regiments when the U.S. entered World War I; the 1st was in Philadelphia, the 2nd in Haiti, and the 3rd and 4th in the Dominican Republic. The 5th Regiment was the first of ten to be organized during the war and went to France during the summer of 1917, the 6th following that fall. The 7th, 8th, and 9th never got to France, nor did the 10th, the Corp's first artillery regiment. The Army reluctantly allowed Marine infantry regiments to fight in France but drew the line at an artillery regiment. Three other infantry regiments were formed in the last months of the war but also saw no action, the 13th, 14th, and 15th. No one knows why there was no 12th Regiment, but one was formed in 1927 to fill the gap.

Most of the regiments were deactivated after the Armistice. In fact, only the 4th saw continuous service between the wars, stationed for most of the period in Shanghai. From time to time, the 2nd was in Haiti, the 1st, 3rd, and 15th were in the Dominican Republic, the 5th and 11th in Nicaragua, and the 6th and 12th in China. In 1930 the Corps started designating its regiments as "Marines," a colloquial term that originated in World War I to distinguish Marine regiments from Army regiments.

The Fleet Marine Force was organized in 1934 for the purpose of carrying out amphibious operations as an integral part of the U.S. fleet. The 5th Marines formed the nucleus of the 1st Marine Brigade, which in turn became the East Coast contingent of the Fleet Marine Force. Similarly, the 6th Marines formed the nucleus of the 2nd Marine Brigade on the West Coast. Through the rest of the 1930s, this was the strength and structure of the Corps.

In the two years before Pearl Harbor, the Marines nearly tripled in size—the 8th and 10th Marines were reactivated in 1940; the 1st, 2nd, 7th, and 11th early in 1941. When America entered the war, this expansion picked up momentum. Twenty-nine infantry, artillery, and engineer regiments saw duty in the war, and all but the 16th Marines participated in at least one campaign. In addition, there were a number of specialized regiments, including raider, parachute, and service regiments.

The 4th Marines, transferred from Shanghai to the Philippines, were forced to surrender to the Japanese at Corregidor, the first and only time a Marine unit of battalion size or larger was captured. With the capture of the 4th Marines, the only unit with uninterrupted service since 1914 temporarily dropped from the rolls. Units of the 1st Raider Regiment were used to reconstitute the 4th Marines in February 1944. The 4th Marines were later integrated into the 1st Provisional Marine Brigade, which in September 1944 was redesignated as the 6th Marine Division.

All Marine divisions date from World War II. The first two divisions were created in February 1941 by the redesignation of the 1st and 2nd Marine Brigades; by the summer of 1944, the Corps had six divisions. All were patterned after the Army's triangular division, three infantry regiments of three battalions each. But a Marine division is unlike any army division in the western world. It carries its own tanks, air force, ground transportation, artillery, supply, engineering and medical battalions. It is self-sufficient, a small army. At the end of the war, twenty-four infantry and artillery regiments were on active duty.

The Marine Corps attempted to maintain a skeletonized version of the wartime Fleet Marine Force, although some regiments were down to one or two battalions while others existed only on paper. An infantry "regiment" might consist of three rifle companies plus a headquarters and service company. The structure was reorganized in 1947 and only 1st through 11th Marines survived. This perpetuated the historical lineage and honors of the oldest regiments in the Corps. The Corps shrank again in 1949 and only the 2nd, 5th, 6th, 10th, and 11th Marines survived, but in traditional form: three infantry battalions plus headquarters and service elements.

Marines were sailing to Korea less than three weeks after the North Koreans crossed the 38th Parallel. The first to leave was the 1st Provisional Brigade, quickly built around the 5th Marines. Only four regiments saw

OPPOSITE PAGE: An LAV armored vehicle can maneuver over rough terrain to bring its firepower to bear on the enemy. Most Marine vehicles have been introduced since Vietnam.

combat, all part of the 1st Marine Division, although eight regiments were reactivated, along with the 4th Battalion, 10th Marines.

After the war, all twelve regiments were kept on active duty and were grouped into three Marine divisions. The Army changed the structure of its divisions in the late 1950s, but the Marine divisions stayed essentially the same, making them the largest and heaviest infantry divisions in the world today.

In Korea, a regiment rarely had been deployed for special operations; those tasks usually fell to a reinforced battalion or a battalion landing team. That was the case, too, in Lebanon in 1958 and the Dominican Republic in 1965.

Full regiments did deploy in Vietnam, but they usually didn't remain intact, as they had in previous wars. The war in Vietnam was fought mostly on a company or even a platoon level. Marines called it a "chevron war." Because of this, a change came in Marine field organization. A regiment had operational control of a number of elements which were not its own, and the old lines of command and communications simply didn't work anymore.

Ten regiments of infantry and artillery plus half of another regiment engaged in combat in Vietnam. The 1st Force Service Regiment also served there, although not as a separate regiment but as part of the Force Logistic Command. The 13th, 26th, and 27th Marines were reactivated in 1966, the 28th Marines the following year. The 26th and 27th Marines and two battalions of the 13th Marines saw action. The demands of the war caused the reactivation of the 5th Marine Division. After Vietnam, the division and all of its regiments were deactivated.

Nine infantry and three artillery regiments are currently on active duty. They comprise the 1st Division at Camp Pendleton, the 2nd at Camp Lejeune, and the 3rd at Okinawa. Of these, the 5th Marines has by far the longest continuous existence. In addition, there are four regiments, three infantry and one artillery, in the Marine Corps Reserve. A major reorganization of the Reserve was undertaken in 1962; one result was the formation of the 4th Marine Division and the 4th Marine Air Wing, both headquartered in New Orleans. Later the 14th, 23rd, 24th, and 25th Marines were reactivated on a Reserve basis. The lineage and honors previously earned by earlier regiments with the same designations are carried by the Reserve regiments and their battalions.

Marines invariably identify themselves by battalions and regiments. Ask a former Marine what outfit he served with and he will reply, "Second Battalion, 5th Marines," or simply, "Two-five." A division is too big and rarely acts as a unit anymore. The distinctive division patches were done away with shortly after World War II. Pilots and aviation personnel do the same thing: identify themselves by their squadron, not an air wing. And under the new Marine Corps structure, even battalions and regiments lose some of their identity when they go into a combat situation.

In 1975 a serious, in-depth reappraisal was made of the Marine Corps. It was started by the Senate Armed Forces Committee and was continued by the Corps itself. Commandant Louis H. Wilson appointed a board headed by Major General Fred E. Haynes, Jr. The board addressed itself to these questions.

- ★ Was there a need for a 196,000-troop Marine Corps?
- ★ Should the primary mission of the Corps still be to attack enemy shores from the sea?
- ★ Should the Corps continue to have its own air wings?
- ★ Was the Corps ready to fight a modern war against an enemy equipped with sophisticated weapons?
- ★ What should be the mission of the Corps in the future?

The trickiest of the questions was what should be the future mission of the Corps: a clearly defined purpose would make answering the other questions a relatively simple matter.

For a long time, the Corps had defined itself as a force-in-readiness. Its World War I slogan, "First to Fight," was just one expression of this concept. The Marines' role was to counter and contain aggression, wherever in the world it might occur, until the Army could mount a major land effort. Commandant Wilson told the Senate Armed Forces Committee, "This mission is meant to provide the fleets with a ready capability to project combined-arms combat power ashore."

The problem was that the American mood in the immediate post-Vietnam period was basically isolationist. Foreign commitments were acknowledged, but there was strong opposition to future military intervention. A study of the Marine Corps by the Brookings Institution concluded: "There is a growing public disenchantment with military ventures overseas, particularly those involving the use of ground troops."

The Haynes board countered: "History has demonstrated again and again the cyclic nature of political affairs. It is dangerous to reduce the only viable forcible entry capacity the nation has as long as the U.S. continues to have overseas interests that are both vital and vulnerable."

Commandant Wilson expanded this view in his testimony before the Armed Forces Committee. "Everyone knows we need an Army, we need a Navy, and we need an Air Force. It is difficult to explain why we need a Marine Corps. [With] a country such as ours that has a $180 billion investment overseas and, roughly, overseas trade of some $74 to $80 billion a year, we need a force that can project power overseas. . . . I think it is inconceivable that we should not have this capacity to project power ashore overseas. . . . [The Corps] is not a defensive force but a means of projecting power ashore where we may be required. Of course, that's our mission. . . . I am not concerned about the future of the Marine Corps so long as we have ready forces such as we have today, because I am convinced that when the call comes, they have my telephone number —and I expect a call."

One result of this reappraisal was to increase Marine involvement in the defense of Europe. The United States was questioning the ability of the NATO forces positioned in Europe to withstand a Soviet onslaught, and whether it would be possible to adequately reinforce them from the United States. The Soviet submarine fleet and its missiles would pose a formidable threat to reinforcement.

The Corps already was a strategic reserve for NATO. Under the Joint Strategic Objective Plan, two Marine Amphibious Forces (80,000 men and 1,000 planes) were on standby for NATO. The question was how these forces would be used. The Corps wanted the task of protecting NATO's flanks, not as reinforcements for central Europe. The Marines wanted to stay "light and maneuverable." There are 8,000 miles of coastline between Europe's North Cape and Greece, Commandant Wilson pointed out, and this represented a smart use of the Corps and its amphibious capability.

This new assignment was approved, but not at the expense of the Corps's global responsibilities—a decision that amply justified keeping the strength of the Corps at 196,000, but it did create problems of equipment. The Marines needed more firepower and tactical mobility, and Commandant Wilson promised, "Over the next several years, we are going to modernize the Marine Corps in a very dramatic way."

Coming into service were hovercraft capable of carrying a 60-ton payload at speeds up to 50 knots. With older landing craft, the Marines could land at 20 percent of the beaches in the world; now 80 percent were vulnerable. In 1976 the first *Tarawa*-class supersized amphibious ship was commissioned. In 1981 the keel was laid for the *Whidbey Island,* a new class of Landing Ship Dock. LSDs like the *Whidbey Island* are capable of transporting near to shore a landing force of 340 Marines, four of the new landing craft, helicopters, tanks, and other vehicles. The Navy was short on firepower to support a Marine amphibious assault, and in the early 1980s four *Iowa*-class battleships were coming out of mothballs.

There was a parade of new equipment. In the air came more AV-8A Harriers, the V/STOL (vertical/short-takeoff and landing) craft first tested in Vietnam, and the F/A-18 to replace the F-4 Phantom. The CH-53-E Super Stallion, capable of carrying 16 tons 50 miles, added a much-needed heavy-lift helicopter; a new attack helicopter, the Cobra, was equipped with TOW missiles. On the ground, there were a new tank, the M-60 with a 105mm gun; a new 155 howitzer with a range of 18 miles; and a helicopter-transportable Light Armored Vehicle (LAV).

To increase flexibility, the Corps has reorganized its combat forces on the principle of "building blocks." Units can be made as heavy or light as the occasion calls for. For example, an expeditionary force can be beefed up by the addition of tank and AA battalions. In this way, the Corps can give a Marine Amphibious Force the firepower, mobility, and air cover required in a particular combat situation.

Special attention was being paid to equipping combat units with missiles. Infantry fire teams got the SMAW "bunker buster." Each Marine division would have 144 TOW missiles, and each battalion would have 32 Dragons. In the artillery, the MULE, a portable

Merritt Edson got his first taste of military life in a Vermont National Guard regiment on the Mexican border in 1914. When America entered World War I, he dropped out of college and joined the Marines, winning a commission in France. A captain in Nicaragua in the late 1920s, the redheaded Edson proved himself a daring and resourceful officer. He devised a plan to trap Sandino, the rebel leader, and his men. Edson and thirty-two men went up the Coco River and into the jungle, living on beans, bananas, and monkey meat. They ambushed the rebel camp and took it at the cost of one Marine dead and four wounded. Sandino, however, escaped. For capturing the rebel camp, Edson was awarded the Navy Cross. In Nicaragua he learned the art of raiding tactics, traveling light, and fighting with light weapons of intense firepower.

When World War II came, Edson, now a lieutenant colonel, was assigned to train the 1st Raider Battalion. He first led his Raiders ashore at Tulagi, and in the action earned his second Navy Cross. On Guadalcanal 14,000 Japanese troops attacked Henderson Field in what would be a decisive contest—the Battle of Edson's Ridge. In the center of the Marine defensive line, 800 Raiders and Marine paratroopers, weakened by battle and malaria, held a four-mile stretch of strongpoints and outposts. The first night, the Japanese probed the Raider positions. Edson's right flank was pushed back; he counterattacked but couldn't dislodge the Japanese. A new line was established on higher ground. The next night, a flare dropped from a Japanese plane and a destroyer bombarded Edson's position, and two battalions hit the Marine line. The attackers drove a hole between A and B Companies. Edson called in howitzer fire to within 150 yards of his men. The Raiders were slowly falling back to their last-ditch position. Survivors remember Red Mike shouting over and over, "Raiders, rally to me! Raiders, rally to me!" Despite a severe head wound, Edson led his men in hand-to-hand combat. Fighting off repeated attacks that night, the Raiders finally held their position on the ridge. If the Japanese had broken through, Henderson Field, and probably Guadalcanal itself, would have fallen.

On Edson's Ridge, 40 Marines had been killed and 103 wounded—one in every five who fought there. One survivor said, "Sometimes you love him, sometimes you hate him, but I'd rather fight with Red Mike than anyone." Red Mike Edson was awarded the Medal of Honor.

At Tarawa, Colonel Edson, now the 2nd Division Chief of Staff, landed on the second day and took command of the fierce fighting. He was promoted to brigadier general and led the 8th Marines in the final mopping up of Tinian. At war's end, he had served forty-four months in the Pacific, longer than any other Marine officer.

laser-directed rangefinder for forward observers, can pinpoint targets for laser-guided rounds fired from howitzers. Many military experts believe that in the battlefield of the future, small units equipped with precision-guided antitank and antiaircraft missiles will be the controlling factor, not tanks and manned aircraft. If this prophecy is correct, the Corps is moving in the right direction.

"Smart weapons" have caused the military to revise its thinking. General Haynes predicted: "In ten years,

the infantryman will return to a position of dominance on the battlefield because we will have shoulder-fired, fire-and-forget weapons which will be effective both against tanks and aircraft; and he will be protected by light armored vehicles."

Transport planes and helicopters have solved the problem of getting Marines on the scene quickly. Getting their equipment to them is another matter. In the late 1970s the Navy found that the Sea Services, charged with the responsibility of transport, was critically short of ships. Navy and Marine planners searched for a way to alleviate the situation. In 1979 the Carter Administration identified the need for the rapid movement of substantial forces and the capability to deploy forces at distant locations. This need was dramatized by the revolutionary forces in Iran who forced the Shah from his throne.

The Navy and Marines responded with the innovative Maritime Prepositioning Ships (MPS) program. An interim program was authorized immediately. Seven commercial cargo ships became available because of President Carter's embargo of grain shipments to the Soviet Union, an action taken in response to the Soviet invasion of Afghanistan. In 1980 the ships were deployed to the Indian Ocean carrying enough equipment and supplies for an 11,000-man Marine Expeditionary Brigade. This program of prepositioning ships was specifically designed to work in concert with the Military Airlift Command (MAC). The big MAC jet transports can move the men of a Marine brigade in 250 or fewer sorties; the ships would move the equipment and supplies, an operation that normally would require another 4,500 or so MAC sorties.

MPS does more than relieve MAC of flying thousands of sorties. The Marines determined in the 1981 Operation Bright Star exercise that twenty days were needed to deploy by air a single *battalion* with its equipment and supplies. Equally important, the battalion could not operate at peak efficiency if it had to be resupplied by air.

In late 1981 Congress was asked for a program to convert and charter merchant ships to expand and make permanent the Marine Prepositioning Ship program. Contracts were awarded ten months later. Contracts since have been awarded for additions to the program: two hospital ships (TAHs) and two aviation logistics support ships (TAVBs).

One of the inspirations for the MPS program came from a prior program of prepositioning equipment and supplies on land in Norway for use by Marines participating in the defense of the North Cape. However, an extension of that land program was impractical: such storage would mean a great loss in flexibility from a global point of view, and while the Norwegians are strong allies of the U.S., this isn't the case in most of the other proposed storage points.

As the program worked out, an MPS squadron consists of four or five specially configured merchant ships, under the command of the Navy and protected by an escort of Navy ships. The merchant ships are loaded with combat equipment and thirty days' supplies for a Marine brigade. Shortly before the ships arrive at their destination, the 16,500-troop Marine Expeditionary Brigade and a Navy support element—a cargo-handling battalion, an amphibious construction battalion, an assault craft unit, a beachmaster unit, and a Navy special warfare detachment, nearly a thousand in all—together with the brigade's tactical aircraft, are lifted to one or more nearby airfields. The equipment and supplies aboard the ships are then offloaded. If all goes well, the brigade will be combat ready and on the move in five days or less after the ships arrive.

All of this substantially improves the strategic mobility of the Fleet Marine Force, permitting the rapid deployment of a self-sustaining brigade without overtaxing the limited capacity of the available military airlift and Navy sealift forces. There is a financial saving as well. Merchant ships are less expensive to put into operation and to keep operating than are comparable Navy ships.

Depending on the type of ship, four or five ships comprise a squadron. The crews of the ships are civilian; a Navy captain commands the squadron, assisted by a small staff. They are large, highly capable ships, which can unload themselves either at dockside in three days or offshore onto lighters in five days.

There currently are three MPS squadrons, one each in the Atlantic, Pacific, and Indian Oceans. This means that any potential trouble spot in the world can be reached by a squadron in seven days or less.

The ships can be unloaded in bad weather: five-foot waves, fifty-knot winds, or three-knot currents. They can fuel the hundreds of Marine vehicles stored aboard, and land a large helicopter. Aboard ship are maintenance spaces for inspection and upkeep of the stored items.

Rapid deployment—even the *capacity* for rapid deployment—sharply increases the possibility of resolving a crisis before it becomes a war, or of keeping a small war from escalating. Even the movement of an MPS squadron can send a signal which can deter aggression, even though the squadron in international waters, without troops, probably would not be considered provocative.

The new additions to the MPS squadrons, the hospital ships and the aviation logistics support ships, increase the potential effectiveness of the brigade. On the aviation logistics support ships are some three hundred Marine aviation maintenance personnel, and a helicopter landing pad. This allows helicopters to come aboard from duty ashore, be worked on, and return quickly to action. The hospital ships, which are converted tankers, have twelve operating rooms and 1,000 beds, and carry Navy doctors and medical corpsmen.

But all this is to deploy and support a Marine Expeditionary Brigade, and what exactly is a brigade? In command jargon, it is an integrated, combined-arms team, organized and trained as a ready "force package." Being a Marine unit, it is built around the traditional base of Marine combat power—the infantryman. It consists of three full battalions of infantry, a fourth maneuver battalion equipped with 53 tanks armed with 105mm guns, and a reinforced battalion of field artillery which has 36 medium 155mm and heavy 203mm cannon. To counter enemy armor, there are 96 TOW heavy antitank missiles. The brigade will move in 109 fast, powerful AAV-7 assault amphibian vehicles. Air defense is provided by 80 ground-to-air missile launchers, 6 improved HAWKs, and 72 Stingers.

A Marine Air Group (MAG) is part of the brigade and it has 68 helicopters and 78 fixed-wing aircraft. Among the helicopters are 8 CH-53E Super Stallions and 24 AH-1 Cobras, which can be equipped with TOW and Hellfire missiles, rockets, cannon, and machine guns. In the MAG are two squadrons of F/A-18 Hornets, and either 19 A-4M Skyhawks, the workhorse close air support aircraft, or 20 AV-8B Harriers. There also are a squadron of A-6E all-weather attack planes and a complement of photo-reconnaissance and electronic warfare aircraft.

To coordinate this airpower, the Marines use a fully automated air command and control system, widely acknowledged to be the most advanced tactical air control equipment in the military.

The Navy plays an important role in the deployment of a brigade. It helps unload the ships of the squadron and protects them while this is being done. The Navy's special warfare detachment, for example, provides the ships with anti-swimmer defense—a necessity in these days of terrorism.

The Marine Expeditionary Brigade is not the only

OPPOSITE PAGE: A hard-charging Marine comes around a barricade on the combat course at Camp Lejeune, North Carolina. Units keep in shape working in simulated combat.

size the Marines come in. The smallest and most responsive of the Marine Air-Ground Task Forces (MAGTFs) is the Marine Expeditionary Unit (MEU), nominally made up of 1,900 Marines and 100 Navy personnel. An MEU carries with it fifteen days' supplies and ammunition. Two MEUs are deployed continuously with Navy fleets, one in the Mediterranean and the other in the Pacific. From time to time, MEUs also are deployed in the Caribbean and the Atlantic and Indian Oceans. (Marines call these deployments "floats.")

An MEU is made up of an infantry battalion which is reinforced by tanks, antiarmor, artillery, reconnaissance, assault amphibious vehicles, and combat engineer units. Together they form a battalion landing team (BLT). An aviation combat element provides a reinforced helicopter squadron which contains four types of helicopters, from heavy transports to the attack Cobras. An MEU service support group handles everything from medical and dental treatment to heavy engineer and beach support. The composition of an MEU is flexible and can vary as the tactical situation dictates. For example, a detachment of six Harriers often is added to the aviation combat element.

The largest and most powerful of the MAGTFs is the Marine Expeditionary Force (MEF), and a situation would have escalated to alarming proportions before it would be sent into action. An MEF can unleash the full fury of the Corps. It normally is built around a Marine division, aircraft wing, and a large force service support group, although it might range in size from less than a full division to two or more divisions and air wings. An MEF is capable of a wide range of amphibious operations and subsequent operations ashore. Commanding an MEF is a lieutenant general. Usually a Marine division is composed of three infantry regiments, an artillery regiment, a tank battalion, an LAV battalion, a combat engineer battalion, and a reconnaissance battalion.

In the air, the aviation combat element (ACE) provides more than 300 helicopters and fixed-wing aircraft of various types, the air command and control

elements, and the Marine Wing Support Group. The Force Service Support Group (FSSG) has supplies to sustain the MEF for sixty days, plus maintenance, engineering, motor transport, medical, dental, and landing support for the MEF's 49,700 Marines, 2,600 Navy personnel, and their equipment.

Since its inception prior to the Vietnam War, the MAGTF concept has been put into action twice. Two MEUs attached to the Sixth Fleet, the 32nd MEU (later the 22nd) and the 34th (later the 24th), alternated duty with the multination force in Lebanon in 1982; it was the 24th that was decimated in the terrorist bombing of the Marine barracks in Beirut. The 22nd MEU participated in the 1983 invasion of Grenada. An MEU has been on full alert since American warships began escorting oil tankers in the Persian Gulf in 1987.

Despite Lebanon and Grenada, the Marines who have seen the most action since Vietnam have been embassy security guards. Marines traditionally have protected U.S. embassies when they were threatened. In 1905 Marines were assigned to guard the embassy in St. Petersburg, then the capital of Russia. That same year, Marines from the Philippines relieved an Army detachment guarding the legation in Peking, the beginning of the Corps's long China duty. A company-sized Marine guard protected the embassy in Managua, Nicaragua, during a 1922 uprising. Embassy duty did not become a permanent assignment for the Marines, however, until 1948. By 1972, ninety-seven U.S. embassies and legations had Marine guards, usually a seven- or eight-man detachment commanded by a staff noncommissioned officer. The Marine Security Guard Battalion, headquartered in Quantico, administers the operation.

Security guards are trained in a special six-week school at Quantico. The tour of duty for a security guard is three years: eighteen months in a "good" post like Paris or Rio, eighteen months in a "hardship" post like El Salvador or Moscow. Many Marines enjoy embassy security duty. The hours standing guard are long and usually boring, but there is the camaraderie of the Marine House and the Friday evening cocktail parties they hold for embassy personnel. (The Marines charge for drinks, and the profits go to underwrite one of the most popular events of the embassy social season, the Marine Corps birthday party.) Life is good for Marine security guards—until trouble comes, until they are on the cutting edge.

The final act of American involvement in Vietnam was the evacuation of the embassy in Saigon. Security guards were in the forefront of that surrealistic scene. Other incidents at embassies involving the Marine detachments already have been noted: the 1974 attack on the embassy in Cyprus, the problem the Marines had with Idi Amin in Uganda that year, the attack on the embassy in Taiwan, the seizing of the Teheran embassy and the 444-day captivity of the hostages, and the alleged security breaches in Moscow. These should have been enough. There were others.

In 1977 the Marine detachment in Moscow evacuated the embassy and guarded classified documents whole Soviet firemen fought a fire that raged for eighteen hours. Later that year Marines met the Ethiopian Army with drawn weapons when, in protest of U.S. plans to cut off military aid to that country, an attempt was made to take over the embassy.

Marine security guards in Managua, Nicaragua, helped evacuate 1,423 civilians during fighting in the city in 1979, which accompanied the ouster of President Anastasio Somoza Debayle. The 1979 Iran crisis stirred up trouble for security guards in other countries. The U.S. embassy in Thailand was bombed, the embassy in Libya was attacked. Muslims also attacked the American embassies in the Philippines and Kuwait. In 1981 three Marines were killed and one wounded when the jeep carrying them to the embassy in San José, Costa Rica, hit a mine.

MAGTFs may be used only occasionally, but they are kept in fighting trim through a relentless series of exercises throughout the world. In a typical year, elements of the Corps participate in some ninety exercises overseas with as many as thirty-four allies. Marine Reserve units take part in many of these exercises. The locales are selected to give Marines experience to simulate combat in jungles, the desert, and in cold weather.

The commitment to NATO in the defense of the North Cape has placed a strong emphasis on mountain and cold weather training. The Corps's mountain warfare training center is high up in the Sierra Nevada Mountains north of Yosemite National Park at Bridgeport, California. Here there are schools that teach both individual Marines and units up to the size of a battalion the skills and tactics necessary to conduct successful combat operations in the harsh environments of cold weather and rugged mountains. The Battalion Mountain/Winter Operations Course at Bridgeport is considered by officers and enlisted men to be as tough as any Marine training. They are trained to fight on skis and to camp out in temperatures that often plunge to 20 degrees below zero.

In the summer they are trained in mountain climbing. They use pitons and ropes to scale nearly vertical cliffs, the work made harder by the thin air at altitudes near 10,000 feet. Often a unit is climbing so high on a mountain that observers need high-powered field glasses to track their progress. In an exercise just before graduation, a platoon must scale a steep cliff at night, working against the clock.

In another part of California the Marines prepare for desert warfare, coupled with fire-support coordination training. The world's largest Marine Corps base is at Twenty-nine Palms, some sixty miles northeast of Palm Springs in the Mojave Desert; it covers 932 square miles, nearly the size of Rhode Island. Twenty-nine Palms is the home of the Marine Corps Air Ground Combat Center. (The base also is the home of the 3,660 men of the 7th MEB.) The terrain at the base consists of steeply sloped mountains with intervening flat valleys. The elevations range from 1,800 to 4,500 feet. The average annual temperature is 67 degrees, but that statistic is deceptive; summer temperatures can hit 130; winter temperatures, 15. The average annual rainfall is four inches. All in all, an ideal place to simulate war in the desert, and to live-fire all supporting arms in realistic exercises.

The main training activity at Twenty-nine Palms is Combined Arms Exercises (CAX), during which the units face a Soviet-type threat: an MEU faces a reinforced motorized rifle battalion, an MEB a motorized rifle regiment.

Initial information is given the force commander in a letter of instruction, later information in intelligence summaries. Once the exercise has begun, the enemy is simulated by means of input from the tactical exercise evaluation and control group. The enemy also is represented by ground targets. As H-Hour approaches,

An M-60 main battle tank is brought ashore on an LCM during exercises at Camp Pendleton, California. The M-60 is the only Marine armor that can't be transported by helicopter.

Infantrymen board helicopters in a combat training exercise. Vietnam was a helicopter war and skills perfected there now are standard operational practice for deploying Marines.

eight-inch cannons (representing naval guns) and other artillery commence firing on the objective. Mobile assault companies attack across the line of departure, and helicopter gunships work on the flanks. Jet aircraft fire rockets and make bombing runs, providing close air support. Tanks close in and fire their main guns. Cobras, and TOW missile vehicles also are engaging the enemy. The sights and sounds increase to a level approximating that of actual combat. As the troops advance, naval gunfire, artillery, and aircraft shift to attack deeper targets. Everyone is firing live ammunition; Twenty-nine Palms is the only Marine installation that allows troops to maneuver through ordnance impact areas.

Soon everyone is moving up. Artillery batteries take new firing positions; reserves are brought up; the command post, usually housed in an AAV, comes forward, meeting the challenge of maintaining command and control. The logistic problems in a CAX are real because of the climate, terrain, and the live fire. All of these factors affect men and equipment. Food, water, ammunition, batteries, spare parts, and replacement items continue moving forward. Simulated—or actual—casualties are evacuated to the rear.

The trick is to properly orchestrate the maneuvering force, the supporting arms, the close air support, and the logistic support so that they work in concert. The commander and his staff must not only know and understand fire support coordination doctrine, they also must be able to execute that doctrine using all the available supporting arms on the battlefield. If the commander is successful, if he can bring firepower to bear on the enemy—"steel on target"—then his unit can advance without suffering unnecessary casualties in his ranks.

A CAX lasts several days and nights. As the exercise progresses, there are lulls in the battle. Unlike actual combat, a CAX permits the commander to pause and correct his mistakes. During such pauses it is easy to pick out the experienced Marine enlisted men. Those without tasks are in the shade of their vehicles catching a nap.

All aspects of each CAX are evaluated by a team of observers. The primary emphasis is on the ability of the commander and his staff to coordinate supporting arms. A CAX evaluation is a most important entry in a senior officer's fitness report.

How closely does a CAX resemble actual combat?

During a pause, a master gunnery sergeant, a decorated veteran of Vietnam, gave the question some thought.

"It comes pretty close, closer than you'd think looking around here now," he said. "You can't see the enemy, and he never counterattacks. That's different, of course. But when you get rolling, particularly at night, and the planes are whistling in and everybody is firing at once—you almost believe you're in combat again. And hell, every now and then, somebody gets hurt or killed out here. Now, that's real, isn't it?

"I love it when the firing really gets going," he continued. "It's like listening to a band and being able to pick out the various instruments from their sound. Every gun, every weapon, has a special sound—we call it its signature. Those big eight-inchers make a noise like a bass drum. Boom! Boom! Missiles hiss like a snake. Did you hear the mortars? Thunk! Thunk! Machine guns are nice, particularly the fifties; it's like triple-tonguing on a trumpet. Ta-ta-ta-ta. Now, I don't love it when those suckers are firing at me, but this is nice. Real nice."

CHAPTER 11

A MIRROR OF SOCIETY

A small ceremony at Camp Pendleton on October 2, 1987, marked the end of an era: the retirement of the last of the some 669,000 Marines who served in World War II. The thirty-six-year career of the Marine being honored, Chief Warrant Officer Charles Russell, included combat at Peleliu and Okinawa, Korea and Vietnam, where he was wounded in 1969. Earlier in the year, Sergeant Major Domenick A. Irrera had retired, the last enlisted Marine with World War II service. The number of Marines who served in Korea is now dwindling down to a precious few. Most enlisted Marines still on active duty who saw action in Vietnam now are usually gunnery sergeants or sergeant majors; most officers are majors or above. It comes as a shock to learn that nearly half of the Marines today are teenagers.

The Corps has changed tremendously in many ways

OPPOSITE PAGE: World War II Marines in battle dress march past a group of women reservists. Women Marines were credited with freeing enough male Marines to create the 6th Division.

since Russell and Irrera enlisted. For example, there were no blacks in boot camp then; the few joining the Corps were trained separately and served in segregated battalions. And Russell and Irrera probably were too busy in World War II to take much notice of the influx of women Marines. Now women serve in practically every part of the Corps. There are 10,000 women Marines, and 19 percent of the Corps is black. How blacks and women gained acceptance is an interesting part of the social history of the Corps.

On August 27, 1776, Isaac Walker, Negro, enlisted in Captain Mullan's company of Continental Marines. Later that year another recruit was listed as "Negro," and there may have been others, for the early records were sketchy and incomplete. But when the Marine Corps was reestablished in 1798, the official recruiting regulations clearly stipulated "no Negro, Mulatto or Indian to be enlisted." The Corps was to remain lily white until the eve of World War II.

The first major step toward ending segregation in the armed forces was President Franklin D. Roosevelt's Executive Order 8802 in 1941. Beyond question the order was unpopular at Headquarters Marine

Corps. Shortly after Pearl Harbor, Commandant Thomas Holcomb said, ". . . the Negro race has every opportunity now to satisfy its aspirations for combat in the Army—a very much larger organization than the Navy or Marine Corps—and their desire to enter the naval service is largely, I think, to break into a club that doesn't want them."

Despite the commandant's objections, Secretary of the Navy Frank Knox insisted that the Marines take a thousand black recruits a month. On June 1, 1942, Alfred Masters and George O. Thompson became the first modern black Marines. Two months later the first black unit was activated, the 51st Composite Defense Battalion, at Montford Point, a new camp near Camp Lejeune. Colonel Samuel A. Woods, Jr., a native of South Carolina, was the commander, and all the officers were white.

The early black recruits were of exceptional quality. Charles W. Simmons, later sergeant major of the 51st, held a master's degree from the University of Illinois. George A. Jackson was an ex-Army lieutenant. Gilbert H. "Hashmark" Johnson had been in both the Army and the Navy. There were white D.I.s at Montford Point until early 1943. After that, black D.I.s took over under the direction of Sergeant Major "Hashmark" Johnson.

A second defense battalion, the 52nd, was formed. Black Marines also served in twenty-one depot and twelve ammunition companies. In the beginning, the black units were used as labor and stevedore battalions, freeing other Marine units for combat. Blacks first saw action in the invasion of Saipan, and two black Marines were killed on the first day. After the battle, Commandant Alexander A. Vandegrift announced, "The Negro Marines are no longer on trial. They are Marines, period."

In the invasion of Guam, a former Memphis truck driver, Private First Class Luther Woodard, was awarded the Silver Star, the highest decoration earned by a black Marine in the war. Some black units had exemplary records. The 3rd Ammunition Company was awarded the Presidential Unit Citation at Saipan. The 6th Ammunition Company and the 33rd, 34th, and 36th Depot Companies received the Navy Unit Commendation at Iwo Jima.

Nine black Marines were killed during the war and seventy-eight were injured. A total of 19,168 served in the Corps, 12,738 of them overseas. Blacks accounted for less than 2.5 percent of the wartime Corps.

Near the end of the war, in March 1945, three blacks were sent to Platoon Commanders Class at Quantico. They didn't graduate, but after returning to civilian life they became a doctor, a lawyer, and a college professor. The next three black officer candidates also didn't make it. On November 10, 1945, the 170th birthday of the Corps, Frederick C. Branch of Hamlet, North Carolina, a veteran of the 51st Defense Battalion, became the first black Marine officer. Three more blacks were commissioned from the V-12 program in 1946. Among them was Lieutenant Herbert E. Brewer of San Antonio, Texas, who served in the Korean War and by 1973 was a colonel, the highest-ranking black in the Marine Reserve at that time.

On July 26, 1949, President Truman signed Executive Order No. 9981 which ended segregation in the armed forces. Again, the Marines at first demurred. Commandant Clifton B. Cates said publicly that segregation was a problem to be solved by American society, not the armed forces.

At that time there were some 2,200 blacks among the 75,000 active-duty Marines. First to be integrated were Marine athletic teams. The black boot camp at Montford Point was closed in September 1949, and black recruits were put in integrated platoons at Parris Island and San Diego. That same month Annie E. Graham, of Detroit, and Ann E. Lamb, of New York, became the first black women Marines. The Corps ordered in November 1949 that all individual black Marines be assigned to any vacancies in any unit where they could be used effectively.

The number of black Marines had dropped to 1,502 by the beginning of the Korean War. In the next three years the Corps rose from 74,279 to 249,219; blacks in the Corps to 14,731. Two black Marines won the Navy Cross in Korea, and a number were awarded the Silver Star and Bronze Star. Major General Oliver P. Smith spoke of the thousand black Marines he commanded in Korea: "They did everything, because they were integrated, and they were with good people."

By the 1960s the Marine Corps liked to say that there were no white or black Marines, only "green Marines," although many Marines still made the distinction between "light green" and "dark green." Of the 448,000 Marines to serve in Vietnam, 41,000 were black, and by and large they did themselves

Now a major general and the senior naval aviator, Frank E. Petersen was a fighter pilot in Korea. He has led the way for blacks to senior positions in the Marine Corps.

proud. There were five black Medal of Honor winners, all killed shielding their fellow Marines from exploding grenades. The first black Marine to win the Medal of Honor was Private First Class James Anderson, Jr., of Compton, California, for action on February 28, 1967. The other recipients: Private First Class Oscar P. Austin, of Phoenix, Arizona; Sergeant Rodney M. Davis, of Macon, Georgia; Private First Class Robert H. Jenkins, Jr., of Interlachen, Florida; and Private First Class Ralph H. Johnson, of Charleston, South Carolina.

In Vietnam the senior black officer was Lieutenant Colonel Frank E. Petersen, Jr., of Topeka, Kansas, who had received the Distinguished Flying Cross in Korea. He was named commanding officer of Fighter Attack Squadron 314 in 1968, a unit flying Phantom jets out of Chu Lai. He flew 280 combat missions, was shot down and rescued, and was awarded the Legion of Merit. Until he recently retired Lieutenant General Petersen was the senior aviator of both the Marine Corps and the Navy.

Lieutenant Colonel Hurdle L. Maxwell commanded 1st Battalion, 6th Marines, the first black to command a Marine infantry battalion.

Other black Marines distinguished themselves in Vietnam. One was Sergeant Major Edgar R. Huff, the first black infantry battalion sergeant major. Huff served two tours in Vietnam and was wounded while rescuing a radioman who had been trapped by enemy fire in an open field. For his gallantry Huff received the Bronze Star, and two Purple Hearts for his injuries. He retired in 1972, the first black Marine to complete thirty years of service.

The senior enlisted Marine at the battle for Khe Sanh was Sergeant Major Agrippa W. Smith. James E. Johnson, who had enlisted in 1944, rose to be a chief warrant officer, and after retiring in 1965 became assistant secretary of the Navy for manpower and reserve affairs. In 1969 Major Edward L. Green, a Vietnam veteran, became the first black officer to teach at the Naval Academy.

Despite all this, blacks in the 1960s still had a long way to go in the Marines. There were only 48 black officers in 1964, 282 in 1973 out of an officer corps of 20,000 and only 24 were majors or higher. It was no better in the enlisted ranks. In 1964 there were only 184 blacks in the top three enlisted grades, 1,394 in 1973, out of some 29,000 enlisted black Marines.

During the 1960s, American society was torn by racial violence, and the Marine Corps had its share of ugly incidents. In 1969 alone, Camp Lejeune had 160 cases of assaults, muggings, and robberies that apparently were racially motivated. The night before the 1st Battalion, 6th Marines, shipped out for duty in the Mediterranean, blacks assaulted white Marines at a farewell party. Two white Marines were stabbed and another died of head injuries. Charges were brought against forty-four Marines, and thirteen were convicted. One black Marine was given nine years at hard labor for manslaughter. A board of inquiry was critical of both the militant blacks and leadership at the base.

There was racial violence at Marine bases in Hawaii, Okinawa, and in the rear areas in Vietnam. Several involved "fragging," Marine slang for lobbing a live grenade at people you dislike. In late 1969 Commandant Leonard F. Chapman, Jr., acknowledged that

A rifleman checks his squad's position during field maneuvers at Camp Pendleton. The new M16-A2 is the first rifle that can be fired left-handed.

the Marines had a "problem." After Major Green returned from Annapolis to become special assistant to the commandant for minority affairs, he wrote:

"Although it is doubtful that the influence of racial prejudice will ever be completely eradicated . . . the military has made commendable progress in moving toward this objective. . . . When a commander makes his subordinates aware that discriminatory behavior will not be tolerated within his command, it will not exist."

Racial tensions eased in the 1970s, but, ironically, one of the affirmative action measures designed to correct the underlying problems backfired on the Corps. Secretary of Defense Robert McNamara ruled that the services had to meet sharply increased racial quotas of recruits, whether or not the recruits met educational standards. As the number of high school dropouts shot up, the Marines found themselves with

the highest per capita rates of desertion, absent-without-leave, and drug abuse cases in the armed forces.

Commandant Louis H. Wilson admitted to the Senate Armed Forces Committee in 1975 that the Corps "has had a manpower quality problem" and was starting to do something about it. Four thousand "unsuitable" Marines were ultimately discharged, and a standard quota of 75 percent high school graduates was set among recruits, a sharp increase from the 46 percent the Corps was getting in 1973. This had the effect of lowering the percentage of black enlistments from 19 to 15, and the commandant said, "I think this is about right—15 percent black—because they constitute about 12 percent of the population. I think this would be a good mix."

In 1987, despite the fact that virtually all recruits had to be high school graduates, the percent of blacks in the Marine Corps had risen to 19 percent, a major achievement. True integration was hardly achieved overnight, but it has made the Corps a stronger and a better force.

Russell and Irrera probably got accustomed to serving with American Indians early in their Marine careers. In combat in the Pacific, Navajo Indians created their own legend as Codetalkers, speaking over field telephones in their own language so messages could not be understood by the Japanese. The Codetalkers made possible swift, secret battlefield communication.

Women got off to an earlier start in the Marine Corps, but they too had a long road to real acceptance. (Marine mythology has a woman Marine aboard the U.S.S. *Constitution* during the War of 1812, disguised as a man and using the name George Baker. No evidence supports the delightful story, however.) The true beginning came on August 12, 1918, when the Secretary of the Navy authorized the Corps to enroll women as Reservists. The following day, Mrs. Opha M. Johnson became the first woman Marine. In all, 305 women served as enlisted Marines during the war, performing clerical duties; none rose above the rank of sergeant. "Free a Marine to fight" was the recruiting slogan.

After the Armistice, the Corps began to phase out its women Reservists, but it was late 1922 before they were all gone. These pioneer women Marines suffered more than their share of sexual harassment; "Marinettes" was probably the kindest of their many nicknames. One incident came at a pass-in-review on the White House lawn during the war. Addressing the distinguished visitors, Secretary of the Navy Josephus Daniels, with a twinkle in his eye, turned to the women Marines and said, "As we embrace you in

PORTRAIT IN GREEN:
RODNEY M. DAVIS

Three months after graduating from high school in Macon, Georgia, Rodney Davis was in the Marines. After Parris Island and the School of Infantry at Camp Lejeune, he served with the 2nd Marines, rising to lance corporal. He was a guard with the Marine Detachment in London for three years. In August 1967, Sergeant Davis was sent to Vietnam as a platoon guide with Bravo Company, 1st Battalion, 5th Marines.

On September 6, 1967, the platoon was attacked by a large force of North Vietnamese army regulars. Some of Sergeant Davis's platoon members were in a trench where he was directing their fire. Davis moved from man to man, shouting encouragement, while firing and throwing grenades at the oncoming enemy. A Vietnamese grenade landed in the trench in the midst of the men. Sergeant Davis instantly threw himself on the grenade, absorbing the full force of the explosion. His Medal of Honor citation notes: "Through his extraordinary initiative and inspiring valor in the face of almost certain death, Sergeant Davis saved his comrades from injury and possible loss of life, enabled his platoon to hold its vital position, and upheld the highest traditions of the Marine Corps and the United States Naval Service. He gallantly gave his life for his country."

Two years after his death, his mother, Ruth Davis, was at the dentist's when a friend called and said someone from the Marines was at her house waiting to see her. "My thoughts were, 'My God, maybe he didn't die!'" she said. "Then when I found out it was about the Medal of Honor, at first I was disappointed, but after I got over the shock, I began to realize the magnitude of the honor."

On May 9, 1987, at the Long Beach Naval Station in California, Mrs. Davis and Sergeant Davis's widow and two children watched the commissioning of the U.S.S. *Rodney M. Davis,* a guided-missile frigate, the first warship to be named in honor of a black Medal of Honor winner.

uniform today, we will embrace you without uniform tomorrow."

The Corps dragged its heels forming a woman Reserve unit in World War II; it was the last of the four armed services to do so. Pressed on the issue, Commandant Holcomb reluctantly wrote to the Secretary of the Navy on October 12, 1942: " . . . in furtherance of the war effort, it was believed that as many women as possible should be used in noncombatant billets, thus relieving a greater number of the limited manpower available for essential combat duty."

Holcomb liked to tell the story that when he went home that night to the Commandant's House at Marine Headquarters in Washington and announced his decision to allow women into the Corps, the portrait of Archibald Henderson fell off the wall.

President Roosevelt quickly approved the measure, and on November 7, 1942, the U.S. Marine Corps Women's Reserve was authorized. Its total strength, to be reached by June 30, 1944, was set at 1,000 officers and 18,000 enlisted women.

At the request of the commandant, a committee of distinguished educators compiled a list of twelve outstanding women to be considered for the post of director of the women's reserve. Holcomb chose an amazing woman from the list, Ruth Cheney Streeter, of

World War I reservists called Marinettes put up recruiting posters in New York City. For many years there was stiff resistance to the idea of women being part of the Corps.

Morristown, New Jersey. President of her class at Bryn Mawr College, a specialist in health and welfare for twenty years, and a pilot, Mrs. Streeter was sworn in as a major. For the succeeding thirty-four months she led the women Marines with distinction, eventually rising to colonel.

Mrs. Streeter was amused, and the male officers embarrassed, at her commissioning ceremony when she noticed that her commission read, "Know ye, that reposing a special trust and confidence in the patriotism, valor, fidelity and abilities of RUTH C. STREETER, I do appoint *him* . . ."

"My job was to see that the women fitted effectively into noncombat positions in the U.S.A. and Hawaii," Major Streeter recalled, "making it possible to release enough men to form the Sixth Marine Division." She said that she and her colleagues felt that the Sixth was really theirs. The commandant concurred: "The Sixth Division could not have been formed unless women had taken over the stateside jobs of those 18,000 men and 1,000 officers."

Women officer candidates initially went to Mount Holyoke College in Massachusetts; enlisted recruits went to Hunter College in New York City. Uniforms were adaptions of regulation Marine "greens" and Dress Blues. Lipstick was selected to match the cord on the winter cap, and was marketed under the trade name of "Montezuma Red." Both officer and enlisted training was moved in the summer of 1943 to Camp Lejeune. On the urging of Eleanor Roosevelt, weapons instruction was added to the training.

Unlike the WACs, WAVEs, WAFs and SPARs, the new women Reservists had no acronym and were known to the public simply as Lady Marines. In the Corps they were known as WMs. Male Marines called them BAMs, short for "Broad-ass Marines." Not to be outdone, the women referred to their male associates as HAMs, "Half-ass Marines."

During the war, jobs in the Marine Corps were broken down into four classes to determine how women Marines could best be utilized:

Class I. Jobs in which women are better, more efficient than men. Example: all clerical jobs.

Class II. Jobs in which women are as good as men, and could replace men on a one-to-one basis. Examples: some clerical jobs in which women are especially good, like accounting; also jobs requiring a high degree of finger dexterity.

Class III. Jobs in which women are not as good as men, but can be used effectively when need is great, such as wartime. Example: most of the jobs in motor transport.

Class IV. Jobs in which women cannot or should not be used at all. Example: jobs demanding unusual physical strength.

Despite this apparent pigeonholing, women Marines proved themselves in new situations time after time during the war. For instance, women Marines were handling all Link Trainer instructions and most of the tower air control duties at the air station at Cherry Point by 1944.

Several World War II women Marines are deserving of a particularly snappy salute. Lily Hutcheson Gridley was one of the first twenty women commissioned and later became the Corps's first legal assistance officer. She left the service as a lieutenant colonel. Sergeant Major Ethel M. Wilcox was one of the first women recruiters. Colonel Helen G. O'Neill, a yeoman in World War I, rose to be assistant to the director of women Marines. She was one of the women officers at the unveiling of the "Molly Marine" statue in New Orleans, which honors all of the wartime women Marines.

By the end of the war, 18,460 women Marines were on duty from Washington to Pearl Harbor. At Marine Corps Headquarters 85 percent of the personnel were women. By December 1945 two-thirds of the women Marines, including Colonel Streeter, had been released from active duty. The plan was that they would all be gone by September 1946, but at the last minute it was decided to keep a small cadre of women on active duty.

In 1948 change swept the armed forces; with unification of the services and racial integration came equal status to women in uniform. One result was a buildup of women Marines to a strength, by June 1950, of 100 officers, 10 warrant officers, and 1,000 enlisted women. A historic event came on the birthday of the Corps in 1948 when the commandant swore into the regular Marine Corps ten outstanding women sergeants. One of their number, Sergeant Bertha L. Peters, later became the first Sergeant Major of women Marines.

At the outbreak of the Korean War, thirteen platoons of women Marine reservists were called to active duty, a symbol of the acceptance in the Corps that women had earned. By this time the role of women in the service was quite well defined. Congress had prohibited the use of women in dangerous combat situations, but the dynamics of international conflict were soon to change. No longer would danger be confined to the field of battle.

For example, fifteen women Marines were assigned to embassy duty on a trial basis in 1979. Two, Vicki Lee Gaglia and Betty Jo Rankin, both corporals, were assigned to the U.S. consulate in Karachi, Pakistan. A mob surrounded the consulate, and the women, armed and wearing helmets and flak jackets, stood ready with the other Marines to defend the building. After an all-day standoff, Corporal Gaglia lowered the American flag while two male Marines covered her with shotguns. Other incidents at other embassies convinced the Corps that such duty was too hazardous for women Marines, and they were withdrawn the next year.

The issue of women Marines on hazardous duty and in combat units is bound to be reopened, however. Denmark, a NATO partner of the Marines in the defense of Northern Europe, is experimenting with the use of women in combat units and, unofficially at least, seems pleased with the results. And women Marines have shown an aptitude for the martial arts: in 1987 a woman recruit set a new Corps record in qualifying on the rifle range at Parris Island. And women Marines have fitted successfully into paracombat Military Police.

One possible problem remains. The Marine Corps has the lowest percentage of women of any of the services. Early in 1988 Commandant Alfred M. Gray

Brigadier General Gail M. Reals is the first woman to become a Marine general through the regular promotion process. Women became part of the regular Corps in 1948.

was asked why this was. "Because we have enough women," he replied.

Not too many years ago, marriage spelled the end of a woman's career in the Marines. Now, women Marines marry and have children with a minimum disruption in their working lives. More often than not, they marry other Marines, and the Corps makes an admirable attempt to keep the couple stationed together. Day care centers and schools are part of the modern Marine base, post exchanges stock such things as diapers and nursery furniture. At a recent graduation ceremony at Parris Island, a Marine from the air station at nearby Beaufort and his wife, a sergeant in the public affairs office at the recruit depot, watched their son become a Marine.

There are 10,000 billets in the Corps for women Marines, and no special recruiting efforts are required to fill them; in fact, usually there is a waiting list. Enlisted recruits are trained at Parris Island, officers at Quantico. Their training is remarkably similar to that of male Marines. Some of the exercises are modified for the women, but they are worked equally hard and show the same percentage increases in body strength and endurance. They live under the demanding discipline of women D.I.s, run the obstacle course, rappel from the same tower, and spend equal time in field exercises. They go through the rifle and pistol ranges and earn the same marksmanship badges as the men, firing the same scores from the same distances. For a while a woman held the rifle range record. They receive equal pay and equal benefits. And when a woman Marine falls from grace, she is subject to the same code of military justice and the same consequences of breaking it. Many civilian companies and organizations lag far behind the Marine Corps in observing equal rights and equal opportunities for women, both in the letter and the spirit of the law.

President Jimmy Carter appointed the first woman Marine general, Brigadier General Margaret Brewer. Another Marine milestone came when Gail Reals became a brigadier general, rising through the regular selection process.

The changes witnessed by Russell and Irrera weren't limited to the progress of minorities. Certainly their pay improved; private's pay in World War II was a joke, just a bit more than the prewar $21 a month. Nor did the joke stop as a Marine went up the ladder. A three-star general in 1944 made about $12,000 a year. But for a long time, a Marine could exist on very little money. He had his bunk and three meals a day, and if his trousers, or whatever, wore out, he "surveyed" them—turned in the old gear for new, free. Now a Marine gets a clothing allowance, and if he's not careful he will outspend it in keeping up appearances. So many things were free in the wartime Corps that when payday came he was paid in cash, and it was spending money. It usually went for cigarettes, beer, the pursuit of women, and the other traditional pleasures of liberty.

The bases have changed, too. Gone are the Nissen huts—Quonset huts to everyone but a Marine—and the whitewashed two-story barracks and administration buildings. Everything now is brick and substantial; a modern Marine base looks like the campus of a state university. All continuity isn't lost, though; prisoners from the brig still police the grounds. A jarring element on bases are the Burger Kings and McDonalds, now acceptable alternatives to the mess hall. (Can an Egg McMuffin provide the sustenance of chipped beef on toast? Don't Marines in camies look a bit silly at a salad bar?)

The Corps passed a watershed of sorts a few years ago. There now are more dependents of Marines than there are Marines. Once the saying was "If the Marines wanted you to have a wife, they would have issued you one." Now even PFCs get married, although they usually have a tough time of it financially unless both husband and wife are Marines. Bases give over large tracts to housing for married Marines. Base

clubs cater to their social needs, the hospital to their medical needs. Marine wives fill many of the civilian jobs on the base.

Like Russell and Irrera, many retired career Marines live near a base. There are practical reasons for this: the base hospital, the golf course and other recreational facilities, and the post exchange and commissary. Housing is easy to find near a large Marine base, at least on the East Coast.

Take Camp Lejeune, for example, home of the 2nd Marine Division. There are 35,000-plus Marines and some 800 Navy medical personnel stationed there. Family members of the military personnel number about 32,000, of which one-third live on the base. The retired military population, including family members, accounts for another 33,000.

To service the needs of this large number, the base has 5,000 buildings, which include 11 chapels, 3 commissaries, 12 exchanges, 3 seven-day food stores, 112 auto service stations, 7 schools from kindergarten to high school, 548 officer and 3,472 enlisted family housing units, 112 spaces for mobile homes, a 236-bed hospital, 8 branch clinics and dispensaries, 10 ambulances, 25 service clubs, and a host of recreational facilities including 26 swimming pools. There are 80,000 privately owned vehicles registered aboard the base, which has 400 miles of roads and 50 miles of sidewalks. Despite the number of Marines who eat at home and the attractions of the fast-food outlets, the mess halls serve an average of 22,600 meals a day. Lejeune would be tremendously crowded if it didn't encompass 110,000 acres—170 square miles, with 14 miles of beach on the Atlantic.

By comparison, the town outside the Lejeune main gate, Jacksonville, has a population of about 17,000—less than 10,000, residents say, not counting the Marines who live in town. If to live in Jacksonville is like sleeping next to an elephant, the feeling must be relieved somewhat by the Lejeune payroll of $408,000,000 per year. Counting purchases, construction, and repair work on base, the Marines spend more than a half billion dollars in the area.

There are reminders in Jacksonville of an earlier era in the Corps: an excess of used-car lots and country-and-western bars, a tattoo parlor near the main gate, pawnshops with signs saying "We buy Dress Blues." But the Marine presence is not as readily apparent as it once was. Marines don't wear their uniforms to

town anymore, although a Marine in civilian clothes looks like just that—a Marine in civilian clothes; there is no disguising a high-and-tight haircut, let alone devil-dog or globe-and-anchor tattoos on a muscular forearm.

Once they were called "brown-baggers," the married Marines who lived off base and brought their lunches in paper bags. They are so prevalent now that the nickname has faded away. In the early morning their cars are backed up at the main gate, camie-clad Marines shuttling from one world to another.

On the base, there are an impressive number of joggers. Marines must pass a semiannual physical fitness test and keep their weight within strictly prescribed limits; to "pork up" is to be put on a medically supervised low-calorie diet. Fitness always has been critical to the Corps, but now everyone seems to be jogging or pumping iron. The new commandant, General Gray, has grumbled publicly about Marines in designer warm-up suits. He advocates a return to such traditional exercises as running the length of a football field toting a fellow Marine in the fireman's carry.

Overseas, the married Marine has new problems.

Once the conquering hero with the almighty dollar in his pocket, he is now, at best, a guest who has overstayed his welcome, and in the closing days of the Reagan Administration, the dollar in his pocket has shrunk disastrously. Faced with sharp cost-of-living increases, more and more Marine dependents are reluctantly returning home. "When were you last in Okinawa?" a Marine asks. "Was it when the Americans were driving the good cars?"

Another sign of the times: real estate developers are looking covetously at Marine bases. The Corps does own some beautiful and enormously valuable pieces of American real estate. Camp Pendleton's 100,000-plus acres, with its miles of beach, gets pressure from Los Angeles to the north and San Diego to the south. Expensive condominiums have been built right up to the edge of the base, and the owners are quick to complain when the artillery range is in action or when jets, supporting amphibious exercises, come in low. Commercial interests and civic groups would like to see the El Toro Marine Air Station become the Orange County municipal airport. Weekend and night operations at El Toro have been suspended to alleviate noise complaints. Thousands of homes for commuters

OPPOSITE PAGE, ABOVE: *Woman Marine D.I. struts her stuff as her platoon waits to pass in review. Drill instructor is considered one of the toughest jobs in the Corps, and D.I.s earn extra pay.* THIS PAGE, ABOVE: *It's not easy for a woman to become a Marine but most find it a rewarding life. They enjoy equal rights and equal pay and serve in all fields except those considered "combat."* THIS PAGE, CENTER: *In camies a woman field telephone operator at battalion headquarters relays a message to a unit in the field.*

The educational opportunities for Marines are almost limitless. THIS PAGE, BELOW: *At Parris Island a female recruit rappels from the tower. Boot camp is segregated but basically the same for both sexes. No one says the women have it any easier.*

Four D.I.s at the San Diego Recruit Depot await the start of graduation ceremonies. Recruits at Parris Island refer to their California counterparts as "Hollywood Marines."

to Washington could be built on the sprawling base at Quantico, less than thirty miles south of the capital. A base commander spends much of his time now placating local pressure groups and making sure his Marines are exemplary citizens.

Another concern of a base commander is ecology. Tanks and artillery fire can be hard on the landscape. On one of the beaches used for amphibious exercises at Camp Pendleton is the nesting area of a rare species of seabird. This section of the beach is roped off and scrupulously avoided by the Marines. A similar situation exists at the vast desert training base at Twenty-nine Palms, California. Pre-Hispanic Indian ruins are respected during the large combined-arms exercises held at the base. At every juncture, a modern base commander is asking, "What's the environmental impact of this?"

Coming back to the recently retired Russell and Irrera: economics may provide the rationale for making their retirement near a Marine base, but there is an emotional reason as well. Leaving the Corps is hard, and the longer one has been in, the harder it is. Retirement is an emotional wrench, and some never

get over it. Living near a Marine base ensures a retired Marine the companionship of other retired Marines and the opportunity to participate in Marine-related activities. And that means a lot to a middle-aged man who hasn't been a civilian since he was a teen-ager.

One way in which Russell and Irrera will undoubtedly keep in touch with the Corps and its doings is through membership in the Marine Corps Association. Its some 100,000 members are Marines and former Marines who share a special feeling for the Corps. The association operates out of a handsome new building at Quantico, and its best-known activity is publishing the monthly magazine *Leatherneck,* a fixture of Marine life since its founding in November 1917. The association also publishes *Marine Corps Gazette,* edited primarily for career officers.

Leatherneck describes itself as "the magazine *for* Marines, *by* Marines," and there is no other magazine, military or civilian, quite like it. It contains news of what's happening in the Corps but doesn't touch on controversial matters. It tells about upcoming unit reunions and reviews books about the Marines.

Former Marines wanting to get in touch with lost comrades use its Reader Assistance column. There are personality stories about such people as the new sergeant major of the Corps, or the former D.I. who played the D.I. in the movie *Full Metal Jacket*. It serves up a generous dollop of nostalgia; some recent article titles: "Shanghai—50 Years Ago"; "The Wrestling Match—1918"; "Life in The Corps in The 1920s." The magazine attracts a number of advertisers seeking to sell Corps-related material: books, videotapes, various items emblazoned with the globe and anchor. A T-shirt in a recent issue carries the message "Every Muther Loves a GRUNT," an offering from Grunt Headquarters in Irvine, California.

All of the changes in the Marines are linked to changes in American society; the Corps doesn't exist in a vacuum, it is a mirror of contemporary society. The Corps is conservative by nature, every military organization is, and it may react slowly to societal changes—but it does react. The subject came up with Brigadier General Joseph P. Hoar, commander of the recruit depot at Parris Island, in a discussion of the improved quality of recruits.

"Isn't it fair to say that the Maine Corps is a mirror of society?" he was asked.

"Well, we are affected by changes in society to some degree," the general replied. "But I reject the analogy of the Corps as a mirror." He paused and smiled. "You see, we like to think of ourselves as a bit better than society."

A modern Marine family at a Parris Island graduation: Master Sergeant Maxx Palmer and his wife, Staff Sergeant Linda, proudly pose with son Richard, a new Marine.

CHAPTER 12

RUFFLES, FLOURISHES AND THE COMMANDANT

The oldest post in the Corps is the Marine Barracks, an enclosure of red brick at Eighth and I Streets, just north of the Navy Yard in Washington. Stationed here are 52 officers, 994 enlisted personnel, and the Corps's mascot, Lance Corporal Chesty VIII, a three-year-old red brindle-and-white English bulldog. The Marine Barracks consist of several buildings enclosing a drill field. A long two-story barracks on one side and the houses of senior officers on the other define the length of the field. At either end are the Band Hall and the Commandant's House, a handsome structure of Georgian-federal design which is believed to be the oldest public building in continuous use in the capital.

The house is now the home of Alfred M. Gray, Jr., a fifty-nine-year-old four-star general and his wife, Jan. Until 1901 the barracks was also the Marine Corps Headquarters, and at various times it has been a re-

OPPOSITE PAGE: General Alfred M. Gray, Jr., addresses troops soon after becoming commandant. He has instituted a "back-to-basics" program to increase the combat readiness of the Corps.

cruit depot and an officers training school. Now the commandant commutes to the headquarters near the Pentagon in Arlington, Virginia.

The original purpose of the barracks was to house a force of Marines to protect Washington. On March 31, 1801, President Thomas Jefferson and Lieutenant Colonel William Burrows, the second commandant, rode out to locate a site for the barracks "within easy marching distance of the Capitol building." A few days later a Washington newspaper ran a notice offering "a premium of 100 dollars . . . to any person who will exhibit the best plan of barracks for Marines, sufficient to hold 500 men, with their officers, and a house for the commandant." George Hadfield, an Englishman, won the prize and is assumed to have been the architect, although the original plans haven't been found.

Construction was completed in 1806, and the Commandant's House was one of the few buildings the British didn't burn when they sacked the capital in 1814. There are several versions as to why. One has it that the commander of the British troops used the house as his headquarters and neglected to torch it when forced to make a hasty withdrawal. Another says

The Marine Corps flag dips in salute in a ceremony at the Marine Barracks in Washington, D.C. This Marine Barracks has been in service since 1801.

that the stand of the Marines at the Battle of Bladensburg so impressed the British that they spared the barracks and house as a gesture of soldierly respect.

Both the barracks and the Commandant's House have seen their share of rebuilding and remodeling over the years but they still retain an uncanny sense of the past. Few visual reminders of the modern world intrude here. Military reviews and ceremonies have been performed at the Marine Barracks from the beginning, and over the years they became more and more formalized. In 1934 a formal parade was conceived, a pageant that would match the splendor of the setting. The parades were open to the public and provided a showcase for the ceremonial prowess of the Marines and the musical eminence of the Marine Band. The planners stopped short of fancy theatrics; the parade adhered to strict regulations, with no trick drills or Queen Anne salutes which were popular then. In 1957 this became the Friday Evening Parade, held

weekly in the summer to celebrate the dignity and pride of the Corps. The ceremony is similar to the one at the Iwo Jima Monument, but larger and more involved. And it features the mascot and the Marine Band.

The barracks is the home of the 143-member Marine Band, a unique institution in itself; it is not only the oldest military band in the United States, but the only musical organization whose primary duty is to provide music for the president. The band made its White House debut on New Year's Day, 1801, at a reception given by President John Adams and has played for every chief executive since. It has played for every inauguration since that of Thomas Jefferson, who gave the Marine Band the title "The President's Own." The band's music opened the first inaugural ball, for James Madison, in 1825. President Martin Van Buren instituted the formal outdoor concerts on the Capitol grounds. The band traveled to Gettysburg with Lincoln in 1863 for the dedication of the National Cemetery and was present when he gave the Gettysburg Address.

John Philip Sousa became leader of the band in 1880 and increased its fame by taking it on annual national tours. Before the band left on its 1891 tour, President Benjamin Harrison gave each band member a cigar. President Calvin Coolidge was unable to attend a special concert in 1924 and sent the band flowers with a note saying, "The Marine Band has earned for itself a unique place in the affections of the American people . . ." President John Kennedy once remarked, "The Marine Band is the only force that cannot be transferred from the Washington area without my express permission, and let it be hereby announced that we, the Marine Band and I, intend to hold the White House against all odds." At the request of Jacqueline Kennedy, the Marine Band led the funeral procession of her slain husband.

The Marine Band played the wedding march as Alice Roosevelt went down the aisle at the White House on the arm of her father, President Theodore Roosevelt. In 1949 Winston Churchill addressed the Massachusetts Institute of Technology's Mid-Century Convocation. As he was about to leave the platform, he turned to the audience and said he would like to "ask one favor"—that the Marine Band play the "Marines' Hymn." To the delight of all, Churchill sang all the words to each verse.

Like all military bands, the Marine Band is an outgrowth of "field musics," the fifes and drums and bugles that once led men into battle. Besides inspiring the troops, field musics had a practical use in battle. Commands were relayed by bugle calls and drum rolls. Field musics wore tunics of opposite colors, or "facing colors," from the combat troops to be readily identifiable as communicators. Each company of Marines once had a bugler who doubled as the commander's message runner. Now the Marine Barracks is the only post that doesn't depend on recorded bugle calls.

Band members are Marines but with a difference. Candidates audition when openings arise, and, if selected, bypass boot camp and go directly to the band, where they receive an appropriate amount of military training, and stay throughout their career. The musicians play some six hundred performances a year, ranging from a solo pianist or harpist to the full concert band. Band members need to be versatile; there are a number of performing ensembles, including the concert and marching bands, chamber orchestra, string ensembles, a dance band, and a Dixieland band. Some members are proficient on more than one instrument. Besides the performing members, there are support personnel who staff the music library, recording laboratory, and instrument repair shop.

In addition to the band, the barracks houses the other Marine ceremonial units—the Silent Drill Platoon, the Color Guard of the Marine Corps, the Drum and Bugle Corps, and two companies of Marines who take part in a number of ceremonies each year. In fact, the primary mission of the barracks is "to provide Marines for ceremonial functions as directed." Some 1,200 of these occur each year, including numerous joint-services ceremonies for arrivals and departures of honored guests at the White House and the Pentagon, and wreath ceremonies at Arlington National Cemetery. Barracks Marines also provide security for the president at the White House and Camp David, and are responsible for the execution of the White House Emergency Plan.

(Another important service the Marines perform for the president is to provide him with helicopters. This is the responsibility of HMX-1, a squadron based at Quantico with aircraft at Anacostia Naval Station, a few minutes' flying time from the White House lawn.)

The Marine Corps Institute is also at the barracks. This unique institution was founded in 1920 to provide correspondence courses in technical and general military subjects for all ranks, from private first class through senior officers. More than five million Marines and members of the other services have taken courses through the Institute over the years. Currently some 220,000 active and Reserve Marines are enrolled, taking one or more of the 203 available courses.

Barracks Marines are constantly being trained to meet their ceremonial and security tasks. In addition to ceremonial protocol, marching, and weapons and flag drills, they participate in civil disturbance training, rifle and pistol qualification, gas chamber drills, and leadership training. As ceremonial commitments permit, they do field training at Quantico: the stamina course, circuit course, speed march, reaction course, confidence course, small unit tactics, and weapons firing.

Keeping the ceremonial units up to scratch is a

When John Philip Sousa was thirteen, he decided to run away from home and join the circus. His father, a member of the Marine Band, found out what his son was planning and discussed the problem with the commandant. Mr. Sousa thought his son needed the training and discipline of the Corps. The commandant agreed, and John was enlisted as an apprentice, a common practice in 1868.

John had begun his musical education on the violin at the age of six under John Esputa and G. F. Benkert, who felt that he was "a boy born to music." Besides military training, the Corps taught the young Sousa "to read, write and cypher as far as the single rule of three." One dollar a month was deducted from his pay to defray the cost of his schooling. His musical, scholastic, and military training quickly dispelled any ideas he had of running away. He discovered that martial music and parades provided all the excitement he had looked forward to in the service.

John and his father served together in the Marine Band until 1875. Then John became a civilian bandmaster, touring the country. His father stayed in Washington and worked for the commandant as a cabinetmaker.

Five years later the commandant was unhappy with the Marine Band and asked John Philip Sousa to become its fourteenth leader. Under his direction the band played concerts at the White House, the Marine Barracks at Eighth and I, and on the Capitol Plaza. In 1891 Sousa received President Benjamin Harrison's permission to take the band on a national tour, an annual event ever since. Sousa's showmanship and executive musical ability made the band a success from coast to coast.

Sousa was beginning to become famous as a composer of marches; the public called him the March King. He wrote "Semper Fidelis," which later was adopted as the official march of the Marine Corps. When President Chester A. Arthur announced his dislike of "Hail to the Chief," Sousa wrote his "Presidential Polonaise." March followed march. Among his most famous compositions are "Stars and Stripes Forever," "Washington Post March," "Liberty Bell," "High School Cadets," "Invincible Eagle," "El Capitan," "The Thunderer," "Hands Across the Seas," and "On the Campus March."

Sousa later composed "The Royal Welsh Fusiliers" to commemorate the association of the Marine Corps with the British regiment. In 1930 he was at Tidworth, England, when the score of his march was formally presented to the Fusiliers.

His last appearance with the Marine Band was in Washington in 1932. As a distinguished guest at a concert, he took the baton and led the musicians in "Stars and Stripes Forever." Tears were reported on the cheeks of Sousa, the musicians, and most of the people in the audience.

year-round job. In December the commanding officer of the barracks holds a conference to review the past year's parade season with an eye to possible improvements, and to plan the next season. In January the ceremonial companies conduct individual training, both in classrooms and on the drill field. Parade staff tryouts for officers and noncommissioned staff officers come in February. When the selections are made, parade staff drills begin and continue through September. Also in February, the Silent Drill Platoon and the Drum and Bugle Corps undergo three weeks of intense, mission-oriented training away from Marine Barracks, Washington. The units make a one-week tour performing at Marine bases before returning to the barracks.

Platoon and company-level drills are a daily routine,

beginning in March. If the weather is bad, they train in a local gymnasium or armory. The parade practice routine quickens in April. Battalion drills begin to get the companies working together. Finally, the parade season begins.

By June a routine is established. Monday and Wednesday mornings the ceremonial companies hold practice sessions. Tuesdays there are rehearsals at the Iwo Jima Monument in the morning and the Sunset Parade there in the evening. There are rehearsals as needed on Thursdays. Friday mornings mean rehearsals at the barracks for the Evening Parade. Nor is that the end of it. About half the weekends find the ceremonial units performing in local street parades, musical concerts, dedication ceremonies, and other events, often outside of Washington.

This schedule, both routine and erratic, continues through late September. The last parade of the season honors the Sergeant Major of the Marine Corps. The final event of the year is one of the most important ceremonial and social occasions of the Corps, the Marine Corps Birthday on November 10. During the fall the barracks prepares for the birthday ceremony at the Iwo Jima Monument and the ceremonial functions at the Birthday Ball.

Bachelor officers at the barracks have an opportunity to become White House social aides. About ten or so Marine officers are on call to go to the White House in dress uniforms and medals to mingle with the guests at the predinner cocktails and escort them to their places. Their duties end there; the officers don't stay for dinner.

The ceremonial duties and social obligations of the men at the Marine Barracks contrast sharply with the problems the commandant must wrestle with daily. And it is ironic that the commandant is not particularly empathetic to the ruffles and flourishes, the pomp and circumstance, of military life. His Marines call him the "Grunt General." And with reason.

Al Gray joined the Marines in 1950. He was an infantry sergeant in Korea, where he was selected for Officer Candidate School. He spent two years in Korea, five in Vietnam. Throughout his career he has angled to go, as he puts it, "where the sound of thunder is." He attracted attention in Vietnam by his skillful participation and leadership in the final evacuation of Saigon. When tapped to succeed General P. X. Kelley as commandant, he was a lieutenant general

commanding Fleet Marine Force Atlantic and the II Marine Amphibious Force. General Gray was a popular choice of the Corps to be commandant, although many felt he would be passed over as too unpolitic. They were delighted to be proven wrong.

Announcing the appointment of General Gray, Secretary of the Navy James Webb likened him to George C. Patton, the Army's legendary "blood-and-guts" general. General Gray is short, stocky, hard as nails, and chews several packs of Red Man tobacco a day. Uncomfortable in Dress Blues, he usually goes to the office in camies. Spit and polish doesn't interest him much. He roams the corridors of Marine Headquarters with a camouflage-painted baseball hat, ready to do battle with "the little old ladies in tennis shoes who stand in the way of progress." "Al Gray is a warrior," says former Secretary Webb. "He knows how to fight, and he knows how to teach people to fight."

The first objective the new commandant set for himself was a return to the basics of the Corps. He is determined to return the Marines to a basic mission: the ability "to go to war tonight."

General Gray in early 1988 ordered that all Marine recruits, regardless of their intended military occupations, attend the School of Infantry, a practice that had been done away with in the early 1970s. Enlisted Marines who did not attend the School of Infantry are receiving compensatory training at their bases. "The world has changed; combat situations have changed," he says. "Rear-area security is now a major problem for all the military forces. It has been for some time. We simply must have a standard of excellence for *all* of our people who perform operations in the military. There is no longer a rear and a front, as there was in World War II."

This is something the general knows from bitter experience. Having commanded the 2nd Division when the bombing occurred in Beirut killing 220 Marines from the division and 21 from other services. Speaking at a Camp Lejeune memorial service, which was attended by President Reagan, he said that mourners from across the country had sent the Marines a message. "It says to hang tough. It says it is high time we stood up and got counted. And it says make sure the Marines . . . stand ready to do what has to be done."

"I believe that every Marine, regardless of rank or grade, male or female, must consider themselves to be a rifleman first," the commandant told Marines at the

Yuma, Arizona, Air Station. "You have got to be able to defend yourself. You have got to be able to shoot, move and communicate. Pick it up, lay it down, get moving, whether you're on the flight line, in supply, in the infantry, or whatever. One Marine Corps. That's the kind of Marine Corps you thought you were going to join. That's the Marine Corps that I believe you want. And if it isn't the Marine Corps that you want, then you should leave."

Boot camp is being toughened up. Classroom instruction on such subjects as "how to write a check" have been eliminated and replaced by more hand-to-hand combat training and the resumption of throwing live grenades, a practice that had been stopped after several recruits were injured. General Gray has ordered more training in stealth tactics, night rescues, and infiltration. The tight rein on drill instructors has been eased somewhat, and the regular exercises and drills are being performed with new vigor. "I don't think boot camp is tough enough," he says. "I think we pamper them too much."

General Gray wants to develop "streetwise" Marines. "We need to teach these high school graduates from East Cupcake, Nebraska, the tricks of the trade. A high school diploma doesn't make you a warrior, it doesn't make you a leader, it doesn't make you a gunslinger—but Marine training can. I used to say in Vietnam that we should recruit kids from the South Side of Chicago. They look around, they watch, they don't trust anybody at first. They never shuffled into booby traps, or walked into punji sticks. They were streetwise, and all Marines should be streetwise."

Commandant Gray makes it clear that the Marine Corps is not a democratic institution. In an extemporaneous speech to infantry officers, he said, "I don't run a democracy. I train troops to defend democracy, and I happen to be their [the troops'] surrogate father and mother as well as their commanding general. And all of you are assistant mothers and fathers. That is an awesome responsibility." Yet the commandant has some surprisingly democratic ideas. From the start, he has told his troops that he wants their thinking. One Marine suggested getting rid of rank insignia on field covers (camie caps and helmets), and it was. A young Reserve captain, says Commandant Gray, made "many outstanding recommendations concerning placing our young Marines in a field environment during

Standing guard at a U.S. embassy, Marines know the threat of terrorism. Some 1,000 serve in the Security Guard Battalion; many have been killed or wounded in attacks.

training, and these are being studied." A pipeline to the top has been opened.

Several things in today's Corps nettle the commandant. One is obsessive joggers. "At around ten o'clock at Marine Corps Headquarters, they get into their silk shorts and $200 Adidas shoes and run to the Eastern Shore, or wherever the hell they go, and don't come back until three in the afternoon. We're going to be the best looking outfit that ever got run off the hill. I'm not against running; I run myself. But I'm a hell of a lot more interested in a Marine being able to carry a wounded Marine a hundred yards across a battlefield, or forced marches under combat conditions, than Marines training for a marathon. If they want to do that, fine. But they will damn well do it on their time, not mine."

Another source of irritation is careerism. "What do I mean by careerism?" asks Commandant Gray. "I mean leaders—officers and noncommissioned officers alike—who care more about themselves, where they're going to go and their career path, than they do about the people they are privileged to lead. It's rampant throughout the Corps, and I think we have to stamp it out. *I'm* going to be the career planner for the officers, and the Sergeant Major of the Marine Corps is going to be the career planner for noncommissioned officers."

Speaking to Marines on the West Coast, the commandant spelled out his new policy. "From now on, you and others like you are going to go where *I* want you to go, do what *I* want you to do, and do it for the length of tour that *I* prescribe. It's all based on three simple things: needs of the country, needs of the Corps, and *last*—what you'd like to do. If you happen to go where you want to go, you've lucked out.

"Now, it's human nature and it's the American way to want to get ahead. I don't have anything against someone being proud of the idea he's going to make corporal, sergeant, colonel, whatever. That's common sense, but, by gosh, when we concern ourselves so much with getting ahead that we stomp on our fellow Marines . . . that's terrible, and it's going to stop.

"We need to get back to some of the basic fundamental things. We need to get back to leadership. We need to take care of our people and let them grow, and make damn sure that they're better physically, morally, and mentally when they leave than when we got them. That's what this military profession is all about. Nothing else."

A handmaiden of careerism is what the Marines call homesteading, finding an attractive base and contriving to stay there for years. Commandant Gray is pledged to stamp out homesteading, too. "You know we've got homesteading in the Marine Corps. Everybody says we've got an East Coast Marine Corps, West Coast Marine Corps, this Marine Corps, that Marine Corps. Now, it has been our life's blood to be able to take a unit from the Atlantic and one from the Pacific —sock em together and go. No other service in the world can do that except us. Now, I tell the staff NCOs: 'You've been somewhere for three years, you're okay; but if you've been there five or six years, you'd better not send out your laundry. You're on your way somewhere else.'

"We're going to shake up our staff NCOs," he continued. "We're going to elevate them and treat them with the dignity and respect they deserve, and permit them to do what they are supposed to do. The ball is going to be in their court. I can take care of getting them more running room, more latitude. I can take care of getting them treated with dignity and that sort of thing. But they have to earn it, deserve it, keep it, and they can't rest on their laurels. This is a tough ball game we're in. You've got to hustle to stay ahead of this crowd we've got running around in Marine green today."

The other pet peeve to the commandant is what he calls "zero defect mentality," the belief that making no mistakes is the measure of performance. He tells his staff NCOs, "We're killing ourselves. You are oversupervising the sergeants and the corporals because you're afraid to make a mistake. The officers are oversupervising you because *they're* afraid of making a mistake. The young officers don't know what the hell they're doing, and the old officers aren't much better. We've got to let our people do things; that's directly related to combat preparedness. Because that's one thing that all of you know, because you've been around—the one thing in combat you can bet on is uncertainty, the so-called 'fog of war.' It never goes the way you want it to go. How in the hell do you deal with that? Well, you mold people by letting them do things.

"Some people are born with initiative, boldness, and all that. A rare handful. Most people have to learn it through the experience of others, and they learn it through the process of doing things. It's a lousy carpenter who doesn't hit his thumb with a hammer once in a while. He's not driving any nails. Now, you show me a guy that isn't making any mistakes and I'll show you a guy who, one, isn't doing anything, and two, I don't want. Now, I'm not talking about going out and doing dumb things and getting people killed—forgetting to put fuel in airplanes or something like that.

"You guys know exactly what I mean. We are so goddamn uptight about how we look that we don't let people do things. I don't give a shit how you look, I care how you are. If you are good, you're going to look good."

Despite all this, Commandant Gray does not agree with the critics in the media who have implied that the Marine Corps is broken and needs fixing. "What I feel," he told an interviewer, "is that, from the standpoint of the nation and the security problems we have, we are very vulnerable in our overseas locations—embassies and the like. We are up against a massive hostile intelligence threat in terms of manpower, technology, and resources. Our Marines—indeed all

A company passes in review at a ceremony at the "8th and I" Marine Barracks. The barracks is the oldest post in the Corps and was the Marine headquarters for years.

Americans overseas—are extremely vulnerable to this hostile threat. We've got to get everybody's attention and improve our aggregate capabilities against this threat. This aspect appears to me to be broken and needs to be fixed . . . and it *is* getting fixed!

"In many ways, the Marine Corps in recent years has been a real success story. We think that one of the great stories that needs to be told is that in the middle and late 1970s, when we weren't getting any funding support for modernization or anything else, the greatest thing the Marine Crops did was to keep its brainpower turned on.

"We acted like we had money and we did our homework through mission-area analyses and studies. We had a long-term strategic and tactical mobility study that we carried on through that period. We studied the Arab-Israeli War. We studied armor and light armored vehicles. We reviewed our structure in great detail, and we examined all of our operational and materiel concepts. We knew what we needed and we did the required documentation.

"When we got the first supplement budget, and had the continuing support from the present [Reagan] administration and the Congress, we struck like Genghis Khan. We had our approved requirements documentation and we went after what we needed. That is why we were able to reequip all the infantry units. We modernized all three Marine divisions and we brought in new aircraft as well. We enhanced our command-and-control capability and added a whole family of new mobility

equipment and other enhancements. Combat service support elements were improved and logistics sustainability was improved. It was indeed a success story!

"Having said that, let me also say that we need to take a hard look at ourselves and make sure that we're prepared to do whatever our country may require of us. We pride ourselves as being the nation's force in readiness—capable of moving out on short notice and taking on any task. That obviously is an ambitious mission, but one that we must be capable of performing. In a dynamic international environment, we must never be comfortable that the answers or priorities that were acceptable yesterday are still correct today.

"We want to take a hard look at all aspects of the Marine Corps—structure, missions, personnel, training, and equipment—to make sure we're properly responding to today's requirements as well as those of the future. If that look tells me we're on track and where we need to be—that's great! If we find areas that need redirection, reorientation, rethinking—I guess you could call that fixing—it's best to know that now and get started on what we need to do. I'm convinced that this nation's Marine Corps is a first-rate fighting organization, and we want to make sure that we keep it honed to a fine edge."

Commandant Gray has a crystal-clear definition of the mission of the Marine Corps: to be ready at all times for sustained power projection. "If you want to go somewhere and project power long enough to win —or get a successful political decision—you've got to come from the sea. The reason is very simple. You can load up all the airplanes of the free world—America, NATO, everybody—and you can fly soldiers and Marines for thirty days and thirty nights to some trouble spot. When you get done, you'll have a small amount of combat power, and you won't be able to sustain it. At the same time, four or five ships could carry more than that airlift, and do it a helluva lot faster than thirty days. And when it gets there, it can sustain itself.

"So you have to come from the sea. That's why we use airlift and sealift in combination. We fly our aircraft to war, we move Marines and materiel by ships, by a prepositioned force. This means we not only play a vital role, we play the *crucial* role in power projection. From the standpoint of stabilizing a trouble spot, it's only when that force on the horizon has Marines on it who can come ashore and help people when they need help—that's when you have a truly credible stabilizing policy.

"The nation expects us to be prepared to go anywhere tonight. Whether it's an amphibious operation or not, that doesn't matter. Fighting and winning is what matters. The basic capability that the Marines have—our forte—must be preparedness, nothing else.

"I believe the nation loves our Marine Corps. I believe they support us. I believe the nation prays for us. They provide the money for the Marine Corps through taxes. But in exchange for that, they place some special demands on the Corps. They demand that their Marines be a little bit special. They demand that we be the premier fighting force in the world. They demand that we be the most prepared force on earth to fight to keep the peace and to do whatever else must be done. And indeed, that we be the best trained, best led, best disciplined force on this planet. That's the way they see it. I don't know if we're that good now. But you damn sure better understand that that's the way we're going to be."

Marine Corps traditions include spit and polish and a precision on the parade ground that is matched by few military organizations in the world.

SEMPER FIDELIS

Observing the Marines going about their business for a number of months in a variety of situations and locales has led to certain conclusions. One is that the Corps today is a flexible, mobile strike force ready to go into action at a moment's notice anywhere in the world. Marines can be sealifted or airlifted into a trouble spot. Once there, prepositioned ships can sustain them until either the situation is well in hand, or reinforcements arrive. Furthermore, the Marines are prepared to respond appropriately to whatever situation they encounter. This may involve keeping the peace, an all-out assault, or anything in between.

Never in its long history has the Corps, in peacetime, been as large or as well equipped. Nor have its ranks been filled with recruits of such exceptional quality. Marine training, always tough and demanding, has taken on a new intensity under a new commandant, an old-school warrior who himself is the stuff of legends. Beyond question, today's Marine Corps continues to be America's military elite.

There is another reason why this is so. The factor that always has been so special about the Marines remains undiminished: their spirit, their esprit de corps. History records that, time after time, the Marines have prevailed in spite of small numbers and hand-me-down equipment. The Corps is living proof that a few good men can make the difference.

Esprit de corps can't be put on a scale and measured, certainly not in peacetime. The only true test is performance in combat. No one knew that the French Army's *esprit* had died in the trenches of World War I until Germany attacked in 1939. No such collapse of nerve ever happened to the Marines. There is no evidence that even the agony and frustration of Vietnam in any way impaired the Corps spirit. It is as gung ho and hard-charging as ever.

In *The Red Badge of Courage,* Stephen Crane wrote of "a mysterious fraternity born of smoke and the danger of death." He might well have been writing about the Marines. True, military life anywhere involves male bonding, and male bonding is intensified sharply by the experience of combat. Men who fight together are, indeed, brothers in a mysterious fraternity. As Shakespeare wrote in *King Henry V:* "We few, we happy few, we band of brothers; For he today that sheds his blood with me shall be my brother."

Nowhere has this spirit of brotherhood been so intense for so long as in the Marines.

Esprit de corps grows out of training, but it goes beyond training. A recruit can be trained to be a good rifleman and adept at squad tactics. But he can't be trained to fall on a live grenade that lands among his squad. If he falls on it, it is because protecting his fellow Marines matters more at that instant than does his own life.

What makes some men so brave? The question nags; even the brave themselves can give no satisfactory answer. By its very nature, bravery is irrational. Normally, self-protection is man's strongest instinct. What instinct, what feeling, takes over in the brave?

An answer that satisfies comes from a former Marine, a decorated veteran of World War II. Writing about the intense fighting on Okinawa where he was wounded, William Manchester spoke for all Marines down through the years: ". . . Those men on the line were my family, my home. They were closer to me than I can say, closer than any friends had been or ever would be. They had never let me down, and I couldn't do it to them. . . . Men, I now know, do not fight for flag or country, for the Marine Corps, glory or any other abstraction. They fight for each other. Any man in combat who lacks comrades who will die for him, or for whom he is willing to die, is not a man at all. He is truly damned."

★

APPENDIX

THE MARINES' HYMN

From the Halls of Montezuma,
To the shores of Tripoli;
We fight our country's battles
In the air, on land, and sea;
First to fight for right and freedom
And to keep our honor clean;
We are proud to claim the title of
United States Marine.

Our flag's unfurled to every breeze
From dawn to setting sun;
We have fought in every clime and place
Where we could take a gun;
In the snow of far off northern lands
And in sunny tropic scenes;
You will find us always on the job—
The United States Marines.

Here's health to you and to our Corps
Which we are proud to serve;
In many a strife we've fought for life
And never lost our nerve;
If the Army and the Navy
Ever look on Heaven's scenes;
They will find the streets are guarded by
United States Marines.

CASUALTIES AND STRENGTHS DURING WARS AND MAJOR ENGAGEMENTS

	DEAD	WOUNDED	OFFICERS	ENLISTED	TOTAL
Revolutionary War	49	70	131	2,000	2,131
Quasi-War with France	6	11	41	1,044	1,085
Barbary Wars	4	10	26	453	479
War of 1812	46	33	93	2,622	2,715
Creek-Seminole Indian War	8	1	58	1,086	1,144
Mexican War	11	47	71	2,170	2,241
Civil War—Union	148	131	90	3,791	3,881
Spanish-American War	7	13	116	4,700	4,816
Samoa	0	2	124	3,614	3,738
Boxer Rebellion	9	17	187	5,520	5,707
Nicaragua	5	16	319	9,739	10,058
Mexico	5	13	341	9,888	10,229
Dominican Republic	17	50	874	26,621	27,495
Haiti	10	26	1,167	18,310	19,477
Nicaragua	47	66	1,211	18,172	19,383
World War I	2,457	8,894	2,462	72,639	75,101
World War II	19,733	67,207	37,664	447,389	485,053
Korea	4,267	23,744	19,536	241,807	261,343
Vietnam-Cambodia-Laos	13,067	88,633	24,994	289,923	314,917

COMMANDANTS OF THE MARINE CORPS

Samuel Nicholas	Pennsylvania	1775–1781
William Ward Burrows	South Carolina	1798–1804
Franklin Wharton	Pennsylvania	1804–1818
Anthony Gale	Ireland	1819–1820
Archibald Henderson	Virginia	1820–1859
John Harris	Pennsylvania	1859–1864
Jacob Zeilin	Pennsylvania	1864–1876
Charles G. McCawley	Pennsylvania	1876–1891
Charles Heywood	Maine	1891–1903
George Elliott	Alabama	1903–1910
William P. Biddle	Wisconsin	1911–1914
George Barnett	Wisconsin	1914–1920
John A. Lejeune	Louisiana	1920–1929
Wendell Neville	Virginia	1929–1930
Ben H. Fuller	Michigan	1930–1934
John H. Russell	California	1934–1936
Thomas Holcomb	Delaware	1936–1943
Alexander A. Vandegrift	Virginia	1944–1947
Clifton B. Cates	Tennessee	1948–1951
Lemuel C. Shepherd, Jr.	Virginia	1952–1955
Randolph McCall Pate	South Carolina	1956–1959
David M. Shoup	Indiana	1960–1963
Wallace M. Greene, Jr.	Vermont	1964–1967
Leonard F. Chapman, Jr.	Florida	1968–1971
Robert E. Cushman, Jr.	Minnesota	1972–1975
Louis H. Wilson	Mississippi	1975–1979
Robert H. Barrow	Louisiana	1979–1983
Paul X. Kelley	Massachusetts	1983–1987
Alfred M. Gray, Jr.	New Jersey	1987–

DIRECTORS OF MARINE CORPS WOMEN'S RESERVES

COLONEL RUTH CHENEY STREETER
February 13, 1943–December 8, 1945

COLONEL KATHERINE A. TOWLE
December 8, 1945–June 14, 1946

COLONEL JULIA E. HAMBLET
June 14, 1946–October 18, 1948

DIRECTORS OF WOMEN MARINES

COLONEL KATHERINE A. TOWLE
October 18, 1948–May 1, 1953

COLONEL JULIA E. HAMBLET
May 1, 1953–March 2,1959

COLONEL MARGARET M. HENDERSON
March 2, 1959–January 3, 1964

COLONEL BARBARA J. BISHOP
January 3, 1964–January 31, 1969

COLONEL JEANNETTE I. SUSTAD
January 31, 1969–January 31, 1973

COLONEL MARGARET A. BREWER
January 31, 1973–June 30, 1977 (Post abolished)

MARINE CORPS BATTLES AND DEPLOYMENTS

WAR OF THE REVOLUTION 1775–1783
Raid on New Providence, Bahamas	March 2–3, 1776
Alfred and *Cabot* vs. British *Glasgow*	April 6, 1776
Second Battle of Trenton (Assanpink Creek)	January 2, 1777
Battle of Princeton	January 3, 1777
Reprisal vs. British *Swallow*	February 5, 1777
Hancock vs. British *Fox*	June 27, 1777
Raleigh vs. British *Druid*	September 4, 1777
Randolph vs. British *Yarmouth*	March 7, 1778
Boston vs. British *Martha*	March 11, 1778
Raid on Whitehaven, England	April 22, 1778
Ranger vs. British *Drake*	April 24, 1778
Penobscot Expedition—July 24 to August 14, 1779	
Battle of Banks Island	July 26, 1779
Battle of Majarbiguyduce Peninsula	July 28–August 13, 1779
Bonhomme Richard vs. British *Serapis*	September 23, 1779
Trumbull vs. British *Watt*	June 2, 1780
Alliance vs. British *Atlanta* and *Trepassy*	May 28–29, 1781
Congress vs. British *Savage*	September 6, 1781
Hyder Ally vs. British *General Monk*	April 8, 1782
Alliance vs. British *Sybylle*	January 20, 1783

FRENCH NAVAL WAR 1798–1801
Constellation vs. French *L'Insurgente*	February 9, 1799
Experiment vs. Haitian picaroons	January 1, 1800
Constellation vs. French *La Vengeance*	February 2, 1800

WAR WITH TRIPOLI 1801–1805
Enterprise vs. Tripolitan *Tripoli*	August 1, 1801
Raid on Tripoli	May 20, 1803
Capture of *Philadelphia* by Tripolitans	October 31, 1803
Constitution, Siren, Argus, Scourge, Vixen, Nautilus, Enterprise, and gunboats vs. Tripolitan vessels	August 3, 1804
Capture of fortress at Derne, Tripoli	April 25–27, 1805

WAR OF 1812
Essex vs. British *Alert*	August 13, 1812
Constitution vs. British *Guerriere*	August 19, 1812
Wasp vs. British *Frolic*	October 18, 1812
United States vs. British *Macedonian*	October 25, 1812
Constitution vs. British *Java*	December 29, 1812
Hornet vs. British *Peacock*	February 24, 1813
Battle of Fort George (Canada)	May 27, 1813
Chesapeake vs. British *Shannon*	June 1, 1813
Battle of Craney Island (near Norfolk)	June 22, 1813
Essex and *Greenwich* vs. British *Seringapatam*	July 14, 1813
Enterprise vs. British *Boxer*	September 4, 1813
Battle of Lake Erie	September 10, 1813

Peacock vs. British *Epervier*	April 29, 1814
Battle of Bladensburg (Maryland)	August 24, 1814
Battle of Lake Champlain	September 11, 1814
Battle of New Orleans	January 8, 1815
President vs. British *Endymion, Majestic, Pomona,* and *Tenedos*	January 15, 1815
Constitution vs. British *Cyane* and *Levant*	February 20, 1815
Hornet vs. British *Penguin*	March 23, 1815

BATTLE OF TWELVE MILE SWAMP (FLORIDA)
September 11, 1812

BATTLE OF QUALLAH BATTO (SUMATRA)
February 6, 1832

FLORIDA INDIAN WAR 1835–1842
Relief of Fort Brooke (Florida)	January 22, 1836
Battle of Wahoo Swamp (Florida)	November 21, 1836
Campaign in the New River Country (Florida)	October 22–December 15, 1836
Battle of Hatchee-Lustee (Florida)	January 27, 1837

MEXICAN WAR 1846–1847
Battle of San Pasqual (California)	December 6, 1846
Battle of Santa Clara (California)	January 2, 1847
Battle of San Gabriel (California)	January 8, 1847
Battle of La Mesa (California)	January 9, 1847
Battle of Veracruz (Mexico)	March 9, 1847
Battle of Tabasco (Mexico)	June 15, 1847
Battle of Chapultepec (Mexico)	September 13, 1847
Battle of Guaymas (Mexico)	November 17, 1847
Battle of San Jose (California)	November 19, 1847

BATTLE OF SHANGHAI (CHINA)
April 4, 1854

BATTLE OF TY-HO BAY (CHINA)
August 4, 1855

BATTLE WITH INDIANS NEAR SEATTLE (WASHINGTON)
January 26, 1856

BATTLE OF THE BARRIER FORTS (CHINA)
November 16–22, 1856

BATTLE OF WAYA (FIJI ISLANDS)
October 6, 1858

CAPTURE OF JOHN BROWN (HARPER'S FERRY, VIRGINIA)
October 18, 1859

CIVIL WAR 1861–1865
First Battle of Bull Run (Manassas, Virginia)	July 21, 1861
Destruction of Confederate privateer *Judah* (off Pensacola)	September 14, 1861
Destruction of Confederate armed schooner *Royal Yacht* (off Galveston)	November 7–8, 1861
Battle of Port Royal (South Carolina)	November 8, 1861
Battle of Hatteras Inlet (North Carolina)	February 7–8, 1862
Battle of Fort Cobb (near Elizabeth City, North Carolina)	February 10, 1862
Battle of Winston (North Carolina)	February 19, 1862
Cumberland and *Congress* vs. Confederate ironclad *Merrimac*	March 8, 1862

Minnesota vs. *Merrimac*	March 9, 1862
Battle of Slocum's Creek	March 13, 1862
New London vs. two Confederate steamers (near Pass Christian, Virginia)	March 25, 1862
Battle of New Orleans	April 24–28, 1862
Battle of Fort Macon	April 25, 1862
Battle of Drury's Bluff (near Richmond, Virginia)	May 15, 1862
Expedition up Santee River	June 24, 1862
Admiral Farragut's fleet vs. Confederate batteries (at Vicksburg, Mississippi)	June 28, 1862
Admiral Farragut's fleet vs. Confederate ram *Arkansas* (near Vicksburg)	July 15, 1862
Keystone State vs. two Confederate ironclads (near Charleston)	January 31, 1863
Expedition up Red River (Louisiana)	March 10–April 14, 1863
Battle of Port Hudson (Mississippi)	March 14, 1863
Attack on Fort Sumter	September 8, 1863
Capture of Stono (South Carolina)	December 28, 1863
Wabash vs. Confederate torpedo boat (off Charleston)	April 18, 1864
Four U.S. vessels vs. Confederate ram *Albemarle* (near New Bern, North Carolina)	May 5, 1864
Kearsage vs. Confederate *Alabama* (off Cherbourg, France)	June 10, 1864
Battle of Mobile Bay	August 5–23, 1864
Battle of Boyd's Neck and Honey Hill (South Carolina)	November 28–30, 1864
Battle of Derang's Neck or Tullifinney Cross Road (South Carolina)	December 6–9, 1864
Battle of Fort Fisher (North Carolina)	December 23–25, 1864
Capture of Fort Fisher	January 13–15, 1865

WYOMING VS. THREE JAPANESE SHIPS AND SHORE BATTERIES IN STRAITS OF SHIMONOSEKI, JAPAN

July 16, 1863

BATTLE OF THE SALEE RIVER FORTS (KOREA)

June 10–11, 1871

WAR WITH SPAIN—APRIL 21 TO AUGUST 13, 1898

Battle of Manila Bay	May 1, 1898
Battle of Guantanamo Bay (Cuba)	June 11–14, 1898
Battle of Cuzco Well (Cuba)	June 14, 1898
Battle of Santiago (Cuba)	July 3, 1898

PHILIPPINE INSURRECTION—JUNE 30, 1898, TO JULY 4, 1902

Battle of Novaleta (Luzon)	October 8, 1898
Battle of Sohoton River (Samar)	November 5, 1901
Battle of Sohoton Cliffs (Samar)	November 17, 1901
March across Samar	December 28, 1901–January 18, 1902

BATTLE OF TAGALII (SAMOA)

April 1, 1899

CHINA RELIEF EXPEDITION (BOXER REBELLION)—JUNE TO AUGUST 1900

Battle of Tong-Ku (near Tientsin)	June 19, 1900
Battle of the East Arsenal (near Tientsin)	June 21, 1900
Battle of Tientsin	June 24, 1900
Battle of the Imperial Arsenal (near Tientsin)	July 9, 1900
Recapture of Tientsin	July 13–14, 1900
Battle of Yangtsun	August 6, 1900
Battle of Peking	August 15–19, 1900

NICARAGUAN CAMPAIGN OF 1912

Battle of Masaya	September 19, 1912
Battle of Coyotepe and Barranca Hills	October 3–4, 1912
Battle of Leon	October 5, 1912

CAPTURE OF VERACRUZ (MEXICO)

	April 21–22, 1914

OCCUPATION OF DOMINICAN REPUBLIC—MAY 5, 1916, TO SEPTEMBER 17, 1924

Battle of Puerto Plata	June 1, 1916
Battle of Las Trencheras	June 27, 1916
Battle of Guavacanas	July 3, 1916
Battle of Las Canitas	April 7, 1917

OCCUPATION OF HAITI—JULY 28, 1915, TO AUGUST 31, 1934

Battle of Grosse Roche	October 24, 1915
Battle of Fort Dipite	October 24–25, 1915
Battle of Fort Capois	November 5, 1915
Battle of Forts Selon and Berthol	November 8, 1915
Battle of Fort Riviere	November 17–18, 1915
Battle of Hinche	April 4, 1919
Battle of Port-au-Prince	October 7, 1919
Capture of Charlemagne Peraltte	October 31, 1919
Battle of Port-au-Prince	January 14–15, 1920

WORLD WAR I—APRIL 6, 1917, TO NOVEMBER 11, 1918

Battle of Les Mares Farm (near Belleau Wood)	June 3–4, 1918
Battle of Hill 142 (near Belleau Wood)	June 6, 1918
Battle of Bouresches (near Belleau Wood)	June 6–7, 1918
Battle of Belleau Wood	June 6–26, 1918
Battle of the Aisne-Marne (Soissons)	July 18–20, 1918
Battle of St. Mihiel	September 12–16, 1918
Battle of Blanc Mont	October 2–9, 1918
Battle of the Meuse-Argonne	November 1–11, 1918

OCCUPATION OF NICARAGUA—JANUARY 6, 1927, TO JANUARY 3, 1933

Battle of La Paz Centro	May 16, 1927
Battle of Ocotal	July 16, 1927
Battle of Telpaneca	September 19, 1927
Battle of Camino Real	December 30, 1927
Battle of Sapotillal Ridge	January 1, 1928
Battle of Quilali	January 1–8, 1928
Battle of El Chipote	January 25, 1928
Battle of Bromaderos	February 27–28, 1928
Battle of the Cua River	May 13, 1928
Battle of the Coco River (near Ililihuas)	August 7, 1928
Battle of Cuje	December 6, 1928
Battle near Octal-Apali	December 31, 1930

WORLD WAR II—DECEMBER 7, 1941, TO AUGUST 15, 1945

Pearl Harbor–Midway	December 7, 1941
Guam	December 8–10, 1941
Wake Island	December 8–23, 1941
Bataan and Corregidor (Philippines)	December 8, 1941–May 6, 1942
Battle of Badoeng Strait (East Indies)	February 19, 1942
Battle of the Coral Sea	May 4–8, 1942
Battle of Midway	June 3–6, 1942
Guadalcanal-Tulagi Landings	August 7–9, 1942
First Savo Battle (Naval-Air)	August 9, 1942
Capture and Defense of Guadalcanal	August 10, 1942–February 8, 1943
Makin Island Raid (Gilberts)	August 17–18, 1942
Battle of the Eastern Solomons	August 23–25, 1942
Battle of Cape Esperance (Naval)	October 11–12, 1942
Battle of Santa Cruz Island (Air)	October 26, 1942
Battle of Guadalcanal (Naval-Air)	November 11–15, 1942
Battle of Tassafaronga (Naval)	November 30–December 1, 1942
Battle of Komandorski Island (Aleutians)	March 26, 1943

New Georgia Group

New Georgia-Rendova-Vandunu Occupation	June 20–August 31, 1943
Battle of Kula Gulf (Naval)	July 5–6, 1943
Battle of Kolombangara (Naval)	July 12–13, 1943
Vella Lavella Occupation	August 15–October 16, 1943
Cape Gloucester (New Britain) Operation	December 26, 1943–March 1, 1944
Green Islands Landing	February 15–19, 1944

Treasury-Bougainville Operation

Treasury Island Landing	October 27–November 6, 1943
Choiseul Island Diversion	October 28–November 4, 1943
Occupation and Defense of Cape Torokina	November 1–December 15, 1943
Tarawa Operation (Gilbert Islands)	November 20–December 8, 1943
Occupation of Kwajalein and Majuro Atolls (Marshall Islands)	January 31–February 8, 1944
Occupation of Eniwetok Atoll (Marshall Islands)	February 17–March 2, 1944
Capture and Occupation of Saipan	June 15–August 10, 1944
Capture and Occupation of Guam	July 21–August 15, 1944
Capture and Occupation of Tinian	July 24–August 10, 1944
Capture and Occupation of Peleliu	September 15–October 14, 1944
Leyte (Philippines) Landings	October 20, 1944
Battle of Leyte Gulf (Naval-Air)	October 24–26, 1944
Iwo Jima Operation	February 19–March 16, 1945
Assault and Occupation of Okinawa Gunto	April 1–June 21, 1945

ENGAGED IN UNITED NATIONS ACTION, KOREA—JUNE 27, 1950, TO JULY 27, 1953

North Korean Aggression	June 27–November 27, 1950
Inchon Landing	September 13–17, 1950
Communist China Aggression	November 3, 1950–January 24, 1951
First U.N. Counteroffensive	January 25–April 21, 1951
Communist China Spring Offensive	April 22–July 8, 1951
U.N. Summer–Fall Offensive	July 9–November 27, 1951

Second Korean Winter	November 28, 1951–April 30, 1952
Korean Defense, Summer–Fall, 1952	May 1–November 30, 1952
Third Korean Winter	December 1, 1952–April 30, 1953
Korea, Summer–Fall, 1953	May 1–July 27, 1953

LANDING IN LEBANON　　　　　　　　　　　July 15–September 30, 1958

LANDING IN THAILAND　　　　　　　　　　　May 16–August 10, 1962

CUBAN MISSILE CRISIS　　　　　　　　　October 24–December 31, 1962

DOMINICAN REPUBLIC INTERVENTION　　　　April 28–January 6, 1965

**THE WAR IN VIETNAM—MARCH 15, 1962,
TO JANUARY 28, 1973**

Vietnam Advisory Campaign	March 15, 1962–March 7, 1965
Vietnam Defense Campaign	March 8–December 24, 1965
Vietnamese Counteroffensive Campaign	December 25, 1965–June 30, 1966
Vietnamese Counteroffensive Phase II	July 1, 1966–May 31, 1967
Vietnamese Counteroffensive Phase III	June 1, 1967–January 29, 1968
Tet Counteroffensive	January 30–April 1, 1968
Vietnamese Counteroffensive Phase IV	April 2–June 30, 1968
Vietnamese Counteroffensive Phase V	July 1–November 1, 1968
Vietnamese Counteroffensive Phase VI	November 2, 1968–February 22, 1969
Tet 69 Counteroffensive	February 23–June 8, 1969
Vietnam, Summer–Fall, 1969	June 9–October 31, 1969
Vietnam, Fall–Winter, 1970	November 1, 1969–April 30, 1970
Sanctuary Counteroffensive	May 1–June 30, 1970
Vietnamese Counteroffensive Phase VII	July 1, 1970–June 30, 1971
Consolidation I	July 1–November 30, 1971
Consolidation II	December 1, 1971–March 29, 1972
Vietnam Cease Fire Campaign	March 30, 1972–January 28, 1973

OPERATION EAGLE PULL (PHNOM PENH, CAMBODIA)　　　　April 1975

**OPERATION FREQUENT WIND
(SAIGON, SOUTH VIETNAM)**　　　　　　　　　　　　　April 1975

**MAYAGÜEZ RESCUE OPERATION
(KOH TANG, CAMBODIA)**　　　　　　　　　　　　　　May 1975

**IRANIAN HOSTAGE RESCUE ATTEMPT
(DESERT ONE, IRAN)**　　　　　　　　　　　　　　　April 1980

GRENADA LANDING (GRENADA, CARRIACOU)　　October–November 1983

LEBANON DEPLOYMENT (BEIRUT, LEBANON)　　August 1982–February 1984

THE BATTLE COLORS OF THE MARINE CORPS

WHAT THE STREAMERS REPRESENT

Presidential Unit Citation (Navy) Streamer with six silver and two bronze stars

Presidential Unit Citation (Army) Streamer with one silver oak leaf cluster

Navy Unit Commendation Streamer with nineteen silver stars

Valorous Unit Award (Army) Streamer

Meritorious Unit Commendation (Navy-Marine Corps) Streamer

Meritorious Unit Commendation (Army) Streamer

Revolutionary War Streamer

Quasi-War with France Streamer

Barbary Wars Streamer

War of 1812 Streamer

African Slave Trade Streamer

Operations Against West Indian Pirates Streamer

Indian Wars Streamer

Mexican War Streamer

Civil War Streamer

Marine Corps Expeditionary Streamer with eleven silver stars, two bronze stars, and one silver "W"

Spanish Campaign Streamer

Philippine Campaign Streamer

China Relief Expedition Streamer

Cuban Pacification Streamer

Nicaraguan Campaign Streamer

Mexican Service Streamer

Haitian Campaign Streamer with one bronze star

Dominican Campaign Streamer

World War I Victory Streamer with one silver and one bronze star, one Maltese Cross, and Siberia and West Indies Clasp

Army of Occupation of Germany Streamer

Second Nicaraguan Campaign Streamer

Yangtze Service Streamer

China Service Streamer with one bronze star

American Defense Streamer with one bronze star

American Campaign Streamer

European-African-Middle Eastern Campaign Streamer with one silver and four bronze stars

Asiatic-Pacific Campaign Streamer with eight silver and two bronze stars

World War II Victory Streamer

Navy Occupation Service Streamer with one Europe and Asia Clasp

National Defense Service Streamer with one bronze star

Korean Service Streamer with two silver stars

Armed Forces Expeditionary Streamer with two silver and three bronze stars

Vietnam Service Streamer with three silver and two bronze stars

Philippine Defense Streamer with one bronze star

Philippine Liberation Streamer with two bronze stars

Philippine Independence Streamer

French Croix de Guerre Streamer with two palms and one gilt star

Philippine Presidential Unit Citation Streamer with two bronze stars

Korean Presidential Unit Citation Streamer

Republic of Vietnam Armed Forces Meritorious Unit Citation of the Gallantry Cross with Palm

Republic of Vietnam Meritorious Unit Citation Civil Actions Streamer

★

BIBLIOGRAPHY

The American Heritage History of World War I, narrative by S. L. A. Marshall (New York: American Heritage Publishing Co., 1964)

And Brave Men, Too, Timothy S. Lowry (New York: Crown Publishers, Inc., 1985)

And They Thought We Wouldn't Fight, Floyd Gibbons (New York: George H. Doran Co., 1918)

At Belleau Wood, Robert B. Asprey (New York: G. P. Putnam's Sons, 1965)

The Battle for Guadalcanal, Samuel B. Griffith, II (Philadelphia: J. P. Lippincott Co., 1963)

The Big Yankee, The Life of Carlson of the Raiders, Michael Blankfort (Boston: Little, Brown & Co., 1947)

Boot, Daniel Da Cruz (New York: St. Martin's Press, 1987)

Conflict: The History of the Korean War, 1950–53, Robert Leckie (New York: G. P. Putnam's Sons, 1962)

Coral and Brass, Holland M. Smith and Percy Finch (New York: Charles Scribner's Sons, 1948)

Creating a Legend, Captain John B. Moran, USMCR (Ret.) (Chicago: Moran/Andrews, Inc., 1973)

The Fighting Elite: U.S. Marine Air Wings, Ian Padden (New York: Bantam Books, Inc., 1986)

The Fighting Elite: U.S. Marines, Ian Padden (New York: Bantam Books, Inc., 1985)

Fire in the Lake, Frances FitzGerald (New York: Vintage Books, Random House, 1966)

Goodbye, Darkness: A Memoir of the Pacific War, William Manchester (Boston: Little, Brown and Company, 1979)

History of Marine Corps Aviation in World War II, Robert Sherrod (Washington, D.C.: Combat Forces Press, 1952)

A History of the United States Marine Corps, Clyde H. Metcalf (New York: G. P. Putnam's Sons, 1939)

History of the U.S. Marines, Jack Murphy (New York: Bison Books Corp., 1984)

Iwo Jima, Richard F. Newcomb (New York: Holt Rinehart & Winston, 1965)

Marine Corps Aviation: The Early Years 1912–1940, Lt. Col. Edward C. Johnson (Washington, D.C.: History and Museums Division, Headquarters, USMC, 1977)

Marine! The Life of Lt. Gen. Lewis B. (Chesty) Puller, USMC (Ret.), Burke Davis (Boston: Little, Brown & Co., 1962)

Militarism, U.S.A., James A. Donavan (New York: Charles Scribner's Sons, 1970)

Old Gimlet Eye: The Adventures of Smedley D. Butler as told to Lowell Thomas (New York: Farrar & Rinehart, 1933)

Once a Marine, Alexander A. Vandegrift as told to Robert B. Asprey (New York: Norton & Co., 1964)

Once a Marine—Always a Marine, Ben Finney (New York: Crown Publishers, Inc., 1977)

Progress and Purpose: A Developmental History of the United States Marine Corps 1900–1970, Kenneth J. Clifford (Washington, D.C.: USMC, 1973)

The Reminiscences of a Marine, John A. Lejeune (Philadelphia: Dorrance & Co., 1930)

Ribbon Creek: The Marine Corps on Trial, William Baggarley McKean (New York: The Dial Press, 1958)

Soldiers of the Sea, Robert Debs Heinl, Jr. (Annapolis: U.S. Naval Institute, 1962)

Strong Men Armed, Robert Leckie (New York: Random House, 1962)

The United States in Vietnam, George McTurnan Kahin and John Wilson Lewis (New York: The Dial Press, 1969)

The United States Marines, E. H. Simmons (London: Leo Cooper, Ltd., 1974)

U.S. Marine Corps Aviation, Peter B. Mersky (Annapolis: The Nautical & Aviation Publishing Company of America, 1983)

The U.S. Marine Corps Story, J. Robert Moskin (New York: McGraw-Hill Book Company, 1977)

The U.S. Marines and Amphibious Warfare, Jeter A. Isely and Philip A. Crowl (Princeton: Princeton University Press, 1951)

Victory at High Tide: The Inchon-Seoul Campaign, Robert Debs Heinl, Jr. (Philadelphia: J. B. Lippincott Co., 1968)

Where Does the Marine Corps Go From Here? Martin Binkin and Jeffrey Record (Washington, D.C.: The Brookings Institution, 1976)